THE CHIEF HR OFFICER

Defining the New Role of Human Resource Leaders

Patrick M. Wright, John W. Boudreau,
David A. Pace, Elizabeth "Libby" Sartain,
Paul McKinnon, Richard L. Antoine, Editors

A National Academy of Human Resources Book

N | A
H | R

JOSSEY-BASS
A Wiley Imprint
www.josseybass.com

SOCIETY FOR HUMAN
RESOURCE MANAGEMENT

Published by Jossey-Bass
A Wiley Imprint
989 Market Street, San Francisco, CA 94103–1741—www.josseybass.com

Jossey-Bass books and products are available through most bookstores. To contact Jossey-Bass directly call our Customer Care Department within the U.S. at 800-956-7739, outside the U.S. at 317-572-3986, or fax 317-572-4002.

Jossey-Bass also publishes its books in a variety of electronic formats. Some content that appears in print may not be available in electronic books.

Library of Congress Cataloging-in-Publication Data

The chief HR officer: defining the new role of human resource leaders /
editors, Patrick M. Wright . . . [et al.].
   p. cm.
 Includes bibliographical references and index.
 ISBN 978-0-470-90534-0 (hardback); ISBN 978-1-118-02322-8 (ebk);
ISBN 978-1-118-02323-5 (ebk); ISBN 978-1-118-02324-2 (ebk)
 1. Personnel management. 2. Personnel departments. I. Wright, Patrick M.
 HF5549.C44794 2011
 658.3—dc22

                                         2010046805

Printed in the United States of America
FIRST EDITION
HB Printing   10 9 8 7 6 5 4 3

CONTENTS

N|A H|R

The National Academy of Human Resources (NAHR) is an honorific organization where individuals and institutions of distinction in human resources are recognized for exceptional professional achievement by election as "Fellows of the NAHR." In addition, the NAHR furthers the HR profession through the Chief Human Resource Officer (CHRO) Academy and other philanthropic and educational activities. For more information, visit www.nationalacademyhr.org.

SOCIETY FOR HUMAN RESOURCE MANAGEMENT

The Society for Human Resource Management (SHRM) is the world's largest association devoted to human resource management. The Society serves the needs of HR professionals and advances the interests of the HR profession. Founded in 1948, SHRM has more than 250,000 members in over 140 countries, and more than 575 affiliated chapters. Visit www.shrm.org.

THE AUTHORS

Richard L. Antoine is president of the National Academy of Human Resources and a consultant on talent management and CEO/senior management succession planning working with CEOs and CHROs. Prior to this he held a number of line positions at Procter & Gamble during a thirty-nine-year career, the last eleven of them as the global HR officer reporting to the CEO.

He has a degree in chemical engineering from the University of Wisconsin and an M.B.A. from the University of Chicago. He has served on many nonprofit and university boards and is currently the vice chair of the University of Wisconsin Foundation and a member of the Human Resource Policy Institute Advisory Board.

James Bagley has been with Russell Reynolds Associates for nearly twenty-five years and has held key leadership roles within the firm. He is currently the global leader of the firm's corporate officers sector, which works with clients across all industries, including industrial, consumer, technology, financial services, health care, and executive assessment. Bagley previously founded and led the firm's HR practice and co-managed the New York office.

Prior to rejoining Russell Reynolds Associates in 1998, Bagley was senior vice president of human resources at MasterCard International, where he had global responsibility for the company's comprehensive HR activities, including compensation and benefits, staffing, employee relations, and professional learning and development. He was recruited to MasterCard from Russell Reynolds Associates, where he focused on assignments for senior-level HR executives across a broad range of industries. He joined the firm in 1984 as HR director. Earlier, he was a benefits and compensation consultant with Alexander & Alexander Services and worked with State Mutual Life Assurance.

He received his B.A. from Fordham University.

Sid Banwart has had a broad range of successful business experiences during a forty-two-year career with Caterpillar Inc. He served in two joint ventures before being named manager of engineering and quality for a new start-up facility in Monterrey, Mexico, in 1985. Returning to the United States in 1990, he held key positions at plants in Illinois before being named Product Manager with global P&L responsibilities, where his business success led to a position as general manager for Caterpillar's Large Engine Division.

He was appointed a corporate officer in 1997, and served as the responsible officer for four different business functions. As corporate vice president, these roles were chief technology officer, head of the components business, chief information officer, and for the most recent five years, chief HR officer.

In his position as chief HR officer, he was responsible for global HR and Labor Relations, global succession planning, compensation and benefits, public and governmental affairs, Caterpillar University, the Caterpillar Foundation, Global shared services, and a variety of other corporate administrative functions.

In 2007, he was inducted into the National Academy of Human Resources. He also served as a board member at the HR Policy Association in Washington, DC. He is currently an executive advisor with Challenger, Gray and Christmas.

Banwart received a B.S. in engineering from Iowa State University and an M.B.A. from the University of Illinois. His recent board responsibilities include Knox College, the Weitz Company, the Fayette Companies, the Heartland Partnership, and the Peoria Symphony Foundation.

John W. Boudreau, professor of management and organization at the Marshall School of Business at the University of Southern California, is recognized for breakthrough research on human capital, talent, and sustainable competitive advantage. His large-scale and focused field research studies the future of the global HR profession, HR measurement and analytics, decision-based HR, executive mobility, HR information systems, and organizational staffing and development. He has published more than fifty books and articles, and his research has been featured in *Harvard Business Review*, the *Wall Street Journal*, *Fortune*, and *Business Week*. Boudreau serves as research director for Marshall's Center for Effective Organizations. He advises numerous organizations, including early-stage companies, global corporations, government agencies, and nonprofit organizations.

Ken Carrig is the former executive vice president of human resources for Comcast Cable, where he was responsible for all people-related functions. He has been recognized as one of the top HR professionals in his field and brought extensive experience to Comcast.

He came to Comcast in 2009 from Sysco Corporation, which he served as executive vice president and chief administration officer. Before joining Sysco, he was global human capital leader for Andersen Consulting/Accenture. Prior to that, he was vice president of global human resources for Continental Airlines, where he was the HR lead for a successful turnaround of the airline during the mid- to late 1990s. Before this, he held multiple HR positions with PepsiCo.

Carrig is coauthor, with Patrick M. Wright, of *Building Profits Through Building People* (2006).

A graduate of Cornell University with a B.S. in labor economics, Carrig serves on the advisory board of Cornell University's Center for Advanced Human Resource Studies. He was elected a National Academy of Human Resources fellow in 2004 and in 2010 received the Distinguished HR Executive Award from the Academy of Management.

L. Kevin Cox is the executive vice president of human resources at the American Express Company. He is the chief architect of the company's human capital plan and related strategies for American Express. He is a member of the American Express Operating Committee, which develops the strategic direction for American Express and determines policies affecting the company overall.

Under Cox's leadership, American Express has been recognized globally as a top place to work. Awards include *Fortune Magazine*'s America's Most Admired Companies, 100 Best Companies to Work For, and Top Companies for Leaders; *Business Week*'s World's Most Innovative Companies; and DiversityInc's Top 50 Companies for Diversity. American Express is also recognized with awards in India, Hong Kong, Malaysia, Argentina, Japan, China, Italy, Poland, Sweden, and the United Kingdom.

Cox has been a leader in human resources for more than two decades, serving in a variety of specialist and generalist roles. His HR expertise lies in the fields of organizational effectiveness, executive compensation, and driving large-scale complex change.

He joined American Express in 2005, after sixteen years at Pepsi-Cola and the Pepsi Bottling Group. He is a former member of the board of directors of Virgin Mobile USA and served as a member of both the audit and compensation committees. He is also a member and the former chairman of the board of directors at Ability Beyond Disability, a rehabilitation institute located in Brookfield, Connecticut.

Cox is involved in a number of professional HR organizations. He serves as chairman of the Advisory Board at Cornell University's Center for Advanced Human Resources Strategy; member of the board of directors of the HR Policy Association; member of the advisory board of Cowdrick; and member of Hewitt's Human Capital Advisory Board. In 2008, the Corporate Leadership Council presented him with its Member of the Year Award. In 2009, the National Academy of Human Resources recognized him by inducting him as a fellow.

Cox is a frequent speaker on strategy, building organizational capability, and increasing the role and influence of human resources in global businesses. Kevin holds a master's of labor and industrial relations from Michigan State University and a bachelor's of arts from Marshall University.

Michael L. "Mike" Davis is senior vice president, global human resources, with responsibility for all HR functions at General Mills. Previously he was vice president, human resources, U.S. retail and corporate, for three years, and prior to that served for nine years as vice president of compensation and benefits. Before joining

General Mills, he worked for fifteen years as a compensation consultant with Towers Perrin. When he left Towers Perrin in 1996, he was the firm's worldwide practice leader for executive compensation.

Davis is a frequent speaker and author on executive and director compensation and benefits issues. He has served on four National Association of Corporate Director Blue Ribbon Commissions on the Compensation Committee, Director and CEO Performance Evaluation, Director Compensation, and Director Professionalism. He has been interviewed or quoted in *Fortune, Business Week, Newsweek, Time,* the *Wall Street Journal,* and the *New York Times* on various resource matters.

He has spoken on executive and director compensation issues at many HR, legal, financial, and corporate governance conferences, and has lectured on these topics at Harvard, University of Chicago, Columbia, Dartmouth, University of Southern California, Cornell, and University of Minnesota business schools. In 2004, Davis was series editor for the newly published *Executive Compensation: The Professional's Guide to Current Issues and Practices.* Davis is also an adjunct professor in the graduate HR program at the Carlson School of Management at the University of Minnesota.

Davis is on the board and is the vice chairman of the Employee Benefits Research Institute, is a board member of the Human Resource Policy Association, and is a board member of the National Committee for Quality Assurance (in health care). He is a member of the Institute of Medicine Roundtable on Health Literacy, a current board member and former board chair of the National Business Group on Health, and has served on the board and has been board chair of WorldatWork.

Davis has two B.S. degrees from Purdue University in industrial management and computer science and an M.B.A. from the University of Chicago. He is also a Certified Public Accountant.

Ursula O. Fairbairn has been chief executive officer and president of Fairbairn Group LLC since April 2005. She served as head of human resources and executive vice president of human resources and quality at American Express Company from 1996 to 2005. Prior to joining American Express, she served as senior vice president of human resources of Union Pacific

Corporation. From 1990 to November 1996 and prior to that, she held numerous marketing and human resource positions at IBM Corporation.

Fairbairn currently serves as a director of Air Products and Chemicals, VF Corp., and Sunoco, Inc. She has previously served on the boards of Centex, Circuit City, Armstrong World Industries, General Signal, and Menasha.

Fairbairn holds a bachelor's degree in mathematics from Upsala College and received a master's degree from Harvard's Graduate School of Education.

Ellie Filler is a partner and the head of the European HR practice for Heidrick & Struggles. She specializes in assignments covering senior management positions in the life sciences sector, including research and development, as well as sales and marketing, and is also responsible for the HR functional area. She serves chemical, pharmaceutical, and consumer health care organizations, focusing on international assignments. Prior to joining Heidrick & Struggles, she worked with an international executive search firm based in Sydney, Australia, focusing on assignments across the Asia Pacific region. Previously, she spent over twelve years in HR with some of Australia's largest organizations in financial services, telecommunications and IT, in learning and development, performance and reward, and operational type roles.

Over the years, she has contributed to implementing diversity practices in organizations—work that has been recognized with multiple awards for best practices.

Filler holds a degree in industrial relations (labor law) and political science from New South Wales University and has partly completed her M.B.A. from Heriot-Watt University in Scotland. She is fully accredited as a practitioner and trainer in targeted selection interviewing.

Jay Galbraith is an internationally recognized expert on global organization design. He is the president and founder of Galbraith Management Consultants, an international consulting firm that specializes in solving strategy and organizational design challenges across corporate, business unit, and international levels. His firm also assists with international partnering arrangements, including joint ventures and network-type organizations. Working with companies ranging from small manufacturing firms to large global firms, his theories on gaining a significant competitive advantage through customer-centricity have been implemented by top-level executives throughout the world.

More than forty years of research and practical applications give Dr. Galbraith a breadth of experience that few, if any, management consultants can claim. His thorough understanding of the fast-changing world of global competition is exactly what today's companies need in order to stay ahead of their competitors. As the author of numerous publications, including more than a dozen books and a long list of research papers, Galbraith is regularly asked for his expert opinion by the media, including *BusinessWeek*, the *Wall Street Journal*, *Fortune*, the *Economist*, and the *Financial Times*.

Galbraith is an affiliated research scientist at the Center for Effective Organizations at the University of Southern California and professor emeritus at the International Institute for Management Development (IMD) in Lausanne, Switzerland. He has previously served as a business school professor on the faculty of the Wharton School at the University of Pennsylvania and the Sloan School of Management at Massachusetts Technical Institute (MIT).

Mirian M. Graddick-Weir is executive vice president, human resources, with responsibility for all HR aspects for Merck's over 100,000 colleagues worldwide. She joined Merck in 2006 from AT&T, where she was executive vice president of human resources and employee communications. Prior to that role, she held numerous positions at AT&T, including chief human resources officer for the Consumer Services Company, vice president of human resources for business effectiveness, and vice president of human resources for multimedia products and services. She also led a major line operations team where she supported over twelve thousand customer sales and service representatives in the Consumer Communications Services Division.

Among her many awards, Graddick-Weir received the Distinguished Psychologist in Management award in 2003, the HR Executive of the Year in 2001, and the AT&T Catherine B. Cleary

Woman of the Year in 1990. In 2009, she was named one of *Black Enterprise* magazine's 100 Most Powerful Corporate Executives in America. In 2010, she was named one of *Black Health* magazine's 25 Most Influential African Americans in Healthcare, Medicine, Pharmaceuticals & Health Foods Industries. *Black Enterprise* magazine also named her to its 75 Most Powerful Women in Business and 100 Most Powerful Executives in Corporate America lists.

She is a member of the board of the Harleysville Group Insurance Company, Jersey Battered Women's Services, Human Resources Policy Association, Cornell Center for Advanced Human Resource Studies, and the Personnel Roundtable. She is also a National Academy of Human Resources fellow.

She earned a bachelor's degree in psychology from Hampton University, a master's degree in industrial/organizational psychology from Penn State, and a Ph.D. in industrial/organizational psychology from Penn State.

Amy Kates is managing partner with Kates Kesler, a organization design firm based in New York City. She works with leaders and their teams to assess organizational issues, reshape structures and processes, and build depth of management capability. She is a skilled diagnostician and designer and helps her clients to understand organizational options and their implications and to make sound decisions.

In addition to her consulting work, she teaches organization design in the MBA program at the Executive School of Business in Denmark through Cornell University. Kates is also an editor of the journal *People & Strategy*.

Kates is the co-author, with Greg Kesler, of *Leading Organization Design: How to Make Organization Design Decisions to Drive the Results You Want* (Jossey-Bass, 2010). She is also the coauthor with Jay Galbraith of *Designing Your Organization: Using the Star Model to Solve Five Critical Design Challenges* (Jossey-Bass, 2007) and with Jay Galbraith and Diane Downey of *Designing Dynamic Organizations: A Hands-On Guide for Leaders at All Levels* (Amacom, 2002). She has published numerous articles and book chapters on the topics of organization design and talent management including "The Challenges of General Manager Transitions" in *Filling the Management*

Pipeline and "Matrix Structures and Virtual Collaboration" in *The Handbook of High-Performance Virtual Teams.*

Her article, "(Re)Designing the HR Organization," was awarded the 2007 HRPS Walker Prize. Her ideas on emerging models for human resources have been used by leading companies around the world as the basis for the design of their HR functions.

Pamela O. Kimmet is senior vice president, human resources, for Coca-Cola Enterprises (CCE). With more than twenty-five years of leadership experience in human resources, she is responsible for the development and implementation of global HR initiatives for CCE's seventy-three thousand employees.

Prior to joining CCE, Kimmet was senior managing director and global head of human resources at Bear, Stearns & Co. From 2001 to 2006, she served as senior vice president, human resources, for Lucent Technologies. She was responsible for developing and implementing a range of initiatives focused on the company's global talent strategy, including staffing, development, and reward programs. At Lucent, Kimmet also held the role of vice president of compensation, benefits, and health services. Before joining Lucent, she held positions at Citigroup and General Motors.

Kimmet serves on the board for Cornell University's Center for Advanced Human Resources Study and the National Business Group on Health and is a member of the Personnel Roundtable. She is a former member of the Conference Board's Executive Compensation Council and Rutgers University's Board for the Center for Human Resources Strategy and the school's Executive Master's in Human Resources Leadership Board.

She holds a B.S. in industrial and labor relations from Cornell University and received an M.B.A. from Michigan State University.

Edward E. Lawler III is Distinguished Professor of Business and director of the Center for Effective Organizations in the Marshall School of Business at the University of Southern California. He joined USC in 1978 and during 1979 founded and became director of the university's Center for Effective Organizations. He has consulted with over one hundred organizations on employee involvement, organizational change, and compensation and has been honored as a top contributor to the fields of organizational development, organizational behavior, corporate governance, and human resource management. The author of over 350 articles and 43 books, his articles have appeared in leading academic journals, as well as *Fortune* and *Harvard Business Review,* and leading newspapers, including *USA Today* and the *Financial Times.* His most recent books are *Rewarding Excellence* (2000), *Corporate Boards: New Strategies for Adding Value at the Top* (2001), *Organizing for High Performance* (2001), *Treat People Right* (2003), *Human Resources Business Process Outsourcing* (2004), *Built to Change* (2006), *America at Work* (2006), *The New American Workplace* (2006), *Talent: Making People Your Competitive Advantage* (2008), and *Achieving Excellence in HR Management: An Assessment of Human Resource Organizations* (2009).

J. Randall "Randy" MacDonald joined IBM in 2000 as senior vice president of human resources. He is responsible for the global HR practices, policies, and operations of the organization and reports to chairman, president, and chief executive officer Sam Palmisano. Prior to joining IBM, MacDonald was the executive vice president of human resources and administration for GTE (now Verizon Communications). Before joining GTE, he held HR positions at Ingersoll-Rand Company and Sterling Drug.

In 2009, MacDonald received the Distinguished Human Resources Executive Award from the Academy of Management for his significant contributions to the science and practice of human resources, including HR-related research and education. He is the first executive to receive this award twice. Among many other awards, MacDonald was named *Human Resource Executive* magazine's HR Executive of the Year in 2008.

He is a member and past chair of Cornell University's Center for Advanced Human Resources Study and a past chair of the Personnel Roundtable. He is also a member of the HR Policy Association, which he serves as chairman of its board of directors.

In 1998, MacDonald was named a fellow of the National Academy of Human Resources, the HR profession's highest honor for outstanding achievement. He was elected to the academy's board of directors in 2000 and serves as its vice chair. He also was a member of the President's Advisory Commission on Consumer Protection and Quality in the Health Care Industry.

MacDonald has a bachelor's degree from St. Francis University; he received the St. Francis University Distinguished Alumni in Business Award in 1999 and was a trustee of the institution. MacDonald also serves as a trustee of Bucknell University and as vice chairman of the board. He is a member of the board of managers of Delphi Corporation and a former member of the board of directors of Covance.

Paul McKinnon is head of human resources at Citi Corporate Center, which he joined in 2008 with twenty-five years of experience in HR management, consulting, and education. He is responsible for all HR for Citigroup and all talent management programs. Prior to this assignment, he was head of talent management for Citigroup.

Until early 2007, McKinnon was senior vice president of the Human Resources Group for Dell, with responsibility for all aspects of the function. During his ten years with Dell, he was instrumental in the company's Winning Culture initiative, which included all Dell's training and development activities, winning external and internal awards, including the coveted award from the U.S. Department of Labor for secretary's equal opportunity programs. He also was chairman of the Dell Foundation.

During the twelve years before that, McKinnon developed a leadership development practice at three separate management consulting firms: McKinnon Consulting, Novations, and Harbridge House. Previously he was an assistant professor at the Darden Graduate School of Business at the University of Virginia, where he taught organizational behavior.

McKinnon has served on the board of directors of the HR Policy Association and the National Urban League. He was inducted as a fellow into the National Academy of Human Resources in 2002.

He has a bachelor's degree in history and a master's degree in organizational behavior from Brigham Young University, and a Ph.D. in organizational studies from the Sloan School of Management at MIT.

Hugh Mitchell was appointed HR director of Shell in 2005. He became a member of the executive committee in October 2007 and chief HR and corporate officer of Royal Dutch Shell in 2009. He is responsible for all aspects of HR strategy, planning, and support in Shell. He also has responsibility for internal and external communications, real estate, health, global security, and Shell Aircraft. He is as well regional director for sub-Saharan Africa.

Mitchell graduated from Edinburgh University with an M.A. in modern history in 1979. Later that year he joined Shell and over three decades with the company has held a variety of HR and business roles in the United Kingdom, the Netherlands, and Brunei.

Mitchell is a member of the board for the Center for Advanced Human Resources at Cornell University and a foundation board member of IMD business school in Lausanne, Switzerland. He was appointed a fellow of the National Academy of Human Resources in the United States in 2009.

Sandy Ogg has been the CHRO of Unilever since February 2005. He started his career in Unilever in January 2003 as senior vice president of human resources in the Foods Division.

Prior to Unilever Ogg worked for Motorola in the change management/organization effectiveness role. He was responsible for leadership, learning, and performance in the division. Before Motorola, he spent fifteen years as a leadership development and change management consultant for clients that included Johnson & Johnson, PepsiCo, General Electric, and Motorola. He also held positions of president at Centre for Leadership Studies, managing director of Dove Associates, and founder of Via Consulting Group.

Ogg started his professional life as a line officer for the U.S. Coast Guard. He was part of search and rescue missions and became a highly decorated commanding officer.

Ogg is an active member in several professional HR organizations, including HR50, Human Resources Roundtable, and FrED (Future of Executive Development), where he is a frequent contributor to its lectures and seminar series. In support of Unilever's corporate social responsibility agenda, Ogg serves as vice chairman of the European Academy for Business in Society, an organization that works in cooperation with the European Union, key global businesses, and business schools.

Ogg has a B.S. in mathematics from the U.S. Coast Guard Academy, an M.B.A. from the James L. Kellogg School of Management at Northwestern University, and an M.A. in education and human development from George Washington University.

David A. Pace is currently executive vice president and chief resource officer for OSI Restaurant Partners, Inc. where he leads teams responsible for human resource management as well as real estate and development. Before, Pace had been a management consultant, entrepreneur, and not-for-profit leader. He was previously CHRO for Starbucks Coffee Company and YUM Brands International, having lived overseas for six years in both London and Nicosia, Cyprus. He is an adjunct faculty member in Southern Methodist University's Cox Graduate School of Business and has been cited in publications including the *Wall Street Journal, Fortune Magazine,* and the *Dallas Morning News.* Pace is currently a board member of Up2US, a rapidly expanding national nonprofit focused on improving the environment for sports-based youth development, which was recently recognized by the White House and Department of Education for its success in launching Coach Across America. Pace has previously served on the boards of Cornell's Center for Human Resource Studies, University of Southern California's Center for Effective Organizations, and the Human Resource Policy Association.

Bill Rosner recently retired as CHRO for the PNC Financial Services Group. Prior to joining PNC in this position in 1995, he worked as the HR director for various businesses of Chase Manhattan Bank. In 1989, he was named HR executive for the Europe, Africa, and Middle East area, located in London, and a senior vice president in 1991. Rosner transferred to New York in 1993 and assumed responsibility for managing Chase's efforts to become an employer of choice.

Rosner is currently engaged in executive coaching and HR consulting and works with New Directions as a managing director focusing on the portfolio life product. He has written on preparing senior staff for the CHRO role and working with the board of directors. He serves on the board of directors for the Boy Scouts of America and the Kellogg Alumni Council at Northwestern University. He also serves on the advisory board for Soundboard Review Services. He recently finished his term on the advisory board for the Center for Advanced Human Resources Studies at Cornell. Rosner is also a graduate of the Directors' Consortium.

Rosner received his bachelor of science degree in industrial engineering from Northwestern University and master of business administration in organizational behavior and finance from Northwestern's Kellogg School.

Eva Sage-Gavin is executive vice president, global human resources and corporate affairs, at Gap Inc. In her role as chief people officer, she sets strategy for the company's communications, government, and public affairs, and HR operations worldwide. Her responsibilities include staffing, diversity, rewards, recognition, employee benefits, learning and development, strategic change, social responsibility, government relations, public affairs, and internal and external communications.

Prior to joining Gap Inc. in 2003, she worked at Sun Microsystems, where she was senior vice president of human resources, and at Disney Consumer Products, a division of the Walt Disney Company, where she also was senior vice president, human resources. She has served in various other senior HR leadership positions for the PepsiCo Corporation, including its Taco Bell division, and for Xerox Corporation.

In 2005, Sage-Gavin was recognized as one of the twenty-five most influential and prominent women leading HR organizations today. In 2006, she received the distinguished honor of fellow from the National Academy of Human Resources in recognition of her lifelong professional achievements in the field of human resources.

A supporter of several educational and nonprofit organizations, Sage-Gavin is active in her community and serves on a number of industry group boards, including the Cornell Center for Advanced Human Resources Studies Board, the President's Council of Cornell Women, the University of Southern California's Center for Effective Organizations, and the Human Resource Policy Association, where she chairs the Education and Training committee. She holds a bachelor's degree in industrial and labor relations from Cornell University.

Elizabeth "Libby" Sartain is now an active business advisor and board member. As CHRO of both Yahoo! Inc. and Southwest Airlines, she led significant business transformation initiatives as a member of executive leadership teams and guided global HR efforts focusing on attracting, retaining, and developing employees. Her focus has been growth companies, where she developed employment brand strategies that helped increase the workforce exponentially while establishing company reputation as a leading employer of choice. She serves on the boards of directors of Peet's Coffee & Tea and Manpower and advises several start-ups and mature organizations on HR, employer branding, and talent management.

Sartain served as chairman of the board of the Society for Human Resource Management in 2001 and was named a fellow of the National Academy of Human Resources in 1998. *Human Resources Executive* named her one of the twenty-five most powerful women in HR in 2005. She holds an M.B.A. from the University of North Texas and a B.B.A. from Southern Methodist University.

Sartain has coauthored *HR from the Heart: Inspiring Stories and Strategies for Building the People Side of Great Business; Brand from the Inside: Eight Essentials to Connect Your Employees to Your Business;* and *Brand for Talent: Eight Essentials to Make Your Talent as Famous as Your Brand.* She is a frequent speaker and is often quoted as a thought leader in human resources.

Laurie Siegel is senior vice president of human resources and internal communications for Tyco International. In this role, she has global responsibility for leading the company's strategies in the areas of leadership development, organizational effectiveness, compensation and benefits, staffing, diversity, learning, HR systems and processes, and internal communications.

Siegel joined Tyco in January 2003 after eight years at Honeywell International, where she served in various roles in the HR area. During her tenure at Honeywell, she held leadership positions in the aerospace division, the specialty materials division, and at the corporate headquarters. Prior to joining Honeywell,

Siegel was director of global compensation at Avon Products and a principal at Strategic Compensation Associates.

Siegel holds a bachelor's degree in general studies from the University of Michigan and received a master's degree in business administration as well as a master's degree in city planning from Harvard University.

Siegel is a member of the Personnel Roundtable and is on the advisory boards of the Cornell Center for Advanced Human Resource Studies and the Rutgers Business School. She also serves on the board of directors and chairs the compensation committee for CenturyLink, a leading provider of voice, broadband, and video communication services.

In 2008, Siegel was named a fellow of the National Academy of Human Resources, the profession's highest honor for outstanding achievement.

Mark Stewart is a senior consultant at Management and Personnel Systems where he develops and delivers assessment centers for companies in the oil and gas industry. He conducts psychological assessments for positions ranging from the professional to senior executive. For more than ten years, he has worked as an internal or external consultant for businesses in a variety of industries. He formerly headed up the assessment and development group for Global Industries, an international offshore construction company headquartered in Houston. Among other accomplishments, he and his team created a succession management process for the top positions in the corporation and a leadership development program for the Americas and Asia Pacific targeting high-potential employees, and he designed and implemented the company's first global, corporate-wide employee survey. He currently serves as an advisor and content contributor for the Organization Development panel of the Society for Human Resource Management.

Charles G. Tharp is the executive vice president for policy of the Center on Executive Compensation. In that role, he is responsible for setting overall policy positions and research initiatives undertaken by the center and representing the center in public forums.

Tharp has over twenty-five years of corporate experience, including key HR positions with General Electric, PepsiCo, Pillsbury, CIGNA, and Bristol-Myers Squibb, where he served as senior vice president of human resources. Most recently Tharp served as the interim executive vice president of human resources for Saks, Incorporated. He has also served as an executive compensation consultant for the global consulting firm Towers Perrin. Tharp has held teaching appointments at Cornell University and Rutgers University and has taught graduate-level courses in executive compensation and HR leadership. He is also a fellow and research scholar at Boston University's Human Resources Policy Institute.

Tharp holds a Ph.D. in labor and industrial relations from Michigan State University, a J.D. from the Quinnipiac School of Law, an M.A. in economics from Wayne State University, and a B.A. from Hope College. In 1998 Tharp was elected a fellow of the National Academy of Human Resources. He previously served as president of the academy, is currently a member of its board of directors, and has served as a past vice chairman of the board of directors of HR Policy Association.

Dave Ulrich is a professor of business at the Ross School of Business, University of Michigan, and cofounder of The RBL Group. He has written fifteen books covering topics in HR and leadership, is currently on the board of directors for Herman Miller, is a Fellow in the National Academy of Human Resources, and is on the board of trustees of Southern Virginia University.

Ulrich emphasizes defining organizations through the capabilities they possess. His work has helped define and shape key capabilities such as change, learning, collaboration, accountability, talent, service, innovation, and efficiency. The outcomes of leadership and HR are the capabilities that an organization possesses that deliver value to customers, investors, and communities.

Although he has been involved in large-scale research projects, most of his writing is characterized by synthesizing complex ideas into frameworks and tools that executives can use. He is a well-traveled speaker, working with groups of all sizes in which he is known for engaging the participants and helping to translate the ideas into actions that work for them. His motto is that good teaching is not what he knows but how his knowledge helps participants do what they do better.

Ulrich has been ranked the number one management educator and guru by *BusinessWeek*, selected by *Fast Company* as one of the ten most innovative and creative leaders, named the most influential person in HR by *HR Magazine* for three years, and has been on the World's Top 50 Business Thinkers List since 2007. He is also the 2010 recipient of the Kirk Englehardt Exemplary Business Ethics Award.

Elease E. Wright is the senior vice president, HR, for Aetna Inc. In this role, she is responsible for the development of all HR strategies, and the delivery of HR services and programs.

Ms. Wright has specialized in HR for more than twenty years. During that time, she has held many key positions, including head of HR reengineering implementation and head of HR finance and administration. She has also served in senior positions in the education, pension, and employee relations departments.

An expert in strategic education models, staffing, employee relations, reengineering, and organizational and leadership development, Ms. Wright has led many critical and successful human resources initiatives. Recently, she has managed the transformation of HR into a strategic business partner, the development and launch of a comprehensive and leading-edge benefits strategy and creation of a comprehensive talent management system.

Ms. Wright's community involvement includes leadership roles for her alma mater, the University of Connecticut, for which she serves both on the board of advisors for the UConn School of Business and the board of directors for the UConn Foundation. She also serves on the board of directors for HR Policy Association, advisory board for Cornell University's Center for Advanced Human Resource Studies, and is past president of the Hartford Region YWCA board of directors. In addition, she serves on the board of directors for the Bushnell, Connecticut's premier performing arts center.

She is a member of the Executive Leadership Council, was named one of *Savoy Professional* Magazine's "Top 100 Most Influential Blacks in Corporate America," one of the Top 25 Most

Influential Black Women in Business, and one of Black Enterprise's Top 50 Blacks in Corporate America. She was also installed in the National Academy of Human Resources (NAHR) 2007 Class of Fellows and inducted into the UConn School of Business Hall of Fame in 2008.

Ms. Wright holds a Bachelor of Science degree in Education from the University of Connecticut.

Patrick M. Wright is the William J. Conaty GE Professor of Strategic Human Resources in the School of ILR at Cornell University. He teaches and conducts research in the area of strategic HR management, with a particular focus on how HR practices, the HR function, and how HR leaders can affect firm performance.

He has recently conducted two large-scale surveys of CHROs in the United States and for the past three years he has designed and led an executive program to develop future CHRO talent. He has more than sixty refereed publications, more than thirty book chapters, and has coauthored or coedited more than fifteen books and volumes.

He sits on seven journal editorial boards and has served on the board of directors for Human Resource Planning Society, World at Work, and the Society for Human Resource Foundation. He has served as a Distinguished Academic Visitor for the Ministry of Manpower in Singapore, as a Senior Research Fellow in Taiwan, and currently holds a secondary position at Tilburg University in the Netherlands as a Senior Research Fellow.

Ian Ziskin is president of Executive Excellence Group LLC, a consulting firm he founded following a twenty-eight-year career as a business executive. Executive Excellence Group builds individual and organizational credibility through human capital strategy, leadership and talent development, and organizational transformation. His global leadership experience includes serving in CHRO and other senior roles with three Fortune 100 corporations: Northrop Grumman, Qwest Communications, and TRW.

Ziskin's writings and commentaries have been featured in a wide variety of books and professional journals. He speaks regularly at universities, associations, and companies. He is a current and past member of multiple boards and executive committees, including vice chairman, HR Policy Association; vice chairman, University of Southern California Marshall School of Business; executive committee and program chair, Personnel Round Table; USC Center for Effective Organizations; Cornell University Center for Advanced Human Resource Studies; HR50; and CHRO/Board Academy.

He has a master's degree in industrial and labor relations from Cornell University, where he held a research and teaching assistantship based on scholastic achievement, and a bachelor of science degree in management from Binghamton University.

In 2007, he was elected a fellow of the National Academy of Human Resources, considered to be the highest honor in the HR profession.

CHAPTER ONE

THE EVOLVING CHIEF HUMAN RESOURCE OFFICER ROLE

Patrick M. Wright, Paul McKinnon, Richard L. Antoine, Elizabeth "Libby" Sartain, John W. Boudreau, David A. Pace

The chief human resource officer (CHRO) role has become one of the most important roles on the executive leadership team. Jack Welch, in his book *Winning* (2005), states of the CHRO role, "Without a doubt, the head of HR should be the second most important person in any organization. From the point of view of the CEO, the director of HR should be at least equal to the CFO" (pp. 99–100).

This has by no means always been the case. The HR function in general and the CHRO (albeit previously the director of personnel), traditionally played a largely administrative role in most organizations. However, over the past thirty years, the HR function, and especially the head of the function, has been elevated. With this increased status has comes increased pressure.

This chapter examines the trends that have led to the current state of the CHRO role and explores the current pressures that provide opportunities and challenges for those who hold the role. It also presents a guide to the rest of the book. Thus, we will first describe the evolution of HR from the 1980s to now, noting some of the major trends and events that have affected the profession

and the CHRO role. Then we will provide an overview of the rest
of the book.

TRENDS IN HR

THE 1980S: HR GOES STRATEGIC!

The 1980s saw the emergence of the concept of strategic HR.
Right around the turn of the decade, James Walker (1980) revised
his book on human resource planning in which he noted that one
consideration in developing an HR plan was the strategy of the
business. However, at that time, little knowledge of strategy existed
in the HR community (even in the general manager community,
strategy had only recently become a hot topic).

Over the course of that decade, the HR profession sought
to align its activities with strategy, but it did so largely in a
siloed manner. In fact, in one of the foundational books on
aligning HR with strategy, Fombrum, Tichy, and Devanna (1984)
organized the chapters around such concepts as strategic staffing,
the appraisal system as a strategic control, and the strategic design
of reward systems. This approach implicitly assumed that each
area of HR should align itself around the strategy of the business
and that the role of the CHRO was to ensure that this vertical
fit existed and to coordinate across these areas to ensure their
activities did not conflict with one another, thus creating the
horizontal fit.

THE 1990S: HR AT THE TABLE

Whereas the 1980s saw HR leaders talking about the need to be
"at the table" (meaning part of the executive leadership team
with responsibility for developing strategy), in the 1990s HR leaders increasingly achieved this position. Dave Ulrich's book *Human
Resource Champions* (1996) defined the major paradigm that would
guide most HR professional thinking during the decade. In
particular, the role of strategic partner gained unprecedented
popularity. Although this was not necessarily new in terms of
defining the activities through which HR leaders could work with
business leaders for the success of the enterprise, labeling the

role caught the attention of those within and outside HR. In addition, Ulrich described a basic HR operating model structure that consisted of the business partners (field generalists), centers of expertise (such as functional specialists from the various HR silos), and shared services (the more transactional aspects of HR).

Although this model provided the foundation on which CHROs could build their organizations, the latter part of the decade saw the emergence of the war for talent, which would become the springboard for the increasing importance of the HR organization, and the CHRO more specifically. Michaels, Handfield-Jones, and Axelrod's book, *The War for Talent* (2001), suggested that CHROs would become as important as chief financial officers to the extent that they could forge a link between business strategy and talent, act as the thought leader in understanding what it takes to attract great talent, facilitate the talent review and action plans, and become the architect of the development strategy for the top fifty to one hundred HR managers. Almost prophetically, they stated, "Today many more CFOs than HR leaders are on division management teams or corporate executive committees. Now that talent is so crucial to competitive success, look for that to change" (p. 33).

THE 2000s: FAILINGS FORWARD

While the previous two decades saw the CHRO role increase in visibility and importance for competitive reasons, the 2000s saw its visibility and importance increase because of a number of organizational failings. In the early 2000s, the dot-com bubble burst, and this was quickly followed by a rash of corporate scandals. No other company better exemplifies this transformation than Enron. In the late 1990s, Ken Lay, chairman and CEO of Enron, had stated, "The only thing that differentiates Enron from our competitors is our people, our talent" (quoted in Michaels, Handfield-Jones, and Axelrod, 2001, p. 2). By the mid-2000s, Enron was in bankruptcy, and Lay, his CEO successor, Jeff Skilling, and CFO Andrew Fastow had all been indicted and convicted. Company scandals at Enron, MCI-WorldCom, Qwest, and Adelphia Communications led to increasing regulatory pressure on companies' financial reporting requirements, particularly as exemplified by the Sarbanes-Oxley Act. This legislation, enacted in 2002, increased the public financial reporting requirements, created personal criminal liabilities for misreporting, and increased the required board governance.

Almost like a bookend, a second set of scandals rocked the business world at the end of the decade with the financial crisis spurred by the collapse of the subprime mortgage market. Massive government bailouts of the financial and auto companies increased government oversight over many aspects of firm operations, not the least of which was executive pay. This government interventionism was mirrored, and to some extent spurred, by a public distrust of large institutions in general and corporate executives in particular. In addition to the existing TARP (Troubled Assets Relief Program) regulations, the Dodd-Frank Financial Reform and Consumer Protection Act of 2010 imposed additional regulation of the financial industry.

Both of these traumatic events have further vaulted the CHRO role into the spotlight. The early company scandals resulted in increased board oversight of the succession, compensation, and performance management of senior executives. The more recent scandals have increasingly focused board attention on CEO pay and risk assessment. Consequently, the time that CHROs spend with board members has increased, and the critical role they play has amplified the risk inherent in their role. Those who effectively manage this new role can achieve new heights in status and impact; those who fail to do so will quickly be asked to leave the company.

SUMMARY

This recap highlights some of the major trends and events that underlay the changing role of the CHRO. Although these events existed at discrete points in time, their impact endures. They have been responsible for creating the requirements for today's CHRO. Although they certainly enlarged the responsibilities, visibility, and impact of the role, they also created a set of pressures that make the role both challenging and difficult. We next discuss these pressures, which serve as the organizing framework for this book.

PRESSURES ON TODAY'S CHRO

As the CHRO role has evolved, the expectations and demands on it have risen dramatically. Today CHROs face five general pressures that make the job both critical and exceedingly difficult. The first two deal with pressures from outside the organization, and the last three emanate from within the firm. These are depicted in Figure 1.1.

First, the competitive pressures are the forces that have changed the competitive landscape over the past few decades. Globalization has resulted in an increasing number of competitors from all over the globe, each with its own unique strength—for example, low-cost labor, highly innovative talent, greater local knowledge, or something else. Globalization also has increased cost competition, which results in CHROs' having to find ways to increase productivity for their firms. Whereas cost competition

FIGURE 1.1. PRESSURES ON THE CHRO

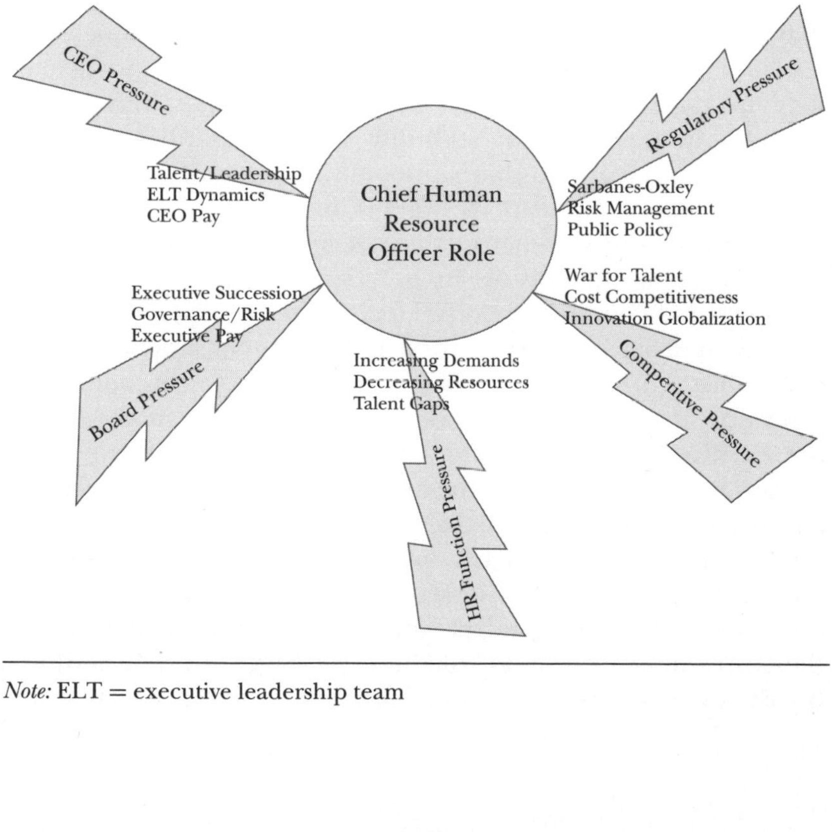

Note: ELT = executive leadership team

requires getting cost out of the organization, building a growing revenue stream requires a focus on innovation. Finally, all of these pressures play a part in the development of a global war for talent.

Second, regulatory pressures describe the increasingly hostile regulatory environment that continues to have an impact on firms, particularly in the United States. In the early 2000s, Sarbanes-Oxley increased the reporting and governance requirements for firms. The financial meltdown of 2008–2009 placed an increased emphasis on risk management from both governmental watchdog agencies and shareholder groups. This also resulted in a more activist public policy as the U.S. Congress, the executive branch, and the regulatory agencies felt a need to exert greater control over corporate decision making in order to avoid another crisis. Finally, the health care reform act passed in 2010 will increase government regulation of a number of aspects of health insurance and health care delivery.

Third, one of the greatest pressure sources within the firm is the CEO. As the CHRO role has grown in importance, these officers increasingly interact with the CEO and do so in a way that is unique relative to some of their C-suite colleagues. The war for talent has caught the attention of most CEOs today, and they are demanding that the CHRO ensure that the company succeeds in this area. In addition, when a number of highly intelligent and highly ambitious people are put together, as on the executive leadership team, conflict is unavoidable. Thus, CHROs face the pressure to react to these team dynamics and manage them in a way that results in functional decision making and interpersonal communications. Finally, after a number of leaders in the financial industry earned large compensation packages right before the industry's collapse, executive pay has come to the forefront of public discussions. Certainly CEOs may pressure the CHRO to ensure that the CEO pay package is competitive, but given the subjectivity of the meaning of *competitive,* this creates another pressure for the CHRO.

Fourth, on the other side of the table is pressure from the board of directors. In particular, just as many CEOs and other senior executives want to maximize their pay packages, boards have increasing pressure to hold those packages down. In addition, boards are increasingly examined regarding their governance and risk management roles in representing shareholders. Finally, after a number of high-profile CEO firings, the importance of executive succession has risen dramatically. In all these areas, the CHRO must react to the pressures exerted by the board.

Finally, we cannot forget that at least externally, people view the CHRO as the leader of the HR function, and that function is under increasing pressure. First, with organizations increasingly competing on their human capital, the demands on HR have increased, and HR functions must become more adept in the areas of attracting talent, executive succession, leadership development, and virtually all other aspects of HR processes. At the same time that the demands are increasing, the function is being asked to meet these demands with fewer resources. Finally, the CHRO must provide for increasing demands with fewer resources, but do so with a function that exhibits significant talent gaps. Thus, CHROs face the pressure of building the talent of the HR organization while simultaneously raising the organization's game.

Overview of the Book

Given these challenges, CHROs must play multiple roles, and it is those major roles that form the structure of this book. Part One describes the CHRO job from a broad perspective. J. Randall McDonald, CHRO at IBM, opens the part by laying out his learnings over almost forty years in HR. In particular he focuses in Chapter Two on what is required to be successful in terms of delivering results and how to develop a perspective and set of skills to perform in the role effectively. In Chapter Three, Eva Sage-Gavin from Gap Inc. describes what she refers to as the art and science of HR. This is the combination of the science in terms of proven tools and frameworks, as well as the art of knowing intuitively how to handle the variety of situations that CHROs face in their role. Richard Antoine, former CHRO at Procter & Gamble and currently the president of the National Academy of Human Resources, describes in Chapter Four the broad responsibilities of a CHRO. In particular, he points out that the critical areas for a CHRO are to deal with ethics, talent, and courage and coaching. In Chapter Five, Patrick Wright and Mark Stewart present the results of the Cornell/CAHRS Survey of Chief Human Resource

Officers. They identify the seven roles of CHROs, five of which comprise the structure of the remainder of the book.

Part Two merges two of the roles that Wright and Stewart identified in Chapter Five. The strategic advisor to the executive team role entails sharing the people expertise as part of the decision-making process, as well as shaping how the human capital of the firm fits into its strategy. It entails the activities focused specifically on the formulation and implementation of the firm's strategy. Playing the role of talent architect requires that CHROs help the executive team see the importance of talent, identify existing and expected future talent gaps, and come to own the talent agenda. In many ways, these two roles are two sides of the same coin, with the only major difference revolving around whether the focus is exclusively on issues pertaining to the high-potential talent and senior leadership versus the issues with regard to the entire workforce.

Part Two begins with former Caterpillar CHRO Sid Banwart's chapter on the intertwined nature of talent and strategic advising. He describes in Chapter Six the importance of employee engagement to the firm's success and the need to have effective leaders who can build that engagement. L. Kevin Cox, CHRO at American Express, then provides a clear path in Chapter Seven and a set of guidelines for optimizing talent management. John Boudreau builds on these concepts in Chapter Eight. He shows how HR leaders can engage leaders from other disciplines by applying the logic of their proven business models to vital questions about talent and human capital. Michael Davis, CHRO at General Mills, describes in Chapter Nine the important work of CHROs in shaping and maintaining culture. Laurie Siegel, CHRO at Tyco, describes in Chapter Ten the strategic advisor and talent architect roles she had to play when taking over this role after the near bankruptcy of Tyco. Northrup Grumman CHRO Ian Ziskin closes out Part Two with a discussion of the unique role that the CHRO plays in talent and strategy when working for a government contractor.

Part Three addresses the issues that those in the CHRO role discuss only among their own in a dark corner of a secluded, nondisclosed location. Senior leadership teams are made up of highly intelligent, highly ambitious, and highly competitive individuals who are expected to work together. Needless to say, each individual has his or her own personal weaknesses, and the dynamic that emerges when all are thrown together can lead to significant conflicts that CHROs find themselves in the middle of. This role is a broad one and can entail anything from behavioral or performance counseling to being the personal sounding board for the CEO.

David A. Pace, the former CHRO at Starbucks and now the CHRO at OSI Restaurant Partners, describes in Chapter Twelve the challenge that a CHRO may find when the chairman, CEO, and other members of the executive team find their agendas, personal or professional, in conflict. Elease Wright, CHRO at Aetna, has served under five different CEOs, and in Chapter Thirteen, she shares some of the tips she has found over the years in adapting her style to the style of each CEO. Similarly, Pamela Kimmet has served as the CHRO at Lucent and Bear Stearns, and currently serves as the CHRO at Coca Cola Enterprises. In Chapter Fourteen, she also shares her insights to how to adapt one's style and agenda to different CEOs. Elizabeth "Libby" Sartain, former CHRO at both Southwest Airlines and Yahoo! describes in Chapter Fifteen the need for CHROs to identify their personal values and brand. Finally, Patrick Wright and L. Kevin Cox discuss the results of the Cornell/CAHRS CHRO Survey again, this time with regard to how CHROs perceive their CEOs' strengths and weaknesses in relation to HR.

CHROs increasingly find themselves involved in interactions with the board of directors, and this is a role that they have indicated as the one they were least prepared for when entering the CHRO role. In Part Four, the chapter authors provide insight into and guidance for how to play this role effectively. Bill Rosner, recently retired as CHRO at PNC Financial, spent over thirteen years in that role during which he saw the his relationship to the board change significantly. In Chapter Seventeen, he describes some of the highs and lows he experienced as a means of showing what and what not to do. Edward Lawler, in Chapter Eighteen, discusses his research examining the role of the CHRO with the board and provides useful guidance for how to strengthen this link. Approximately half of the time CHROs spend with the board is around executive pay issues. In Chapter Nineteen, former CHRO at Bristol-Myers-Squibb and Saks Fifth Avenue

Charles G. Tharp identifies some of the major issues and challenges emerging around executive pay and provides some suggestions for how to succeed in this area. In Chapter Twenty, Ursula Fairbain, former CHRO at American Express, provides her proven strategies for dealing with board around executive pay.

Part Five describes the critical role that CHROs play in leading and transforming the function to deliver value for the firm. Ken Carrig, former CHRO at Comcast Cable (and former CHRO at Sysco Corporation), describes in Chapter Twenty-One a 100-day plan for entering the CHRO role and devising a strategy to transform the function. In Chapter Twenty-Two, Hugh Mitchell, CHRO at Royal Dutch Shell, describes the challenge in transforming a large, institutionalized HR function to meet the new competitive demands of the energy industry. Mirian Graddick-Weir went from CHRO at AT&T to CHRO at Merck. In Chapter Twenty-Three, she describes how to make an effective transition into a new CHRO role in a new company in a new industry. Amy Kates, John Boudreau, and Jay Galbraith provide some examples of innovative HR structures that are being used by successful companies today in Chapter Twenty-Four. Finally, in Chapter Twenty-Five, Sandy Ogg, CHRO at Unilever, describes how the HR function has supported a changing culture and strategy at Unilever over the past few years.

Part Six moves away from the role-based approach to the CHRO to focus on what CHROs must do and possess in order to be effective, particularly from the CEO's perspective. Dave Ulrich and Ellie Filler discuss in Chapter Twenty-Six the challenges that CEOs face today, and suggest how and what CHROs need to be able to do in order to help their CEO succeed. In Chapter Twenty-Seven, James Bagley of Russell Reynolds shares his insights gained over a career in working with CEOs to help them fill their CHRO roles. He describes the changing nature of the CHRO role as well as what it takes to be successful in that role. In Chapter Twenty-Eight, Patrick Wright and Mark Stewart describe their findings from a number of studies examining the demographic characteristics of CHROs in both the United States and globally. Finally, in Chapter

Twenty-Nine, Patrick Wright reviews the previous chapters to provide insight into the four critical knowledge areas that CHROs need to develop in order to be successful.

The CHRO role has been rapidly expanding and transforming over the past twenty years. No one book could exhaustively cover all the aspects of the CHRO's role, and it cannot do so in a way that might not be outdated ten years from now. Nevertheless, the content of this book is based on up-to-date research on the CHRO role and has been developed by those currently most in touch with what defines effectiveness in the role. We hope that you will find it both enjoyable and informative as you pursue your HR career ambitions.

REFERENCES

Fombrum, C., Tichy, N., & Devanna, A. (1984). *Strategic human resource management.* Hoboken, NJ: Wiley.

Michaels, E., Handfield-Jones, H., & Axelrod, B. (2001). *The war for talent.* Boston: Harvard Business School Press.

Ulrich, D. (1996). *Human resource champions.* Boston: Harvard Business School Press.

Walker, J. (1980). *Human resource planning.* New York: McGraw-Hill.

Welch, J., & Welch, S. (2005). *Winning.* New York: HarperBusiness.

PART ONE

TODAY'S CHIEF HUMAN RESOURCE OFFICER

CHAPTER TWO

PERFORM! DON'T RUN!

J. Randall MacDonald

If you are aiming at a top seat in business, I have a simple-sounding piece of advice: "Perform for the office. Don't run for it!" Although it sounds simple, it is hard to do. This is particularly so in the HR function, where for many years our profession had a reputation for being the kind of place where what we like to call "interpersonal skills" seemed to matter more than consistent, measurable results.

That is no longer the case. Today it is not possible to campaign for the top HR job the way a politician runs for office, trying to be all things to all people or simply taking orders from the business. Successful HR leaders now must have a vision for their company's success, make hard decisions based on empirical evidence, and accept responsibility for the results of those decisions.

What I have learned after more than thirty-nine years in HR is that the less you prepare to advance your own career and the more you focus on attaining the business goals of your company, the more likely you are to expand your influence and scope. In short, the best leaders lead, and the promotions take care of themselves. Frankly, it wasn't always that clear to me.

"YOU'VE FAILED"

One of my first real leadership positions was as director of HR for a division of a large company. Being young and ambitious, I threw myself into the race and racked up an impressive list of accomplishments, if I do say so myself.

At a review, I proudly told my mentor all the things I had achieved. When I was finished, he looked at me and said, "Well, that is an impressive list. Very impressive. But you've failed, Randy."

Stunned, I thought he must not have understood me correctly. I began again, going through my presentation even more emphatically. He stopped me and said, "I heard you. You did a lot. But YOU did it. Alone. And that means you failed at the most important part of your job, Randy: building a successful team and influencing others. You didn't bring your people along with you."

It was a defining moment in my career. A person's strongest assets, I realized, can also be his or her most damaging liabilities. Being smart, innovative, a hard worker, even ambitious, were all good qualities to have. But they weren't enough if I did not use them to advance the talents and abilities of my colleagues and the long-term interests of the business.

He was right; I had failed. I resolved then and there to work differently. The lessons I learned that day have never left me.

TODAY'S HR: MORE CHALLENGE, GREATER OPPORTUNITY

In the recent past, the job of even the very best HR leaders was almost exclusively reactive. We reacted to the leadership team's business strategies by finding and hiring the best employees, and then we reacted to employee needs in order to continue attracting and retaining the best talent. Those tasks are still necessary, but they are no longer sufficient.

New technologies and the realities of a worldwide economy have put a wide range of people issues, the domain of HR expertise, on the front lines of business competition. The best HR professionals are those who think like business leaders, not only HR leaders, to influence business strategy and develop programs that drive the whole company forward.

The rapid pace of change means that few businesses can dominate their markets with product or process innovations alone. With information and data flying freely around the world at the speed of light, competitors catch up quickly now to any single advance. Innovation must be ongoing and continuous to maintain market leadership. The only way that happens on a sustainable basis is through a steady supply of the most talented, creative people. The primary factor separating winning companies from the also-rans in this environment is the quality and strategic development of employees. That challenge is at the core of HR's mission at every high-performing company.

The good news for young and aspiring HR professionals is that the desperate need for people willing to take up this challenge makes the function a place of tremendous opportunity. HR is more of a meritocracy than it has ever been before. Bold new HR ideas will yield bold results in this century provided the focus remains on the business and a few guiding principles are kept firmly in mind.

THE VALUE PROPOSITION: BUILDING TRUST AND AN ATMOSPHERE OF INNOVATION

I believe that building a reputation for trust and integrity while encouraging a positive, can-do attitude of innovation and prudent risk taking is key. My job is not to micromanage my team, but to craft a vision based on the business goals of the company and encourage the HR leaders who report to me to be brave, innovative, and proactive in pursuit of that common vision.

It also means setting clear standards. Nurturing an effective and innovative HR environment requires the ability to challenge people intellectually without dampening their enthusiasm or inhibiting their willingness to share ideas.

At IBM HR, we strive to create an environment that has tough, demanding standards for intellectual rigor and performance, but at the same time is open to new ways of thinking. We foster a climate where anyone can throw out any idea, knowing it might not fly, but trusting that it could start a discussion that leads to another idea of real value down the road.

As senior leader, my job is to probe and test, to make certain plans have been thought through to their conclusion. Although we encourage free and open discussion in meetings, I hold feet to the fire when formal presentations for action are being made. This is to uncover any weaknesses in the planning stages. People can become so engrossed in the elegant beauty of what they are creating that they lose sight of real-world utility. We help each other and function best as a high-performance team when we serve as sounding boards and respectfully challenge each other's ideas.

TAKING RESPONSIBILITY FOR MISTAKES

One of the truly great sayings is, "Good judgment comes from experience, and experience comes from bad judgment."

Mistakes and misjudgments are the unavoidable corollary to even prudent risk taking. A senior leader who encourages people to take risks must also guide them in taking ownership of their failures and set the example by acknowledging his or her own.

A few years ago, my team launched a new hiring system at IBM that did not deliver as promised, despite all our efforts and rigor. When discussion of the new system and its flaws came up at the next meeting of IBM's senior operating group, I stood up and said, "Before we begin, I just want to say that we know this program is not working. I apologize for that and take full responsibility. I also want you to know we're shutting the system down immediately. We're going to go back and recreate it, and we'll find the money to do that from our own budget. We won't take a dime from anyone here."

Whatever damage HR's reputation may have sustained from launching a program before it was ready was more than compensated for by the goodwill and trust we gained for standing up and admitting our mistake. It earned us a second chance, and when we rolled the program out a second time, it worked to perfection.

The important point of the story is that we reaffirmed our value proposition to the entire corporation: "You can trust the HR people of IBM to take full responsibility for their programs and do what they say they are going to do—for the business."

JUST THE FAACTs

Creating a value proposition for an entire HR department starts with creating a value proposition for yourself first, as a business professional.

Over the years, I have identified five guiding principles that I believe set apart truly effective HR leaders from the rest. These are the five attributes I do my best to exhibit in my own actions; they are also the qualities I look for when I am considering people for hiring or advancement opportunities. I call this set of principles collectively FAACT, allowing the extra "A" so as to get all five into one tortured acronym. The spelling may not be elegant, but I believe the principles are indispensible to successful business leadership:

Functional knowledge application

Aggressive innovation

Accountability

Continuous learning

Teamwork

FUNCTIONAL KNOWLEDGE APPLICATION

An HR leader cannot anticipate and serve the needs of the business if he or she does not understand the precise skills and abilities the business requires to compete successfully. Truly effective HR leaders take the time to gain a complete understanding of their company's line operations. In fact, the best HR managers develop an expertise concerning their company's products and services to rival that of line managers in all operational areas.

AGGRESSIVE INNOVATION

Striving to be continuously innovative and out in front of the needs of the business is the most consistently productive action any HR leader can take. Doing something is always better than doing nothing. Even when the thing you do doesn't work or turns out to be unnecessary, you can still learn from it. All you can learn from doing nothing is the futility of doing nothing. I am always on the lookout for the new, the creative, and the breakthrough. At IBM we start with the premise, "It can be done, and it can be done differently."

ACCOUNTABILITY

Despite all good intentions, it is sometimes necessary to take actions that contradict previous statements or policies. But if you are consistently open and honest about what is being done and can explain why a change in policy has been made, you can at least make it easier for people to accept the decisions they don't like. We had an issue at IBM a few years ago, and the ultimate resolution was unpopular with many of the affected employees. Members of my staff and I traveled to each of the locations where employees were most concerned. We had no carefully prepared, canned presentation; we took no fancy charts. Instead, we asked for questions. We talked some, and we listened more. If a question was asked and none of us had the answer, we promised to get that information within twenty-four hours—and we did. We took detailed notes on every point of follow-up, no matter how small, and we tracked the completion of each of those open items. We were clearly and visibly accountable, and I believe that made a difference in the way the changes were ultimately accepted.

CONTINUOUS LEARNING

As the business world grows more interconnected globally, leaders must be willing to get outside their comfort zones and heighten their understanding of different cultures. We can do this only by being willing to meet and learn about people different from ourselves.

If I were starting out in HR today, I'd make certain I spent at least a year or two in China, India, South America, or eastern Europe—someplace far outside my home geography and culture. I would also alternate between staff and operational roles to expand my knowledge of the business and gain a better understanding of HR's relationship to accomplishing business objectives.

TEAMWORK

The challenge for top leadership isn't getting the best people; there are many talented and innovative business professionals. The real challenge often lies in encouraging high-performing people to work together as a team. An effective leader must create a collaborative atmosphere at all levels of an organization.

In our shop at IBM, turf wars are unacceptable. I refuse to become involved unless there is a legitimate business issue.

Otherwise I tell the parties to focus on the business and work it out themselves. And they do.

Another challenge to teamwork for HR professionals can be the ingrained tension that often exists between staff and line functions at many companies. At IBM we have instituted a dual top-responsibility HR leadership model to encourage cross-functional cooperation. My direct reports are charged with both a unit, or line, HR responsibility and an enterprise-wide HR responsibility simultaneously. In this way, if conflicting priorities develop, both perspectives are embodied in one senior leader.

Teamwork is the final FAACT principle, and the one on which the other four are most dependent. I know my former mentor would agree that individual efforts at Functional knowledge, Aggressive innovation, Accountability, or Continuous learning will not bear fruit if everyone is not pulling together with a collective focus on the business. In the end, leaders who lead teams most effectively will deliver the greatest value for their business.

ANALYTICS: THE FUTURE OF HR

The job of a leader is to define reality and give hope. The reality of HR is that the role the function plays in achieving business goals has changed dramatically. The time of the solely reactive HR department is gone, and it is not coming back. HR must now function as a full leadership member of the senior strategy team. We have more influence now than in the past, but also more responsibility for achieving superior business results. What gives us hope in the face of these new challenges is knowing that new technologies are providing us with the ability to quantify HR's capabilities and achievements.

Why does the chief financial office (CFO) have the ability to always see the CEO any time she or he wants? It is because the CFO has the numbers—the hard data needed to effectively evaluate the present and create effective strategies for the future. We now have those tools at our disposal as well.

We can use ROI in making the case for our programs and initiatives too—but for us, ROI means not "return on investment" but "return on intangibles." The reactive HR of the past was limited to saying, "People are dissatisfied; we should do something."

The new HR can go much further. We can predict skill needs, quantify skill development, and steer necessary learning toward future needs. We can, in some cases, illustrate links between employee satisfaction and future revenue. We can take the pulse of employee preferences with much greater speed and precision and test possible solutions much more effectively. Indeed, I believe HR has just begun to scratch the surface of what predictive analytics will let us achieve for business in the years ahead.

Just as finance owns the company's financial and physical assets, we now own the human talent asset of the corporation, and we can manage that asset the same way any other asset is managed. We invest in the talent capital and maintain that asset as it continues to become the key productive force for change, differentiation, and competitive advantage for business in this century.

PLAN AND ADAPT

Great challenges and opportunities lay ahead for people who aspire to lead and make a difference for their businesses. The HR function today and in the future needs leaders and visionaries—men and women of talent, persistence, and resolve.

In the end, being an effective HR leader is not about taking my advice or that of my mentor or of anyone else. I can only describe my experience in HR; you must create your own. It is really all about who you are and what kind of HR leader you want to be.

Put the enterprise first, the function second, and yourself last. Don't believe your own press or even read it. It will take your focus off the business.

Finally, build your teams. In the end, you are only as good as the people with whom you work. That may sound like a platitude, but it is the hard truth, and I can illustrate it with the following final story.

A few years ago I had to take a medical leave for a couple of months. When I came back, I noticed that some important decisions had been made in my absence. They weren't the same decisions I would have made. They were better, and it was a wonderful thing to realize. My old mentor would be proud.

CHAPTER THREE

THE ART AND SCIENCE OF THE CHRO ROLE

Eva Sage-Gavin

I often comment to colleagues that there should be a handbook that all new CHROs receive on day one. The reality, though, is that the CHRO's role is not as clearly defined as that of the CEO or CFO.

Throughout the thirty years of my career, I've watched, learned, and participated in shaping the roles, responsibilities, and expectations of the HR field. And today, eight years into my current role as CHRO, I'm amazed by the amount of change in the HR field.

Today's HR leaders face challenges at many turns: a competitive business environment, a changing economy downsizing, globalization, and wary consumers. This in turn creates new challenges for our leaders and employees. These challenges are not insurmountable, but they do demand the right mix of disciplines. Some of our business is science; some is art. We need to balance these two skill sets if we are to be successful.

Although there is no magic handbook, there are important lessons learned on the job. In this chapter, I share some of the pivotal insights I've gained about the art and science of being a successful CHRO.

THE SCIENCE OF BEING A CHRO

Success is yours when you have a clear agenda and address the expectations of your constituents, balancing the four active roles of CHRO:

1. External business leader
2. Internal business partner
3. Employee advocate
4. Team leader

ROLE 1: EXTERNAL BUSINESS LEADER

This is the biggest area of change you will face as a CHRO. External pressures will come from all angles. You need to be deliberate in how you and your company appear to partners, vendors, potential employees, customers, and communities. This means taking a leadership role in when and how its messages are being delivered and perceived—whether they're in advertising, media stories, social responsibility, recruiting campaigns, or the company's annual report.

To succeed in this role, it's imperative to be seen as a brand ambassador, a knowledgeable resource for senior management, an advocate for governance, and a thought leader.

Ambassador of Your Employer Brand

Being an ambassador is not a marketing job; it's serving as an authentic role model for everything your brand represents. At Gap Inc., for instance, creativity and integrity are key values. To be a good brand ambassador requires that you intimately understand your brand, product, customers, and industry. By embodying the brand through your actions and communications, you will motivate employees and create awareness about your positive workplace. Remember that your best ambassadors, your employees, walk in and out of your doors every day.

Resource and Counsel for the Board of Directors

Exhibiting financial acumen and demonstrating a full understanding of how your corporation works will equip you to support the board and present solutions to the complex HR challenges that often face public companies. I like to put myself in their shoes and identify the top three issues they are thinking about. Putting my initiatives in this context is an important way to be valuable to your board of directors.

Leader of Governance for People-Related Policies and Practices

Reputation, integrity, and transparent communication can all cause your stock price to rise—or to fall. The CHRO needs to promote policies, organizational structures, and operating practices that are effective and mitigate risk for the entire enterprise. For example, as a business enters new countries, the CHRO must look at how local laws and customs may align or conflict with the company culture. In some parts of the world, pay and work practices may be locally acceptable, but could have a negative impact on a company's brand. The CHRO must be aware of those issues ahead of time, analyze them, and plan ways to mitigate risks for recruiting, employees, the brand, and customers' perceptions. A CHRO must anticipate business and cultural risks and opportunities even before a new store's doors open in a new country.

The lessons I've learned are to plan ahead, anticipate challenges and threats, and be prepared to make sound, confident decisions. My recommendation to new top seat leaders is, "Think about someday personally certifying documents as a public officer on a global stage with customers, employees, and shareholders all counting on you. Prepare now."

Thought Leader for the HR Profession

What are the top public policy issues today facing your company and industry? Whether they're health care or global challenges, you need to understand and embody what your company stands for. Are you part of leadership groups that are making a difference? It might be time to reinvent your knowledge base by partnering with external and internal thought leaders. The results can be rewarding on many levels. *HR Executive* magazine has recognized my team for leading through tough times and for an innovative flexible work environment program. The Corporate Leadership Council also has honored us for our thought leadership on investing in learning and development experiences that are fully owned and sponsored by frontline leaders by highlighting our program in a publication on best practices.

ROLE 2: INTERNAL BUSINESS PARTNER

Perhaps the most fundamental role for the CHRO is to drive the internal initiatives that enable business strategies, strengthen leadership, and engage the hearts and minds of employees. Think of yourself as both the integrator and the glue that binds the company together. Being deliberate in how you show up and how people perceive you will make a difference in how you are valued and trusted.

CHROs are more than talented HR professionals. They are trusted peers who deliver thoughtful counsel and, more important, are general business managers who understand their business and industry. As such, they know how to build people and HR strategies in ways that directly support business objectives and help drive productivity.

Of course, at the end of the day, you and your team are the experts at talent management and must be able to understand and identify good versus great talent. Having served as the head of HR in very diverse industries, I needed to quickly understand the talent areas most critical to the success of each and focus on them. Identifying critical positions, the great attributes needed to fill them, and prioritizing recruiting strategies accordingly was the key to success, whether I was working with engineers, apparel designers, or international operations management.

Oversight of talent development across the organization is vital in keeping your company competitive, but it can be challenging in larger, more complex organizations. At Gap Inc., with multiple brands, offices, and locations around the world, an ongoing priority is to move talent across the company to ensure business success and support career development. To deliver on this, we have internal placement programs to help employees navigate the opportunities within the company. Equally important is ensuring that the corporation has the executive talent it needs at a vice president level and higher.

Finally, as a CHRO, you are the developer and staunch supporter of your company's culture and values. Culture is an important lever for CHROs and can make or break success depending on how you navigate, embrace, and then support it. Every company I've worked for has had a greatly different culture. An approach that might have worked at PepsiCo might not at Disney. The specialty apparel retail industry is a different story altogether. In approaching any new project at Gap Inc., whether it's a communication strategy or new HR initiatives, we are diligent about upholding the company's more than forty-year legacy and the culture that permeates each of our business divisions. One way we do this is to ensure that our reward and recognition behaviors truly support the culture in ways that are authentic and genuine for employees. We also build culture into our HR and communications programs. For example, when *Ethisphere Magazine* recently included Gap Inc. on its list of the most ethical companies in the world, we made sure employees were aware of this honor because it directly ties to our culture and our value to "do what's right."

ROLE 3: EMPLOYEE ADVOCATE

We often get so busy managing that it can be too easy to forget to be advocates for our employees. You and your team must be a safe place for employees to go, while at the same time making sure that you don't overalign with employees or managers, therefore blurring the lines of objectivity. The balance is delicate. Keep the channels open, and take "open door" (meeting with individual employees) and "roundtable" (meeting with groups of employees). Stay connected and visible.

If you take on your role as a steward and champion for employees, you can better anticipate hot spots and drive change. This was very important during a period of tremendous change at Gap Inc. At the HR helm, I witnessed and helped navigate a full transformational journey from a brand steeped in legacy that lost market share to a turnaround phase and movement toward growth. There's still a long way to go, but we wouldn't have made it without the strong talent at the company and managing it in authentic, honest ways.

ROLE 4: TEAM LEADER

Remember your own team. This can be hard to do given the many other groups that depend on you. But if you aren't leading and inspiring the HR team to excellence, the perception of HR will suffer. As a leader, you want to build an HR community with global business views; a culturally diverse team is more likely to generate creative ideas and high-impact work. As an architect, design and lead initiatives that create high-performing teams. Make sure your HR pipeline is well developed. And as a coach and mentor, empower your leaders to do the same with their own staffs because excellence inspires excellence.

A simple question I ask myself is, "When I turn around, is everyone with me, and am I doing my best to role-model what I expect of others?"

THE ART OF BEING A CHRO

While success with defining your roles and responsibilities and delivering results will get you pretty far, if you don't succeed on the soft stuff, you will fail. After all, the soft stuff is really the hard stuff.

I've learned seven lessons on the job along with the do's, the don'ts, and some questions to consider before you step into the top seat.

LESSON 1: UNDERSTAND THE ROLE OF THE BOARD OF DIRECTORS

Remember that board members are not management or your bosses; they are your colleagues. Getting their approval depends mainly on their confidence in you, not the tactics of your plan. HR needs a seat at the board table, and if you don't have one, you need to advocate for your inclusion. Don't be perceived only as a technical expert or administrator. Your ability to solve the people issues can help the company become more successful, and that, of course, is of critical importance to the board.

LESSON 2: SPEND BALANCED TIME WITH ALL YOUR COLLEAGUES

Your peers will look at you differently in the CHRO role than they will in divisional or departmental roles because you are now both their HR person and the keeper of the rules and culture. The shift to CHRO means you are driving business strategy, mitigating risk, making some tough calls, and managing business pressures.

The tough part is ensuring that you remain the eyes and ears for senior leaders and still maintain trust among your peers. Leaders tend to receive less feedback as they climb up in an organization, and we CHROs are in a position to tell them what others won't or can't say. Build and maintain these peer relationships by giving constructive feedback, along with new ideas and solutions. Over time, most will trust that you are the safe place for those conversations and that your only interest is to help them succeed as individuals and as a team. Providing honest feedback at the highest levels of a company is a privilege and responsibility that takes courage and sensitivity.

You must be democratic and fair about meeting with all of your constituencies. At the beginning of each year or even eighteen months ahead, create a calendar that makes time for each leader and group. Perhaps even color-code it by business group so you can see at a glance that you're balanced in meeting with each constituency.

LESSON 3: BE A BUSINESS EXECUTIVE FIRST

CHROs need to make knowing the business a priority. Although this seems elementary, it can be a shift from the traditional HR role. Develop a clear understanding of product, customers, competition, and financial status. Be sure you can articulate how people strategies tie to business results.

This approach helped me be more effective in many ways and make more direct connections to achieving business results. It also increases credibility. At Gap Inc., my leadership role has expanded to include global social responsibility, government affairs, and public policy in addition to HR, which is giving me the opportunity to oversee important initiatives that are fundamental to our culture, reputation, and business success.

LESSON 4: THINK GLOBALLY, ACT GLOBALLY

Global companies have a unique set of challenges. Having worked for several global brands though the years, I've learned not to take U.S.-centric attitudes with me. I've also had the opportunity to travel to global offices to see firsthand how our reputation and culture are translating across geographical boundaries.

At Gap Inc., we've embarked on a growth strategy that is stretching us all in new ways. Our 135,000 employees around the world are depending on us to keep them informed, engaged, and rewarded as we take the company to the next level.

LESSON 5: DEVELOP A PERSONAL BOARD OF DIRECTORS

How do you prepare the CEO's performance review for the board? Whom do you ask for advice when the board expects you to be an expert? How do you deal with a boss or colleagues who are failing and not responding to coaching? One way is to develop your own external personal board of directors to help you with issues that are hard to discuss internally. This is a safe set of external resources who can give you advice, calibration, and mentoring. Keep these connections strong, and return the favor. Start building that trusted network now. You'll find it invaluable.

I count on three groups to maintain my perspective:

- Leaders who are ahead of me in their careers and lives by ten to fifteen years. This can include people who have retired from long careers and can help me navigate events, make choices, and take a longer-term view.
- Current peers across industries, who can provide safe places to get feedback in the moment.
- People who are up and coming, such as younger HR professionals, students, and interns who can help you keep up with new trends and technology. In fact, spending time with my teenage daughter and her friends has provided me with a window into how young consumers think, socialize, and spend money—a personal joy, of course, and an outstanding insight for a business-focused CHRO.

LESSON 6: MAKE TIME FOR YOUR PERSONAL LIFE

No matter what people tell you, the job of CHRO is 24/7. Every year you get better at balancing it, but you have to be ready emotionally and physically. It's a marathon, not a sprint.

I speak from experience. After seventeen relocations, I've retained learnings from every single one and applied them to my professional and personal lives. Know your boundaries, and let others know them as well. Invest in your emotional and physical health, and never compromise on the things that make you a whole person.

Although you always should plan ahead, understand that sometimes you have to be flexible. I keep a bag packed and my passport up-to-date in case I need to travel at a moment's notice. I'm also willing to interrupt a significant business trip if my family needs me.

Most important, be in the moment: stay fully present in whatever you are doing, and relieve yourself of any guilt that you should be doing something else. My work colleagues and family appreciate the time and effort I put into this delicate balancing act.

LESSON 7: UNDERSTAND AND DEVELOP YOUR PERSONAL BRAND

Developing an authentic brand starts with self-awareness. Be impeccably honest with yourself, and assess your strengths, weaknesses, personality preferences, leadership type, and perceived persona within the company. Make sure you put yourself through the same tools you put everyone else through, such as 360-degree assessments and coaching. Once you find your true North, be deliberate and authentic.

FINALLY

These insights are a starting point. We all should continue to network with other CHROs and ask their opinions and learnings from their own experiences. I challenge you to get started today, whether you are already in the top seat or considering your next move.

CHAPTER FOUR

ETC

Richard L. Antoine

Throughout the chapters in this book, you will read the perspectives and learnings from a series of smart, talented, and experienced HR leaders. These leaders have addressed specific topics like board relations, analytics, supporting the brand, and engaging the organization. This chapter is about none of these specific topics yet it is about all of these.

The title of this chapter is ETC. Undoubtedly when you looked at the title, the common abbreviation *etc.* ("and other things" in Latin) came to mind. It has another common definition, "and other unspecified things of the same class," and this is the definition I address in this chapter: three topics that are critical to the success of any organization and the specific responsibility of the HR officer of that organization.

Although the content of the chapter meets the dictionary definition, the real intent of the three letters is to serve as a reminder of the three critical responsibilities of HR leaders in any organization:

Ethics
Talent
Coaching and courage

ETHICS

HR leaders are responsible for instilling, protecting, and enforcing the ethics of the organization, that is, the set of moral princi-ples that guide behaviors. These ethics, or values as they are frequently called, guide employees and tell them what behaviors are acceptable or unacceptable in the organization. Ethics or values are critical to long-term business success. Common sense tells us that ethical organizations will be successful. In addition, a number of studies have found that organizations with a high purpose and a set of values that are real and guide behaviors in the organization meet with long-term business success.

Merely posting a set of values does not guarantee that these values really guide behaviors, however. There is a huge difference between words on a wall and values that determine the behaviors of an organization. The past ten years of business history is littered with the stories and remains of other companies that failed to follow their ethics.

You may be thinking, *I know it is critically important, but how do we ensure that our employees understand our values and ethics and behave according to them all of the time?* My answer is that here are three steps you must take to institutionalize these ethics. First, develop the list of ethics and values that your organization will use as your guidepost to affect the behavior of everyone in the organization all the time. Perhaps you have these values today. If you do, great. However, I recommend that you spend some time as a leadership team talking about these values and making sure that everyone on the team understands and agrees with them. For most organizations, the list of values and ethics that guide behaviors is no more than five to seven. Values like integrity, passion for winning, and respect for others are among the most common and most appropriate. But you and the senior leadership team need to decide which ethics are critical to the success of your organization.

Second, you need to implement training and education programs that teach these values to everyone in the organization. This education process normally starts with a letter from the CEO to all people in the organization advising them of these values and ethics. Assuming you did that awhile ago, it may be helpful to reiterate this commitment to these values every couple of years. Training programs are critical to the success of companies where values are important and affect behaviors. Since most people learn best through experience, I have found the most effective method of teaching to be case studies. These can be examples of behavior that demonstrate both what you are talking about as well as what you want to avoid. If you use examples from your own organization, make sure they are nonattributable. But real-life examples are the best way to teach what we truly mean about following a set of ethics. You can lay out situations and ask small groups to determine their appropriate handling. When you are doing this training, always ask people to define the specific ethic at play, the principle that is operable, and the appropriate action to be taken. In my experience, even long-service senior employees get value from the rich discussion that occurs when difficult ethical situations are presented to the group. These discussions and annual online training instill the ethics and values that serve as guidelines for your company.

Third, and most important to making sure the ethics statements are not merely words, is what happens when someone violates the ethics. Senior management and the CHRO must always walk the talk. When an employee or group of employees violates the ethics of an organization, appropriate action must be taken every time. The level of the person in the organization or the extent to which the value has been violated does not matter. One could in fact argue that the higher the level of the person who violates ethical standards, the more critical it is to address the violation with the appropriate discipline, which normally includes leaving the organization.

The entire organization looks to the top for indications of how serious everyone is about ethics. The other aspect of this is the extent of the violation. In virtually all organizations, honesty and integrity are values that are mentioned and reinforced many times. Theft of money or proprietary information from a company clearly violates that ethic. I have occasionally been perplexed by the lengthy debates over whether an individual who stole "only $1,000" should be terminated. I have never been able to figure out where the line is between a slap on the hand because it's only a "small" amount of money and the amount where termination is appropriate. Ethics are absolute, not relative. Someone who steals any amount of money or any amount of product or any amount or proprietary information from a company or an organization must be terminated. Clearly define this expectation and outcome in your values and your corporate set of operating principles. Once established, it must be consistently reinforced regardless of the status of the person involved or the amount or extent of the violation that has occurred.

TALENT

Talent management is the second critical responsibility of the HR officer. As with ethics, it is also the responsibility of the line organization, but HR is responsible for the processes that lead to a robust talent management system.

Organizations often spend a great deal of time defining and publicizing the assets that are most responsible for their long-term success. Those assets can include intellectual property like patents, brands that customers trust, or the financial assets that support the business. But most organizations cannot succeed in the long term unless one of their assets is the talent within the organization. Talent determines everything in the end.

The HR leader is responsible for putting in place an integrated talent management system. This system goes from hiring through assignment planning, training, and development to promotion and succession planning. The most critical elements of a robust talent management system follow:

The Building Blocks of Talent Excellence

Success drivers and competencies	Assignment planning
	Talent identification and selection
Performance management	Scorecards
Succession planning	Diversity
Leadership model	Compensation and benefit system
Recruiting and hiring	Employment brand
Onboarding	Workforce planning
Training and development	

I will offer comments about three of these critical elements: competencies, assignment planning, and succession planning.

A robust and successful talent management system starts with a clear list of skills or competencies that determine the success of individuals within the organization. These are commonly called "what counts" factors, "success factors," or "success drivers." I will use the term "success drivers" since I believe that these ten or so skills, capabilities, and competencies drive individual and organizational success. Some of the more common success drivers are leadership, technical expertise, execution excellence, collaboration, and customer orientation. You need to determine those skills or competencies that are critical to your business. Then use them for hiring, performance assessment, promotions, and compensation.

Assignment planning is one of the critical elements of an integrated talent development system. For assignment planning to be effective, individuals within an organization are evaluated to determine the experiences that will qualify them for higher levels. Each organization has to define the experiences that are essential to success at the very top of the organization. For example, General Electric requires all of its top development people to go through Audit because of their heavy financial systems reliance. Procter & Gamble requires that all top managers have both global profit unit experience and country management experience. Companies that are heavily customer oriented like retailing require that all of their senior managers go through a number of customer-facing experiences. Equipped with this understanding of critical experiences, top development candidates can be evaluated to see which experiences they have successfully completed and which remain to be completed.

Determining the experiences necessary for long-term success becomes an important element in the assignment planning process. In addition, successful organizations have found that certain assignments, often called crucible roles, can play an important role in the development of talented managers for higher levels. Crucible roles vary from organization to organization, but they tend to stretch the talents and capabilities of the manager because of the nature of the challenge he or she will face. Examples of crucible roles are acquisition integration, start-up of a business in a new country, start-up of a new product line, and turnaround of an ailing business. From a business standpoint, you want to put your best people against your most important and critical roles. From a development standpoint, you also want to put your most talented people against roles that will challenge them and take out of their comfort zone. Managers who have only a series of incrementally responsible roles within a well-defined structure and with modest expectations for delivery may not exhibit the kinds of successful behaviors that are essential to business prosperity over the long run.

Succession planning is the flip side of assignment planning. In succession planning, the line and HR leaders for organizations take each of the top jobs within that organization and identify successors for the current incumbents. For example, the succession plan for a general manager leading a product line in the United States would start by identifying important criteria for success. What skills, abilities, and experiences should the succession candidate have? Once the criteria are established, you can identify potential candidates to fill this position. A best practice is usually to identify three candidates for each position. Typically one of the candidates will be an emergency successor who could take this role if the current incumbent were hit by the proverbial truck tomorrow. The second and third candidates would be people who could step into the role when the current incumbent moves onto his or her next assignment, whether six months or perhaps a couple of years from now. In the case of CEO succession planning, you could be talking about five years from now. Most best practice companies make sure that at least one of the candidates is a woman or, in the United States, a minority. One caution is to make sure the succession candidates who are identified don't rely heavily on one or two people to fill several roles. While Susie and Charlie may be incredibly talented people, they can't fill more than one position at a time, and if they are listed as successors for multiple other roles, those roles cannot be filled in a timely manner.

COACHING AND COURAGE

The third area in ETC is referred to as coaching and courage or, as some people refer to it, touch and toughness.

Every CHRO is the coach for a number of people—certainly your boss, the CEO, but also members of the senior leadership team. And do not forget the responsibility to coach and develop the top HR people within your organization.

The most effective coaches take this responsibility seriously and devote time and thought to the process of coaching. These elements of time and thoughtfulness are difficult given the many time challenges facing the CHRO. And yet it is increasingly a critical skill. Just like good performance evaluations, effective coaching should emphasize how individuals can use their greatest strengths to drive the business in the organization. In addition, you should work on advising your boss or senior leadership team member on the one quality that can make the most difference in their performance.

Coaching should be timely. The most effective coaching occurs immediately after you see a behavior that is exemplary or problematic. Five minutes of coaching immediately after a behavior you want to see repeated or a behavior that should never be repeated is worth far more than a five-page performance summary delivered six or nine months later. The feedback will be much more relevant or understandable to the person you are coaching if he or she can immediately recall the situation, understand the context where it occurs, and determine what needs to be repeated or corrected in subsequent situations. Written performance feedback that is provided every twelve to fifteen months based on 360-degree feedback is also an important part of the coaching package.

The other part of the CCs is courage. This is why the CHRO job, or almost any other job within HR, is so difficult. On the one hand, you have to have empathy and sensitivity toward people that allows you to know what is going on in the organization and to be an effective coach. On the other hand, an effective CHRO must have the courage to confront bad behavior wherever that may occur in the organization. It is perhaps easier to confront the bad behaviors of people lower in the organization and ensure that the appropriate discipline, including termination, occurs. It is much more difficult and requires a much greater degree of courage to confront bad behavior and ethical lapses on the senior management team or even your boss. One has to wonder where the CHRO was during the Enron, AIG, and WorldCom situations.

Be wary of the expressed concern that "this individual may have done something, but he still is an outstanding performer." That may be true from a results standpoint. But if the individual is getting those results through unethical means or bad behaviors such as abusing subordinates, then the behavior must be confronted and dealt with appropriately. The CHRO must have the courage and personal conviction to deal with such people. In many organizations, the more senior managers are also your colleagues and perhaps your friends. This again requires a great deal of courage and personal commitment to the values and long-term success of the organization to deal with bad behaviors even when they directly affect people you have known for many years.

The CHRO is also responsible for supporting the people with small jobs or small voices. People lower in the organization are counting on him or her to protect and defend them when they are being inappropriately affected by people much higher in the organization. In addition, there are people at every level, including the most senior level, who are reluctant to speak up when more aggressive people in the organization are bullying and making unreasonable demands. You have a responsibility to the long-term success of the organization to support them, defend them, and correct the behaviors that are making their work lives miserable and having a negative effect on business results.

The CHRO is a challenging and yet rewarding role. It is up to you to protect the ethics and values of the organization, build the most critical asset of the organization (its talent), and do the necessary coaching of the top people in the organization to ensure long-term success. All of this requires more courage than most people would attribute to HR leaders, and yet I have seen many CHROs step up to the challenge. Successful CHRO should keep in mind three letters, ETC, as they do their very important roles.

CHAPTER FIVE

ROLES AND CHALLENGES OF THE CHRO
Results of the Cornell/CAHRS CHRO Survey

Patrick M. Wright, Mark Stewart

The increasingly rapid pace of change in the world presents constantly emerging challenges for business organizations. The financial crisis that has driven swift decreases in demand and ensuing increases in unemployment appeared almost without warning. Regulatory changes such as Sarbanes-Oxley resulted in increased reporting and governance requirements, and the financial bailouts of banks and automakers will result in even more government intervention in the decisions of management. These two developments have occurred within the constant transformation stemming from increased globalization and technological change. All of these trends and events have driven changes in the roles of the CHRO, yet little formal research exists regarding this role and how it is changing.

In an effort to address this dearth of systematic knowledge regarding the CHRO role, the Center for Advanced Human Resource Studies conducted the first annual Cornell/CAHRS Survey of Chief Human Resource Officers in 2009. This chapter examines how CHROs allocate their time across a variety of roles and identifies the challenges they face in their position.

Research Methodology

The survey was designed by the lead author (P.W.) with the help of a number of CHROs who comprise the advisory board of the Center for Advanced Human Resource Studies (CAHRS). The research predominantly focused on CHROs at Fortune 150 companies, plus some additional CHROs with whom the lead researchers had relationships. From the list of 165 CHROs, 54 completed the survey, resulting in a response rate of 39 percent, a rate that is unusually high for any survey research, and particularly for a sample of such senior executives. The interest of these CHROs also was evidenced by the fact that they spent a substantial amount of time on it, with the average time to completion at exactly thirty minutes. Many were candid and wrote detailed responses to many of the open-ended questions. The results for the larger survey are available through CAHRS (www.ilr.cornell.edu/cahrs).

The final question on the survey invited the participants to engage in interviews to follow up on the survey, and twenty-three CHROs were interviewed within six months of the survey. Thus, this chapter presents what we learned about the CHRO position from the quantitative questions, qualitative questions, and the interactive interviews.

Roles of the CHRO

The lead author (P.W.) has been studying the CHRO role for the past four years with a combination of confidential interviews with CHROs, public interviews with CHROs and CEOs, brainstorming groups of CHROs, and examinations of archival data. Based on this research, we developed a typology of seven CHRO roles. CHROs were asked to indicate the amount of time they spent playing these roles:

- *Strategic advisor to the executive team*—activities focused specifically on the formulation and implementation of the firm's strategy
- *Counselor/confidant/coach to the executive team*—activities focused on counseling or coaching team members or resolving interpersonal or political conflicts among team members

- *Liaison to the board of directors*—preparation for board meetings, telephone calls with board members, and attendance at board meetings
- *Talent architect*—activities focused on building and identifying the human capital critical to the firm now and in the future
- *Leader of the HR function*—working with HR team members regarding the development, design, and delivery of HR services
- *Workforce sensor*—activities focused on identifying workforce morale issues or concerns
- *Representative of the firm*—activities with external stakeholders, such as lobbying or speaking to outside groups

After reporting the time spent, CHROs were asked two open-ended questions regarding which role they felt had the greatest impact on the business (and why) and which roles they were least prepared for when they took on the CHRO role. In our follow-up interviews, we asked many of these CHROs to describe in greater detail how they seek to perform each role effectively.

The workforce sensor and representative of the firm roles entailed the least amount of time spent. In addition, these were seldom or never mentioned as roles that have the strongest impact on the firm. Therefore, we focus this chapter on the roles of strategic advisor, talent architect, counselor/confidant/coach, leader of the HR function, and liaison to the board because these accounted for a significant portion of time and were also frequently mentioned as roles that were critical or ones that the CHROs were least prepared for when they took over their positions.

STRATEGIC ADVISOR

The strategic advisor role consists of all activities that focus on attempting to influence the strategy of the firm. These activities could be providing human capital information regarding potential business performance issues (for example, increasing turnover among high potentials), playing devil's advocate regarding strategies being discussed, or simply providing credible business-based opinions regarding the feasibility or effectiveness of proposed strategic decisions.

FIGURE 5.1. PERCENTAGE OF TIME SPENT IN ROLES

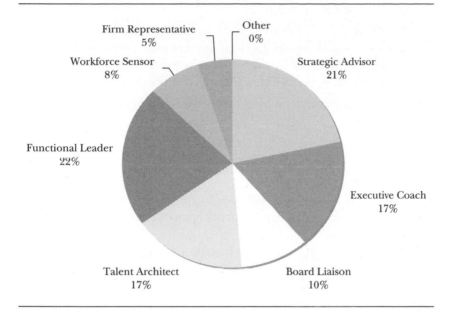

CHROs reported spending the second-most time (21 percent) as a strategic advisor to the executive team (Figure 5.1). This role entails sharing the people expertise as part of the decision-making process, as well as shaping how the human capital of the firm fits into its strategy. This also was the role that was most frequently cited as having the greatest impact on the firm (46 percent of respondents listed this as the most important). Examples of why this role was seen as having the greatest impact are shown in the following comments:

"Influencing key strategic business decisions has the highest leverage in terms of HR influence. Once business strategies are set with a clear talent/employee agenda, the process of implementation becomes self-fulfilling. Engaging with executive decision makers early in the process is critical to being effective in the CHRO role."

"As we gain a stronger voice in the leadership of the enterprise and build credibility, the greatest impact we can provide is driven by our role as a strategic advisor to (and key member of) the executive team.''

''I can influence the talent agenda in a significant way through my interactions with the CEO and senior team. I have a great talent professional who can carry the water and then some—the key is to get the corporate leadership to make it theirs.''

''Shaping strategy drives priorities, resources, and personal influence.''

''Because it helps steer the human component of the company strategy in the right direction, in accordance with the company objectives.''

''Because it is where you will touch the biggest issues and potentially shift the thinking/approach most dramatically.''

Not surprisingly, this role has demanded more time as the financial crisis has emerged, with 44 percent of CHROs saying they spend more time on this relative to twelve to eighteen months ago. One CHRO described the importance of the strategic advisor role in this way:

> HR is critical, but it's a tool in the firm's portfolio. First to truly impact the success of the firm, the CHRO needs to have a broad credibility that only comes from understanding every facet of the business at a level deep enough to be able to add business value in discussions with every leader. That means understanding the firm's economics, customer behavior, products, technology, etc. at a level deep enough to steer and shape decisions in these areas. From that flows the trust and credibility to counter the ''conventional wisdom'' on how best to manage people and shape the firm's talent agenda.

> Without this broader credibility, the CHRO can talk about talent, but risks not having sufficient context to make the right decisions. Second, from the CEO's perspective, the most useful thing is the integration of the people strategy with every other part of the firm's operations. The only way to truly integrate these areas is to be actively involved in the broader discussions as well.

Angie Lalor, the CHRO at 3M, stated in an interview, ''As strategic advisor I have to recognize that what may seem like a small decision can have a big impact on the organization—for instance decisions such as whether or not we decide to make an acquisition or redesign and restructure the organization. These are more point in time decisions but they have a broader impact on the company."

How CHROs influence the strategy seems to be less by being the "expert" and more often by being the person who is asking the difficult questions. Ian Ziskin from Northrup Grumman describes his influence tactics in this way:

> The single biggest thing I do is to ask questions. I ask questions like, "Have we thought about this alternative?" or "What are the implications of doing this?" One of the questions I find myself asking a lot is: "What is it that we are really trying to achieve?" Because I find that if you ask that question enough (sort of like the 5 why questions of Toyota) you are able to peel back the onion and find that the issue is something completely different from where you started. By focusing on asking questions, sometimes you find yourself asking a question that no one has yet asked and it takes the conversation in a different direction.

Talent Architect

The role of talent architect focuses primarily on ensuring that the right people are in the right positions at the highest levels of the firm. As opposed to the strategic advisor, where the focus is on the nature of the business strategies themselves and the broad organization capability necessary to implement them, the talent architect role aims at ensuring that the right leadership is in place to execute the strategy or initiative.

This role takes a significant portion of a CHRO's time (17 percent) and was also frequently (32 percent) cited as the role in which the CHRO has the greatest impact on the business.

Playing the role of talent architect requires that CHROs help the executive team see the importance of talent, identify existing and future talent gaps, and come to own the talent agenda. Interestingly, but not surprisingly, as the economy soured, few CHROs indicated that they are spending more time in this role; rather, the majority (53 percent) reported they currently spent the same amount of time as twelve to eighteen months before.

A number of CHROs described the ways in which the talent architect role affected the business:

"Having the right person in the job has the single highest beta return of all decisions that the CHRO can influence."

"Much of the conversation and activity addressed by the other roles is focused on or involve talent issues."

"Through leveraging human capital, the company is going to drive the innovation and execution to succeed and grow. The talent architecture and tie to the business strategy is how you get the focus on the right talent needs and develop the best solutions."

"People drive firm success. The response to demographic, societal, economic, regulatory factors on talent will be critical for success."

"Talent architect is the most controllable and tangible way for HR to have the strongest impact on the firm."

"Making sure we have the right talent to drive the business strategies and deliver business results is critical."

One CHRO stated it this way: "Keeping the senior team focused on the strategic talent needs of the business allows proper identification of talent gaps and future needs, thus allowing time to develop best talent and design appropriate experiential assignments."

COUNSELOR/CONFIDANT/COACH

The counselor/confidant/coach role is a multifaceted one that entails dealing with all of the conflicts and challenges that happen when a group of highly ambitious people become interdependent on one another as on an executive team. For instance, L. Kevin Cox, CHRO at American Express, said, "When you take ambitious achievement-oriented people, mix with imperfect alignment (rewards), and add a leader that doesn't confront, you have all the ingredients for a dysfunctional team. This is quite common, because senior teams are made up of ambitious people, incentives can never be perfect, and few leaders enjoy confrontation."

Thus, this role focuses on managing the interpersonal dynamics of the executive team in a way that helps them to work together effectively.

Interestingly, CHROs report spending as much time in this role as they do in the talent architect role (17 percent). Also interesting is the fact that this is the role in which the highest percentage of CHROs (45 percent) reported spending more time since the beginning of the economic crisis. Finally, a number of CHROs listed this role as one of the roles with the greatest impact. Twenty percent reported it as the role with the most impact or included it with other roles as those that have the greatest impact.

This role seemingly is a broad one and can entail anything from behavioral or performance counseling to being the personal sounding board for the CEO. Perhaps as pressure mounts on CEOs from investors and analysts, the CHRO is the most trusted advisor who can be counted on to give personal advice or simply to listen to the CEO's problems. Here are some examples of how CHROs perceive the impact this role on the business:

"If done well, it sets you up to be very influential as a strategic advisor. When you start as strategic advisor in the midst of a lot of change, you run the risk of being somewhat removed from the intensity of what senior line managers are experiencing."

"In that role, the CHRO can shape the behavior and actions of the key executives in the company, and thusly shape the future direction of the firm, even more so than in the strategic advisor role."

"I think it has to do with the specific executive who is filling the CEO role. For a CHRO who supports a strong employee-oriented leader, this one-on-one coaching role would not be so prominent. But if you are supporting a leader who is struggling, who is not a natural employee advocate, your coaching role in tough times with the CEO becomes much more pronounced."

One comment regarding this role was:

If I do my job right, I am the copper wire that connects all the outlets of the firm together effectively. This includes OD [organization development] work (which some might put in the strategic advisor category), performance counseling and relationship building, business consulting and the strategic elements of talent acquisition and planning.

So what does this role look like? Jorge Figuerado, the CHRO at McKesson, describes the role in this way: "I don't like to think of my job as providing opportunities for confession or psychological guidance, but I do think that part of my job is helping people work through their thorniest issues, and often the thorniest issues revolve around people."

This role also presents great risk. It does not necessarily mean being the messenger between the CEO and some member of the executive team, but rather ensuring that productive conversations take place between those people. Mirian Graddick-Weir from Merck stated:

> I believe that facilitating discussions between the CEO and his/her direct reports is a more appropriate role than is being the constant messenger. There are unique times when a messenger is called for, but I limit that role to the times when it is the best way to get the two parties to have a productive conversation. I think the messenger role is a tough role, and the problem is that you are rarely able to help the parties build a productive dialogue and relationship. Also, I have seen people get clobbered in the messenger role where they passed along the wrong information or have done it in a way that explodes. I think oftentimes the CHRO has to be very careful because you can end up playing the mediator or messenger role and you're the one that ends up getting shot.

LEADER OF THE HR FUNCTION

Those unfamiliar with the CHRO role would assume that the major responsibility of the head of HR is to lead the HR function. Although conceptually this is true, our work with CHROs suggests that the CHRO role is fulfilled more through delegation and guidance than through hands-on management of the function.

The leader of the HR function role presents some interesting findings. Although it was the role in which they spent the most time, it was not seen as the one with the greatest impact; only 5 percent cited it as such. In addition, this role has twice as many CHROs (35 percent) spending less time in it as report spending more time in it (17 percent) during the economic crisis. It seems that CHROs increasingly rely on their direct reports to design and deliver HR services while they shift their attention to advising and counseling the top executive team. This may be beneficial from two perspectives. First, CHRO expertise can play a vital role in effective decision making during trying times, so delegating HR responsibilities to direct reports can maximize the CHRO's opportunities to contribute to strategy. Second, delegation provides an opportunity for CHROs to assess their direct reports, particularly in terms of their viability as potential successors. Here are two examples provided by those who identified the HR leader role as having the greatest impact on the business:

"For us, right now, getting the outsourcing model right is critical. In addition, since we are in the process of spinning off a significant portion of our business, we are rethinking and refocusing our strategy, vision, and employee value proposition—this will be critical to gaining the hearts and minds of our employees in this transition!"

Laszlo Bock from Google laid out an interesting model for how he sets and communicates the agenda for the HR function:

We have four broad goals within people operations. This is a framework that guides individuals in people operations by helping them get to where you are going as a company. More specifically, our first goal is, "Find them, Grow them, Keep them." The idea is to find great people to work for Google, grow and develop their skills while they are here, and do everything we can to keep them at Google.

The second goal is, "Put our users first." This goal echoes what we do as a company; also it is deeply meaningful in how we think about the users of people operations, which are all the other Google employees.

The third goal is, "Put on your own oxygen mask before assisting others." The thinking behind this goal is, in many organizations,

[that] HR is doing all this work in the company for others, and they forget to grow and develop their own people. Eventually this cripples your ability to serve the rest of the organization because the very best, most talented people get recruited out of HR to go be heads of HR at other companies.

The fourth goal at Google's people operations is, "This space intentionally left blank." In our environment, we find that things change very, very quickly, and that creates a lot of uncertainty. Uncertainty causes people to put less discretionary effort into their work, to be less satisfied, less collaborative, more competitive with fellow employees, as well as making them more likely to leave the company. Hence, this goal is an attempt to explicitly recognize the dynamic nature of our internal and external environment.

Also, we have subgoals within each of four goals previously mentioned for which I am personally accountable. In fact, everyone within people operations has personal quarterly goals that tie back to these four functional goals.

LIAISON TO THE BOARD

In our interviews and working groups with CHROs over the past four years, the unanimous conclusion is that CHROs are spending more time with the board of directors than in the past. However, little research has examined how much time and around what topics this interaction takes place.

In fact, the results of the survey suggest that the liaison to the board is a role that seems to be increasing in importance, although it has a long way to go before equaling the strategic advisor, talent architect, and counselor/confidant/coach roles. CHROs reported spending 10 percent of their time in this role, and roughly a third (32 percent) reported spending more time in it over the past twelve to eighteen months. Most interesting about this role is that it was by far the role most frequently cited as the one CHROs were least prepared for, with 70 percent listing it.

We asked a follow-up question about the topics that they spend time on with the board and found that CHROs spend the bulk of their board exposure on issues of executive compensation. Executive compensation dominates this interaction, with a reported 49 percent of the board interaction revolving around this topic. However, change is emerging as executive pay and governance and compliance become almost inseparable. Kevin Barr of Terex states:

> Today I spend the most time with our board covering governance and compliance issues, second is pay, third is succession and fourth is executive performance. When I first started at Terex nine years ago, number one was pay, number two succession, third was executive performance and governance, and compliance was almost nonexistent. I think boards are currently extremely risk averse. The compensation committee has become equally, if not more, onerous than the audit committee. The audit committee became somewhat nightmarish after the Enron debacle and Sarbanes-Oxley, and it became exhausting in dominating the work of the board, though it did some positive things as well. Compliance, which is related to Sarbanes-Oxley, has now taken over, and boards are concerned about personal liability, and they are extremely concerned about appearance, and they are very much concerned about meeting compliance regulations.

In addition, as a consequence of the financial meltdown and ensuing recession, CHROs spend more time with the board on risk assessment. Laurie Siegel from Tyco states:

> I do a risk assessment for the board every year. It includes everything from the risk of a portfolio that is too fragmented and geographically dispersed, making appropriate oversight problematic to the risk of business continuity if there is a swine flu outbreak. In addition, I think what is really useful, and what the board appreciates, is often times when the CEO and I are traveling on an international flight, we will ask one another questions, such as, "What can go wrong?" and, "What are we not considering that could derail our strategic and operational efforts?" This has become sort of standard airline conversation.

> I think there is tremendous value in taking an out-of-the-box approach and considering what you are not thinking about, and the board appreciates that because a big part of their job involves anticipating the future issues that day-to-day management might not consider. What the board expects from me is the thought process and the reassurance that we are on it.

While this initial glimpse provides some insight into the increasing exposure of CHROs to the board, we believe that this is the role that will see the most change, in both time and substance, over the next five to ten years.

CONCLUSION

CHROs reported how they spent their time in various roles and which roles they felt were most critical to having a positive impact on the business. What became clear from the written comments and the interviews was that success as a CHRO role comes not from performing one role well, but from being able to integrate all, or at least many, of the roles simultaneously. In fact, it seems almost difficult to distinguish among the strategic advisor, talent architect, and counselor/confidant/coach roles in terms of their importance and impact. A number of CHROs combined these in some way as being highly interrelated to one another. For instance, one wrote: "It is critical that the CHRO is intimate in the formulation and implementation of strategy, as the culture, morale, and talent architecture are inextricably linked to the ability to execute strategic plans. The ability to formulate and execute on a strategy is contingent on the quality of senior leadership talent as well as the work environment. . . . The CHRO is right in the middle of the talent and culture/environment equation." Another CHRO described the interrelationships in this way: "If the CHRO does not have a role of confidant/counselor, it is hard to be seen as credible in the strategy discussion and move forward in the talent development with commitment from the CEO and COO."

An additional comment that emphasized the interconnectedness of the roles was, "There is not one role. The impact comes from a combination, primarily strategic advisor combined with counselor/confidant, that leads to doing the right things for talent development." Another CHRO summed up the necessity of being effective in both the strategic advisor and counselor/confidant/coach roles: "That's the difference between a great HR leader and an average one."

Finally, L. Kevin Cox from American Express articulated his own conceptual model of how CHROs attempt to merge these various roles:

> If I were drawing it, there are three layers. The top layer has the strategic advisor at one end running into talent architecture because I just think those are two ends of the same pipeline. I have a very difficult time breaking those two up even though they are different focus areas. You start off having input into the general strategy, but then have to get into the decisions about the actual talent in terms of who can and should lead that area of the business, and that is never a linear process with neat sequential steps.
>
> Underneath that and running across both the strategic advisor and talent architect piece I would say is the confidant role, because in the course of both of those discussions, you are having to identify and manage the interpersonal dynamics: Who is threatened? Who unduly gains what internal conflicts can arise? etc.?
>
> Finally, underneath that is the leader of the HR function. Once the strategy and talent issues have been addressed, you have to get the HR talent and processes in place to make that initiative a success.

Thus, the job of the CHRO continues to evolve. CHROs play many roles and must find ways to balance the time they spend in each, as well as ways to coordinate and integrate the various roles effectively. Those who do this well will have a significant impact on the reputation of the function in the minds of senior leaders.

PART TWO

THE CHRO AS STRATEGIC ADVISOR AND TALENT ARCHITECT

CHAPTER SIX

LEADERSHIP AND EMPLOYEE ENGAGEMENT
A Positive Synergy at Caterpillar
Sid Banwart

To set the stage for this discussion, it is important to provide some context and background about Caterpillar Inc. Caterpillar is one of only 2 percent of companies currently listed on the New York Stock Exchange that has the honor of being on the exchange for eighty or more years. Although it is headquartered in the relatively small city of Peoria, Illinois, it is clearly a global enterprise. In 2008, about two-thirds of sales were outside the United States, and exports from the United States to other countries totaled $16 billion. During the economic downturn in the early 1980s, Caterpillar lost more than $1 million per day for nearly three years. Then during the 1990s, the company undertook a major recapitalization of its U.S. factories, along with a significant struggle with the United Auto Workers union as ways to address issues of competitiveness in the United States. These management challenges have provided valuable case studies for a number of business schools.

This discussion is a synopsis of some of the challenges the company has faced in more recent history, and it outlines how the synergies between leadership and employee engagement have evolved in a purposeful way at Caterpillar.

The views and opinions expressed in this chapter are those of the author, not necessarily Caterpillar Inc.

THE PLAN

In 2004, Caterpillar chairman and CEO Jim Owens appointed a group of company leaders to form a strategic planning committee. This group of fourteen was charged with outlining a corporate strategy to move a good company into the future as a great company.

OUR VALUES IN ACTION

Under Owens's leadership, the group determined that the Caterpillar Code of Conduct, first published in 1974, required an update. As vice president and CHRO, I coordinated and managed the project to interview more than two thousand employees around the globe. This input led to a significant update of the code, which was re-released as "Our Values in Action":

- Integrity: The Power of Honesty
  Integrity is the foundation of all we do.

- Excellence: The Power of Quality
  We set and achieve ambitious goals.

- Teamwork: The Power of Working Together
  We help each other succeed.

- Commitment: The Power of Responsibility
  We embrace our responsibilities.

These four key values translated well into the twelve primary languages in which Caterpillar does business around the world and became the foundation for the new strategy. (The Appendix at the end of this chapter provides a more detailed description of each value.)

CRITICAL SUCCESS FACTORS

Another key feature of the new strategy was the development of seven critical success factors (CSFs)—people, quality, product, velocity, distribution, emerging markets, and trough—which became widely known and understood in a remarkably short period of time. Of note for this particular discussion and analysis are the trough and people CSFs (see Figure 6.1).

FIGURE 6.1. CATERPILLAR STRATEGY PYRAMID

TROUGH CSF

With the launch of the strategy and values, Caterpillar began an effort to develop the trough CSF—a critical effort because it was only a matter of time and circumstance until another down economic cycle occurred. Being ready for such a trough at the bottom of the downturn (defined as a decline in sales and revenues of 25 to 50 percent) was key because of the significant losses the company incurred in the 1980s. It was especially important because Caterpillar had been rewarded with a price-earnings (PE) multiple better than the market up to the 1980s, but had been struggling with a PE below the market ever since in spite of some good financial performance.

Management believed that only by being profitable during a trough period could the company regain a PE multiple consistent with the overall market. This realization led to the strategic goal of delivering profitability during a significant downturn. Leading the effort on achieving profitability in the trough was group president Doug Oberhelman. (Oberhelman became CEO on July 1, 2010, and chairman of the board on October 1, 2010.) His approach was to require each division of the company to develop its own rigorous trough plan and to address those plans each year during annual strategy reviews. He placed emphasis on making sure the plans were thorough and executed at a detailed level.

PEOPLE CSF

The people CSF had two top-tier measures (employee safety and employee engagement) and three second-tier measures (leadership, diversity, and learning). CEO Jim Owens was the corporate sponsor of the people CSF, and I was its corporate owner. I was responsible for global communications, integrating people measures into the personnel evaluation process, integrating people measures into the succession planning process, and conducting scheduled reviews of progress with the entire officer group.

In addition to an extensive communications strategy to cascade information about the new strategy and values, each CSF was assigned an owner and a set of critical measurements for success. The 2010 corporate goals were aspirational in nature so as to motivate changes in behavior and draw the organization together around what was important in implementing the new strategy and moving the company beyond good to outstanding. Corporate goals were also established for each interim year. The CFO and I tracked progress, but the responsibility for execution belonged to the administrative council, consisting of all operating officers of the company.

A RECAP

To summarize, the key elements of the effort put into place in 2005 included a strategy with Our Values in Action as a foundation:

- Critical success factors with 2010 goals and accountability for annual progress
- A detailed, rigorous trough plan
- A positive, proactive people plan

THE RESULTS

Between 2003 and 2008, Caterpillar achieved an impressive record of profitable growth, combined with dramatic improvements in employee safety and employee engagement. Equally impressive, if not more so, was the company's response to the worldwide economic crisis in late 2008. Management's rapid, effective response proved that the company's trough plans were rigorous and well executed. This resulted in sustained profitability in 2009 despite sales 37 percent lower than those of 2008, along with maintaining a mid-A credit rating and sustained dividend payments during the most severe economic crisis since the Great Depression (see Figure 6.2).

It is fair to ask how leadership and employee engagement played a role during the landmark period of record sales and record profits followed by a dramatic, catastrophic decline in demand. (To personalize the journey, I will refer to the Caterpillar leadership team as "we.")

FIGURE 6.2.   FINANCIAL RESULTS, 2003–2008

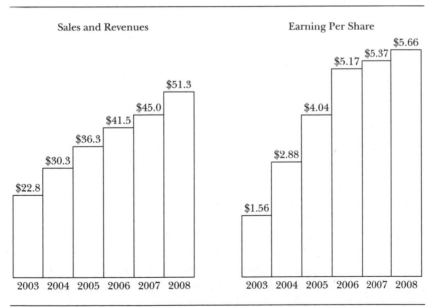

Early in this journey, we asked employees around the world to live Our Values in Action, form relationships with colleagues, and provide quality products and services for customers around the globe. Employee engagement was one of the keys to achieving some very aggressive goals according to CEO Jim Owens: "Our goals for the future require a coordinated, unified effort across our entire company. The only way we'll achieve these goals is with the enthusiastic, passionate commitment of every employee. You can instruct employees to reach certain goals, but you'll only get to the highest levels if you engage your people—their hearts and minds—in achieving them together. That's what it takes to become a great company."

As CHRO, I recognized that every organization has resources and assets, but most of those assets (machines, equipment, and software, for example) depreciate with time. People resources, however, can appreciate with time, given the right leadership. In Caterpillar's eighty-five years of operation, we have always worked to cultivate close connections among our employees and with our dealers and suppliers—aware that these relationships are a key link between our business performance and long-term marketplace potential.

Since the inception of the new strategy, we have worked to create a business culture in which employee engagement is an important component. Part of the vision was to create a more unified Team Caterpillar in which employees worldwide are challenged, motivated, and rewarded for performance and continuous improvement. Although this journey remains ongoing, the data show significant improvement in the talented and dedicated Caterpillar people around the world. What this means to the leadership team is that we must continue to do the right thing, the right way, at the right time—and for the right reasons. This is what employee engagement means to us at Caterpillar.

During our journey, we have found a strong statistical correlation between leadership and employee engagement in every country in which we do business. The facilities with the highest employee engagement scores also were doing the best on a number of key business measures, indicating that employee engagement is a cross-cultural strength for Caterpillar.

THE ANALYSIS

It is fair to ask why there was success with many of the CSFs during the period of growth and why there was success with the trough CSF during the recent economic crisis. The discussion that follows provides some additional information on how we went about executing our strategy. What emerged were a number of documented positive correlations. Although we believe that these relationships are real, we stop short of claiming cause and effect.

My staff and I provided leadership to the analysis of the information. Annually employees across the globe participate in an extensive online survey. Total participation exceeds 90 percent. The survey results are summarized in a number of indexes, including an employee engagement index that is developed for each supervisor, manager, and executive in the company. The employee engagement indexes are then compared with other measures such as profit, quality, leadership, and safety. Some examples follow.

LEADERSHIP BY EXAMPLE

CEO Owens assigned a sponsor and owner to each of the CSFs, but volunteered to sponsor the people CSF himself. As such, he was the personal champion for employee safety (Figure 6.3) and engagement (Figure 6.4). His sincere and continuing communications, both formal and informal, combined with institutional support from my role, were instrumental in dramatic improvements in both areas.

LEADERSHIP IN SUCCESSION MANAGEMENT

I viewed leadership and employee engagement as a business need that must be supported at the top of the company and worked to integrate this relationship between leadership and engagement into the company's succession management processes.

Caterpillar's executive office has the responsibility to select each candidate for the top three hundred positions in the

FIGURE 6.3. EMPLOYEE SAFETY

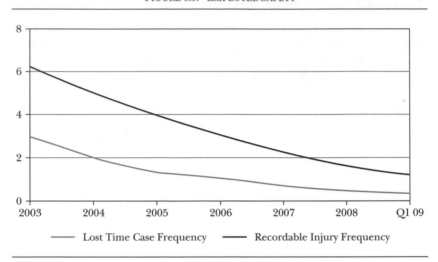

FIGURE 6.4. EMPLOYEE ENGAGEMENT

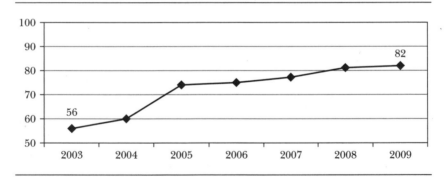

company. Candidates are selected not only on the traditional requirements of performance, potential, and diversity, but also on engagement, leadership, and values as measured by the annual employee opinion survey results. This is an important evolution for a company with a long history of developing leadership talent and filling the CEO position from within. This intensified focus has been implemented at other levels in the organization as well, where future leaders are identified and nurtured.

LEADERSHIP AS A CONTACT SPORT

According to the Hay Group (2001), as much as 35 percent of the variability in discretionary performance is a result of managerial styles and behaviors. Therefore, we make personal contact a responsibility for every leader. In our annual employee opinion survey, we ask participants to respond to two statements that specifically point to this particular area: "The person I directly report to demonstrates genuine interest and concern for me as a person" and a similar question for the senior management with whom they interact.

When we correlate these questions to the engagement of our people, we find more than a thirty-point positive difference in the engagement of employees who believe there is a positive relationship between themselves and their bosses—one that shows genuine interest and concern to the individual as a person, not just as an employee.

LEADERSHIP METRICS

Based on research by the Gallup Organization, about 80 percent of Fortune 500 companies perform an employee opinion-gathering activity (Wagner & Harter, 2006). However, according to the findings of this study, 60 percent of these companies reported that morale and effectiveness went down the year after the survey was conducted.

At Caterpillar, we find that leadership follow-up is a critical part of the process. In 2009, my staff and I discovered that if employees said yes to the question of whether the leader had shared results of the survey, their engagement levels were nineteen points higher than those who said no. Even more impressive, the HR team found that if employees said yes when asked whether they saw tangible action taken as a result of the survey, their engagement levels were twenty-six points higher than those who said no.

Because it is clear that leaders have a direct impact on employee engagement and because of the strong, positive corre-lation with a number of key business indicators, I communicated these findings directly to the entire officer group and to the annual strategic review conference attended by the key 120 leaders from around the globe.

About 60 percent of the questions in our employee survey start, "The person I directly report to..." or "In my immediate work group..." Therefore, each leader has the ability to make a significant impact on the survey and on employee engagement, giving them strong accountability for results.

A specific example that illustrates the manner in which this is made a reality at all levels in the organization comes from John Bolden, formerly HR director for Caterpillar Logistics Services, and Steve Larson, a Caterpillar vice president and chairman and president of Caterpillar Logistics Services. These managers engaged their leadership team by studying the relationship between employee engagement and warehouse operational performance. By proving a positive statistical relationship between the two factors, leadership had all the evidence it needed to support leaders who had fostered strong employee engagement.

ANALYSIS SUMMARY

At Caterpillar, we have seen a broad, statistically significant correlation between employee engagement and business performance factors such as profitability, lower absenteeism, lower attrition, improved safety, improved quality, improved productivity, and faster implementation of the Caterpillar Production System. I stop short of attributing cause and effect, although the correlations provide sufficient evidence to support our leadership approach and selection process.

CONCLUSION

Engagement is about more than the work being performed. It is about the interaction between the leader and the employee. Leaders have the privilege and opportunity to help employees move from compliance to commitment. We believe this journey is worth the effort because of the potential that can come from each employee's willing, discretionary effort. Committed, loyal employees who give their personal best will come together to make the entire company the best it can be.

While we have made a great deal of progress at Caterpillar over the past several years, our journey continues. To review the impact that this effort has yielded, we offer the following:

- Our voluntary attrition has been about half the national average in every country where we did business during the entire decade of the 2000s.
- Our profitability at the peak and our profitability in the trough have set new positive records during this decade.
- We've learned that what and how are not mutually exclusive and that a good leader is a demanding leader, but in the right way.
- We have developed and implemented a year-long employee survey and action planning process, so the leadership effort is continuous and not just an annual event.
- We know from strong and statistically significant correlations between leadership and employee engagement that many other positive business results follow.
- We know that engaged employees do matter, and we will manage in such a way as to continue earning our reputation for good leadership.

Appendix: Our Values in Action

As a result of our efforts to transform the culture at Caterpillar, we developed our Four Values in Action, which describe the critical values that drive all of our decision making.

Integrity: The Power of Honesty

Integrity is the foundation of all we do.

It is a constant. Those with whom we work, live, and serve can rely on us. We align our actions with our words and deliver what we promise. We build and strengthen our reputation through trust. We do not improperly influence others or let them improperly influence us. We are respectful and behave in an open and honest manner. In short, the reputation of the enterprise reflects the ethical behavior of the people who work here.

We put Integrity in action when

- We Are Honest and Act with Integrity.
- We Avoid and Manage Conflicts and Potential Conflicts of Interest.

- We Compete Fairly.
- We Ensure Accuracy and Completeness of our Financial Reports and Accounting Records.
- We Are Fair, Honest, and Open in Our Communications.
- We Handle "Inside Information" Appropriately and Lawfully.
- We Refuse to Make Improper Payments.

EXCELLENCE: THE POWER OF QUALITY

We set and achieve ambitious goals.

The quality of our products and services reflect the power and heritage of Caterpillar—the pride we take in what we do and what we make possible. We are passionate about people, process, product, and service excellence. We are determined to serve our customers through innovation, continuous improvement, and intense focus on customer needs and a dedication to meet those needs with a sense of urgency. For us, Excellence is not only a value; it is a discipline and a means for making the world a better place.

We put Excellence in action when

- We Establish a Work Environment That Supports Excellence.
- We Select, Place, and Evaluate Employees Based on their Qualifications and Performance.
- We Provide Employees with Opportunities to Develop.
- We Accept Nothing But the Best Quality in Our Products and Services.
- We Focus on Delivering the Highest Value to Our Customers, Always with a Sense of Urgency.
- We See Risk as Something to Be Managed, and as Potential Opportunity.
- We Take an "Enterprise Point of View."

TEAMWORK: THE POWER OF WORKING TOGETHER

We help each other succeed.

We are a team, sharing our unique talents to help those with whom we work, live, and serve. The diverse thinking and decision making of our people strengthen our team. We respect and value people with different opinions, experiences, and backgrounds. We strive to understand the big picture, then do our part. We know that by working together, we can produce better results than any of us can achieve alone.

We put Teamwork in action when

- We Treat Others with Respect and Do Not Tolerate Intimidation or Harassment.
- We Treat People Fairly and Prohibit Discrimination.
- We Foster an Inclusive Environment.
- We Conduct Business Worldwide with Consistent Global Standards.
- We Collaborate with Key Entities and Organizations Outside Our Company.
- We Build Outstanding Relationships with Our Dealers and Distribution Channel Members.
- We View our Suppliers as Our Business Allies.

COMMITMENT: THE POWER OF RESPONSIBILITY

We embrace our responsibilities.

Individually and collectively we make meaningful commitments—first to each other, and then to those with whom we work, live, and serve. We understand and focus on the needs of our customers. We are global citizens and responsible members of our communities who are dedicated to safety, care for our environment, and manage our business ethically. We know it is both our duty and our honor to carry the Caterpillar heritage forward.

We put Commitment in action when

- We Take Personal Responsibility.
- We Protect the Health and Safety of Others and Ourselves.
- We Protect Our Hard Assets, Our Brands, and Our Other Intellectual Property.
- We Safeguard Our Confidential Information.
- We Use Electronic Communications Technology Responsibly and Professionally.
- We Recognize and Respect Personal Privacy.

- We Support Environmental Responsibility Through Sustainable Development.
- We Are Pro-Active Members of Our Communities.
- We Make Responsible Ownership and Investment Decisions.
- We Participate in Public Matters in an Appropriate Manner.

REFERENCES

Hay Group. (2001). *Engage employees and boost performance: Provide great leadership, meaningful work, and other benefits that lead to engaged performance.* Philadelphia: Hay Group.

Wagner, R., & Harter, J. (2006). *12—The elements of great managing.* New York: Gallup Press.

CHAPTER SEVEN

FOUR STEPS TO WORLD-CLASS TALENT MANAGEMENT

L. Kevin Cox

I can virtually guarantee that your CEO wants you to develop a "world-class talent management process." Many CEOs, however, have difficulty explaining what they mean by "talent management" and often default to the "I'll know it when I see it" description.

Admittedly much has been written about talent management. Many CHROs have read McKinsey's landmark study, *The War for Talent* (Michaels, Handfield-Jones, & Axelrod, 2001). Most of us are familiar with the GE or the PepsiCo processes for managing talent that became widely known and aggressively copied over the past thirty years.

I have worked for three major corporations in my career, and have identified four practical concepts that I believe help to define world-class talent management. Before you dive right into these four steps, it is advisable to center your efforts around the talent outcomes your executive team wants to drive.

GETTING STARTED: THE OUTCOMES OF TALENT MANAGEMENT

As you engage with your business leaders, I strongly recommend you begin with a discussion of outcomes. Many business leaders are deeply suspicious of process for the sake of process, and they are especially guarded in or around the HR field.

71

Aligning with your business leaders around outcomes provides a useful tonic for their concerns. This alignment will help define success and, done correctly, will suggest a way in which results can be measurable. I believe in dialogue, and I practice the Socratic method of working with business leaders to produce a set of outcomes that are mutually owned by the business leaders and the HR organization. Following are the ten critical questions I ask:

1. Do we want to manage the top 5 to 10 percent of talent separately from all others?
2. How directive are we willing to be in the management of our top talent?
3. How much central direction of talent are we willing to tolerate?
4. What do we believe are the most effective ways to develop talent?
5. Do we want to manage diverse talent in unique ways?
6. What balance do we want to strike between internal talent development and external talent acquisition?
7. What rate of attrition is acceptable by organizational layer?
8. What is the right balance between organizational breadth and depth for our top talent?
9. Where are our key talent gaps (functionally, geographically) relative to our strategy?
10. By organizational layer, how long does it take to reach peak performance in a role?

If you could line up a group of top-tier CHROs, I don't think you would get strong alignment around the answers to all ten of these questions. More important, I don't believe you would fare any better when talking to CEOs, board members, or executive teams. The key, however, is to come to consensus within your executive team. Once you agree on answers to these questions, developing the right measurements for each is a relatively simple step.

Skipping the step of alignment can lead to a slew of organizational problems. Most commonly, it can lead a CHRO to begin to preach or proselytize about the "right way" to manage talent. This can lead to the production of cumbersome processes and scorecards that often produce little change and lots of resentment.

(Do we really need more Dilbert cartoons or *The Office* episodes on the shortcomings of bad HR?)

Alignment with your executive team won't guarantee smooth sailing on talent management, but it will certainly give you a much stronger basis from which to drive change and a much more reliable measurement system to demonstrate outcomes to CEOs, boards, and your organization.

Once you have alignment you can move on to the four steps to world-class talent management.

Step 1: Manage Talent Deployment Centrally

Great talent management has two natural enemies: hoarding (that is, keeping talent to themselves) and incrementalism (that is, not thinking about how to really stretch talent).

Hoarding

Unit leaders are under enormous pressure to deliver results. They quickly learn who in their units are their top performers or producers. The 80/20 rule is one of the first lessons in leadership: 80 percent of the work is done by 20 percent of the people. Like most other business axioms, there are many exceptions. But in general, unit leaders are loathe to take the actions necessary to encourage their top performers to move out of their units, whether laterally or vertically. In most cases, they are acting quite rationally; they are compensated largely on results, and if enterprise-wide goals are used at all, they often comprise only a small portion of the unit leader's compensation.

Their coping mechanisms to resolve this dilemma are cunning and broadly effective. They can downplay or qualify the potential of their top talent in reviews and discussions with their leaders: "She is getting there, but isn't really ready to take on broader responsibilities. Let's keep her in place another twelve to eighteen months."

Unit leaders have many private conversations with their top talent as they seek their leader's advice and counsel on career questions—for example: "Well, you can certainly raise your hand for that transfer to the Consumer Division. But I know the guy that runs that side pretty well, and he shows a lot of favoritism to his cronies who have worked in that group for years."

Hoarding of talent creates an insidious culture where cronyism flourishes and leaders create companies within companies that confuse and limit the potential of the talent unfortunate enough to work for those leaders.

INCREMENTALISM

I once worked for a CHRO who would confront and challenge managers who, during talent reviews, would make a statement that reflected incremental thinking around talent: "He runs a market that sells about 1 million cases per year. He's blown away his numbers for the past three years. So I think we should move him to a market that sells 1.5 million cases per year."

Great CHROs (and great CEOs) understand that talent needs to be developed in thoughtful, but not incremental, ways. Getting the balance right between "stretch" and "in over her head" isn't easy, but it is vital to the success of a world-class talent strategy.

THE SOLUTION

In my experience, the best way to counter hoarding and incrementalism is through central planning of talent deployment. I am convinced that left to their own devices, most unit leaders will stifle the growth of the talent within their own organizations. At best, they will create a unit that is capable but does not produce reliable exports of talent to other units within the organization. Over a few years, that organization will inevitably experience the issue of too much depth and not enough breadth (also known as stovepiping talent).

Most successful companies lay claim to certain talent as corporate assets. It might be the top two hundred performers in a large firm or particular salary bands in another one. Whatever the nomenclature, the key point is to publicly sweep a segment of talent into a centrally managed process.

Once you have identified the stratum of talent you wish to centrally manage, you can apply a different set of rules to those corporate assets. They might be expected to relocate more frequently than the balance of talent within your organization. You might plan or guarantee "return trip tickets" (that is, the ability to return to their previous roles) to those people who accept the career risks of going into turnaround situations or less-than-ideal geographical locations. Or you could accelerate their development through specially developed master class sessions with the senior-most leadership.

Whatever different rules you choose to apply to this select population, you will have taken the most important step to counter your organization's tendency to hoard talent or develop it so carefully so as to stifle your talent's full potential.

Step 2: Engineer Tension into the Talent Management Process

It requires a fair amount of tension to make a talent management process work correctly. In many cases, it also requires heat and time.

The tendency of leaders to manage everyone to the middle has given rise to talent differentiation systems. Many years ago, PepsiCo used labels such as FCP (full category promotable) and VHP (very high potential) to differentiate its talent. GE's vaunted "Session C" and "9-Box" was a similar method aimed at differentiating talent and planning talent movement to align with strategic business requirements.

These are relatively simple concepts, but are quite often poorly implemented. Real or perceived barriers exist to the concepts of talent differentiation. Some may charge the concept is "unfair" or "overly political." Concerns can emerge from the legal community around systemic bias or potential discrimination. In my experience, however, the biggest barrier stems from an aversion to the tension or the conflict that is essential to great talent management.

Although you must certainly develop your systems in conjunction with the organizational culture, the companies best known for excellence in talent management have found ways to become comfortable with tension. They may use cross-business line talent reviews to ensure consistent standards. Some might use external assessment techniques and data to counter intuition and conjecture. Some have a very strong HR presence and set an expectation that the HR professionals in the room have independent opinions and are encouraged to share those freely, even when they conflict with the prevailing wisdom from the leaders of the talent in question. It is important for CHROs to direct questions around talent not just to the leaders of that talent, but to the HR generalists or the talent professionals who are in the talent review meetings.

At American Express, I encourage my HR generalists to get to know the top talent within their organizations personally and to engineer the proper amount of tension into the talent review process. Ideally, this constructive tension can be developed privately, within the confines of the leader's office. But failing that, they are expected to present their own thoughts and observations in talent sessions, even when it is uncomfortable to do so. I work hard to demonstrate this trait personally and to role-model the expected behavior of my HR teams when we have senior-level talent reviews, including those presented to our board of directors.

Whether you use a system or a Ouija board is immaterial. Any forcing device to differentiate talent will do. But without tension that is stoked by courage and built on observations and data, it will be difficult to have a talent management process that will yield extraordinary results.

STEP 3: USE SCENARIO PLANNING TO MODEL YOUR ORGANIZATION'S EVOLUTION

If you want to quiet a room of very talented, very ambitious executives, ask them this question: "What will your organization look like in three years?" There will be some harrumphing. Someone surely will point out, "I don't have any idea what the business will look like in three years, much less the organization." You will hear some complaining. Someone will say, "That's not entirely in my control. My boss gets a big vote in that, and you should ask him."

Of course, no one can tell the future, and there are kernels of truth in these responses. But those perspectives also serve to obfuscate an inconvenient truth about talent management: we do a much better job in planning financial capital than human capital. Ask a CFO what the capital outlay is likely to be over the next three years, and she will tell you with an impressive amount of precision. Of course, it depends, but there is a financial capital strategy at all well-managed companies, and there needs to be a better human capital strategy at most.

Move a little further upstream in the talent supply chain, and you will find frustrated staffing managers who yearn for more clarity around what skills will be needed and where. They will talk about "filling holes" rather than "hiring ahead of the business curve." This certainly isn't true everywhere, as companies with robust workforce planning functions can attest.

I have had some success with a simple technique to break through the resistance of managers who prefer to "manage for today" rather than think through their organizational needs over a multiple-year time frame. I refer to it as Plan A, implying a manager also needs a Plan B and Plan C, since Plan A rarely works out as hoped. In it, I suggest they list their positions and incumbents for their key positions, and age the organization over a three-year period. They need to include categories for talent exports and talent upgrades. They are encouraged to estimate when roles might be combined or eliminated. This simple exercise forms the basis of useful dialogue. If they have made no changes over the three years, it points out the remoteness of the likelihood that things will remain static for that period. It serves as a basis to ask why they believe their talent would be content to remain in role indefinitely.

Plan A in Exhibit 7.1 is the basis of their talent review. It is a wonderful forcing device for dialogue and alignment among multiple levels of the organization. It provides a forum to identify corporate assets, aids in the conversations around standards and whether they are being constantly challenged and raised, and helps with workforce planning because sensitive issues such as retirement horizons can be brought forward in a constructive forum. As a multiple-year view of talent deployment, Plan A also points out the occurrence of incrementalism.

Of course, it isn't perfect. And changes, often unexpected ones, certainly happen. But revisiting their Plan A twice each year can provide leaders the basis of a dynamic, robust talent process.

EXHIBIT 7.1. PLAN A—FINAL

2007	2008	2009	2010	2011
SVP A Mary	SVP A Alyce	EVP A Bob	EVP A Bob	EVP A
SVP B Bob	SVP B Bob			SVP (new) Antonio
SVP C Simon	SVP C Simon	SVP C Sue	SVP C Sue	SVP C Sue
SVP D Jayne	SVP D Jayne	SVP D Jayne	SVP D EXTERNAL	SVP D Sarah
SVP E Anthony	SVP E Marc	SVP E Marc	SVP E Marc	SVP E Andrea
SVP F Malayka	SVP F Malayka	SVP F Malayka	SVP F Bill	SVP F Bill
SVP BENCH Sue, VP G Bill, VP H Alyce, VP I Marc, VP J	SVP BENCH Sue, VP G Bill, VP H Pierre, VP Q Andrea, VP R	SVP BENCH Bill, VP H Pierre, VP Q Andrea, VP R	SVP BENCH Pierre, VP G Andrea, VP R Antonio, VP S	SVP BENCH Pierre, VP G Tom, VP T
SVP Export List Simon, SVP C Anthony, SVP E	SVP Export List Simon, SVP C Malayka, SVP F	SVP Export List Malayka, SVP F Marc, SVP E	SVP Export List Marc, SVP E	SVP Export List
SVP Exit List Mary, SVP A	SVP Exit List	SVP Exit List Jayne (RETIRE)	SVP Exit List	SVP Exit List

Step 4: Link External Talent Acquisition with Internal Talent Development

When I was twelve years old, I was a Boy Scout, and the greatest week of all was the week of Scout Camp. The best part of that week was the snipe hunt, when we would take impressionable Tenderfoot scouts into the woods late at night, armed only with a bag and a flashlight, and tell them all about the elusive snipe, a bird that was very difficult to catch—difficult, of course, because it didn't exist. But every year, in a tradition that I hope continues to this day, thousands of Tenderfoot scouts chase the elusive snipe in woods all over the world.

This final step might well be the snipe of world-class talent management: linking talent acquisition strategies with internal development strategies. Figure 7.1 illustrates how I think about the varying responsibilities for talent acquisition teams, talent development teams, and business leaders to execute effective talent management.

Talent acquisition, defined here as the search for external talent, is alive and well at most well-managed firms. And in most of those firms, talent development—the strategies to increase the capability, performance, and potential of internal talent—also works reasonably well. The problem is that they are often decoupled from one another, making world-class talent management difficult to achieve.

FIGURE 7.1. RESPONSIBILITIES FOR THE VARIOUS ASPECTS OF TALENT MANAGEMENT

Talent Requirements
(Business Leader)

External Hiring   Internal Development
(Talent Acquisition Teams)   (Talent Development Teams)

To illustrate the point, take a look at the goals of the people responsible for talent acquisition and compare them to the goals of those responsible for talent development:

Talent Acquisition	Talent Development
Focus recruitment efforts on leaders who excel at innovation and risk taking	Focus core leadership development on building the capability to better leverage relationships and improve the ability to operate in a matrixed organization
Hire high-potential campus recruits we can quickly mold into leadership roles, with 75 percent of new campus recruits promoted within three years of hiring	Maximize the individual's contribution in the role, with a focus on the development of deep functional experience, with 95 percent of all employees meeting their "time in job" guidelines
Develop an in-depth personalized needs assessment on executive hires; know them well before they enter the organization	With HR business partners, develop a comprehensive ninety-day plan for all new executive leaders
Implement an assessment process to build a fact-based selection process	Implement a 360-degree assessment process to focus the development needs of executive leaders

Are there meaningful points of integration? Are there any shared goals that would drive greater cooperation and knowledge transfer? Is it possible that these two organizations might be approaching your business partners separately, causing many business leaders to complain about the lack of HR integration or strategic thinking?

In many ways, both talent acquisition and talent development are fulfillment shops. They exist to satisfy talent demand, but they do so in very different ways. I believe it is essential, however, to clarify who in your organization has the accountability for defining the talent demand. Is it your business leader? Your HR generalist? The answer can vary as long as all parties agree on roles and responsibilities, and have the capability to execute within those roles.

At American Express, the business leader is responsible for defining the talent demands of his or her unit. These leaders may request particular subject matter expertise (talent scans or organizational effectiveness consulting, for example), but ultimately they own the responsibility for defining their talent demand. Once this demand is defined, it is relatively straightforward to satisfy it using either external or internal talent in some combination.

As a CHRO, you must think this through and develop a personal position on the subject. It is important to seek the input and alignment of your business partners (see question 6 in the list on p. 72) and then translate the clarity of roles and responsibilities throughout your HR organization. I have seen more finger pointing, misunderstanding, and wasted effort in this domain than any other within HR. At the end of the day, it is possible that we fail to deliver against the talent requirements more than any other business need; this is ironic, given that this is where most business leaders expect to find the greatest delivered value from HR. It is also problematic given the intensity around the precise talent needs in today's economy.

Like the snipe, I have seen glimpses of it, but have yet to finally capture it. I know this linkage is important, and though progress has been made, I know my teams and I have a great deal more work to do on this step as we look to lay claim to world-class talent management.

CONCLUSION

The four steps set out in this chapter are essential building blocks to CHROs who are seeking to build a world-class talent management system for their business partners. As is true with much of the HR domain, there remains room for debate, challenge, and disagreement. It is important to reiterate that the ultimate referees are our business partners, which emphasizes the importance of beginning with a robust discussion around outcomes sought.

REFERENCE

Michaels, E., Handfield-Jones, H., & Axelrod, B. (2001). *The war for talent*. Boston: Harvard Business School Press.

CHAPTER EIGHT

RETOOLING HR AND AVOIDING THE SERVICE TRAP

How Proven Business Models Offer Untapped Potential for Strategic Talent Decisions

John W. Boudreau

Why do HR leaders and their constituents work so hard, accomplish so much, and yet still often encounter questions and doubts about their real impact? Undoubtedly the work that leaders do is valuable, so why is HR still struggling with its identity after over fifty years of progress (Lawler and Boudreau, 2009)? How can so much hard work and accomplishment still be achieving outcomes that are less than optimal?

An engineer presented with this paradox of hard work with less-than-optimal outcomes might say these are classic symptoms of failing to target investments where they make the biggest difference. The answer is usually not more effort or investments but better targeting. Better targeting happens when the drivers of the system are clearer, and where the key decision makers have

---

The ideas in this chapter are based on *Retooling HR: Using Proven Business Tools to Make Better Decisions About Talent,* by John W. Boudreau. Boston: Harvard Business Press, 2010.

both accountability and capability to invest where it matters most, and avoid investing where it makes little difference. Disciplines as diverse as finance, operations, marketing, and innovation achieve this with widely shared and consistent proven business frameworks. Frameworks such as net present value, supply chain optimization, and market segmentation lead to better targeting by creating greater accountability and capability among all leaders, not just those in the particular discipline.

This chapter shows how CHROs can tap such frameworks to create the same effect when it comes to investments in talent and human capital.

THE SERVICE TRAP

HR itself can be a barrier to improved decision models when it unwittingly delivers such great "service" that it actually prevents leaders from seeing the full effects of their decisions. This might be called the service trap. For example, unit leaders understandably wish to forgo long-term human capital forecasting and simply wait until vacancies arise to post the requisition and receive high-quality talent immediately and consistently. Indeed, this is often the explicit or implicit definition of strategic staffing. Yet for HR to deliver this service, it may require compromising the talent pipeline, spending far more than would be required with advance planning or making heroic special efforts that are unsustainable. The trap is that the unit leader is often unaware of all of this, because HR is so good at hiding it behind the veil of great service.

More mature disciplines avoid this trap. Instead, they help leaders understand and hold them accountable for the impact of their decisions on costs, pipelines, and optimization. For example, a leader who chooses to save money on inventory by holding too little safety stock and expecting the supply chain organization to deliver at the last minute is held accountable for the cost and process implications of that decision. The implications of such decisions are not merely a supply chain problem. Leaders are expected to optimize the supply chain with strong input and consultation from supply chain experts. This is exactly the same issue as the staffing example, yet the models that leaders are encouraged to use are often very different between staffing and supply chains.

Aiming to get beyond being just the compliance police, HR sometimes focuses on providing great service. However, in addition to compliance and service, HR needs to help managers make smart decisions about talent. If HR focuses only on getting better on service, then critical work on creating a decision science may be ignored. CHROs have long sought to banish the specter of being the personnel police who only say no. Striving to evolve beyond a simple compliance model, CHROs often aim for a services paradigm. In this paradigm, they gauge the success of their HR organizations by the amount of time their leaders spend on human capital–related issues, the diligence with which those leaders engage with HR programs, or the degree to which HR organizations are regarded as delivering value. This paradigm is laudable, but it can work against an important element of making HR a true decision science. Like finance and marketing, a true decision science defines HR success as "improving decisions about talent and human capital wherever they are made" (Boudreau & Ramstad, 2007, p. 4). As in the staffing example, if great service shields HR's constituents from the full implications of their decisions, then what appears to be great HR service can actually impede improvements in the quality of decisions about human capital.

RETOOLING HR TO TEACH, NOT JUST COMPLY OR DELIVER

HR organizations are far more effective in delivering HR services than in educating leaders about the quality of their HR decisions. Yet our research at the Center for Effective Organizations shows that the quality of HR's strategic contribution is correlated more with how well HR educates leaders than how well HR adds value by delivering high-quality services and much more than how well HR adds value by ensuring compliance with rules and guidelines (Lawler & Boudreau, 2009). The irony is that by overemphasizing compliance or services, HR may actually detract from the goal of educating leaders about the quality of their decisions. If HR engages with constituents mostly to say, "That's not allowed because we have a rule against it," that obviously does little to help the leader understand the factors involved in the decision. Less obvious is that overemphasizing HR service to meet the demands of clients can also actually be counterproductive in terms of the quality of the human capital decisions.

The answer for HR is to take a page from business models that have long been used by other functions, such as finance, operations management, marketing, and engineering. These functions often strike a better balance between supporting the needs of line leaders, while holding those leaders accountable for sophisticated decision making. Here are some examples.

PERFORMANCE TOLERANCE LOGIC CAN RETOOL HOW LEADERS THINK ABOUT EMPLOYEE PERFORMANCE

The logical model that line leaders often hold for employee performance is something like, "We must have top performers in every job, and every competency should be maximized." Yet this is not the way performance is seen through typical engineering models. In those models, the connection between performance levels and system performance determines quality tolerances. For example, the hydraulic system of an aircraft is held to very high and tight performance tolerances, but the upholstery inside the cabin is held to a less stringent performance tolerance. Keeping the cabin environment at a sufficient quality standard is important, but that does not mean that "the best performance everywhere" can be the rule. The implication is that HR must help leaders acknowledge where improving talent quality makes a pivotal difference and where good quality is good enough.

The CHRO and other HR leaders often make well-meaning efforts to improve worker performance by setting tough goals on all the key performance indicators for a job or by striving to meet the seemingly laudable goal of "having top performers in every role." Business leaders come to believe that a reasonable and appropriate goal for human capital is to have the best quality of talent everywhere and the highest performance possible on all elements of a job. Strategic HR contribution is defined as delivering on this goal, often through heroic efforts at attraction, selection, and retention. Yet does the chief operations officer approach his or her role this way? What if a manufacturing manager said, "My unit's performance numbers look better if we have all of our machines running at full capacity, so operations provides the greatest value when they make that happen"? The operations group could maximize machine utilization by allowing the manufacturing manager to feed lots of raw materials into the system, and this will indeed improve the utilization rate on the machines with excess capacity. However, the processed materials will pile up as half-finished goods in front of machines that are at the bottleneck. The better decision is to run most of the machines at less than capacity and instead raise the capacity of the one machine that really matters: the bottleneck (Goldratt, 1999).

The parallel in HR is to avoid devoting scarce resources to goals such as "the best people for every job," and instead focus on getting the best people in the job that is the bottleneck—the one where an improvement will have the biggest impact. For example, at Disneyland, making Mickey Mouse a better performer may be far less pivotal than making the sweepers on the street better at addressing the needs of the guests that they encounter. As Boeing transformed itself to build the 787 aircraft through composite technology and a more codependent supply chain, making engineers better at traditional engineering may be less vital than making engineers adept at managing supplier relationships (Boudreau & Ramstad, 2007; Boudreau, 2010).

Targeting the most pivotal performance improvements for workers uses the same logic as targeting machine performance improvements to the bottleneck of a manufacturing process. The bottleneck metaphor in manufacturing is a special case of the engineering principle of performance tolerance optimization. The principle is so fundamental that business leaders naturally encounter it in many business decisions. "Retooling" HR means making such principles a fundamental element of talent decisions as well.

TEACHING OTHERS ABOUT PERFORMANCE TOLERANCE LOGIC

The operations organization doesn't just make decisions about machine use; it is also accountable for helping manufacturing managers learn not to make the mistake of maximizing utilization rates at the expense of excess in-process inventory. Operations management frameworks make leaders smarter about such decisions, so they are more accountable and adept. All leaders are expected to understand the idea of a bottleneck and act appropriately—even if they are not operations experts. The chief operating officer is not accountable simply for delivering what constituents want, but for educating them to make good decisions. High-quality operations decisions take precedence over simply meeting constituents' needs.

When we consider the HR example through this lens, it is clear that it's not just HR leaders at Disney deciding to improve sweepers instead of improving Mickey Mouse. It's HR providing decision frameworks (like performance tolerance logic) so that line managers can make wise decisions about people management. A decision-based HR organization makes leaders smarter about improving worker performance where it matters most, just as they should be smart about improving machine utilization where it matters most.

This means redefining the mandate of the CHRO and the HR organization to deliver the right outcomes and, more important, to educate their clients using professional frameworks that make those clients smarter. In this example, that means helping leaders understand that as attractive as it sounds for every leader to strive for top performance everywhere is not optimal. Where performance improvement does not produce large effects on strategic outcomes, the job of leaders is not to demand that their organization be staffed with A players, but rather to attract and manage B players where their contribution is most appropriate and optimal.

INVENTORY AND SUPPLY CHAIN LOGIC CAN RETOOL HOW LEADERS THINK ABOUT TALENT SOURCING

As a second example, consider the earlier situation where a unit manager saw an unexpected spike in sales activity and decides there is a need for more workers to meet the demand. Unit managers admonish their HR business partners to fill the vacancies immediately, and the HR business partners in turn press their colleagues in the staffing organization to do what it takes to be "strategic," defined as meeting the request. The staffing organization manages to deliver great quality on a moment's notice, and everyone celebrates HR's strategic heroism. Yet this is only part of the story. Behind the scenes, this last-minute heroism can produce exorbitant staffing costs and a higher failure rate for the new employees, perhaps caused by hiring managers' being allowed to cut corners on their interviews. The line manager often never even sees the staffing budget implications: "HR's staffing budget is their job; I have a business unit to run" is not an uncommon attitude. The failure rate of employees hired in a hurry may not become apparent until well after the crisis has passed, and the failure is often not clearly connected to the leader who made the decision to rely on last-minute hiring. Both the high staffing budget and the failure rate may appear in isolation as an "HR problem," but in fact they stem from the decision to forgo advance human capital planning and insist on an instant staffing solution.

This paradox is not unique to HR. In supply chain management, the same thing happens when a sales organization, having collaborated and approved a sales and manufacturing plan for the year, suddenly books massive orders just before year end to make its goals. The result is a spike in demand that ripples back through the supply chain, often wreaking havoc with the carefully laid logistic arrangements that took months to put in place. The costs of filling the orders quickly can be many times as great as any revenue increase that the sales organization achieved, and often results in lower-quality products, returns, or delivery failures. It even has a name: the bullwhip effect (Reddy, 2001).

The difference is that logistics engineers and planners more often hold the sales organization accountable. They may change the commission formula so that salespeople get their bonus based only on sales that are not returned, not late, and meet quality standards. Smart organizations don't tolerate attitudes like, "My job is sales, not manufacturing. Why should I suffer because they can't turn out quality stuff on time?"

It's more than just an admonishment that "we should all get along." It's based on hard-nosed logic that makes sure the full costs of sales decisions get attached where they will motivate the right choices. Everyone is expected to be accountable and adept at this problem, even if they are not logistics planners. Unit leaders in sales and manufacturing know to call their counterparts in logistics planning for help, and when those counterparts arrive, they make the unit leaders smarter, often by saying no to misguided requests.

No one intentionally tries to unbalance manufacturing or achieve their sales goals by decimating the production plan. That kind of misallocation of investments happens when smart and well-meaning people respond to the best signals they have, but those signals are faulty. When the line of sight to the larger issues is fuzzy, it's easy to focus on activities rather than deliverables and to believe you are getting a lot done when you are actually not or when you are even causing harm somewhere else. Leaders and their stakeholders in the disciplines of logistics, manufacturing, marketing, finance, and operations have developed frameworks that guide the logical models of decision makers both inside and outside the functional profession and make them more accountable and more adept.

Holding the sales organization accountable if they up-end the manufacturing plan to make their end-of-year numbers is not that different from holding line managers accountable if they up-end the human capital plan by failing to consider human capital needs far enough in advance. However, in the staffing situation, the unit manager probably never sees the full cost and can be forgiven for assuming that "strategic partnership" from HR means providing top-quality resources at minimum cost on a moment's notice with zero risk. It is as potentially counterproductive as the idea that the sales organization does not have to worry about manufacturing or operations. Why not expect leaders to be as smart about the full cost of their staffing decisions as they are about their sales decisions?

CHROS MUST ADDRESS MISCONCEPTIONS THAT LIMIT THE HR DECISION SCIENCE

Are decisions about talent management and human capital more vulnerable to these logical mistakes because human capital decisions don't matter to organization leaders? No. Indeed, every leader in the world knows that human capital decisions like these, multiplied over tens or thousands of well-meaning leaders, can have effects at least as significant as decisions about manufacturing, supply chains, and logistics.

Are human capital decisions less systematic because human behavior is so random or self-interested that any attempt to be systematic about it is doomed to failure? No. Human nature is just as much at work in manufacturing and marketing as it is in job performance. Indeed, a hundred years of research on work behavior actually has a lot to say about predicting things like performance and turnover (Cascio & Boudreau, 2009).

People are obviously not inanimate widgets. Does respect for free will and humanity make it unfair to use the same logic for workforce decisions as we use for decisions about more inanimate objects like inventories and machines? No. In fact, it's arguably more unfair and disrespectful to employees and job applicants to make important decisions about where to invest in their development, performance, and careers in ways that are logically flawed.

Today's leaders are smart and well meaning, and they believe that good talent management decisions matter. Yet they often pursue seemingly logical decisions but misguided goals like demanding the best performers in all roles or saving time by filling employee requisitions at the last minute. This kind of mistake happens when smart and well-meaning people respond to the best signals they have, but those signals are faulty.

Could leaders in HR and their stakeholders develop frameworks to make human capital decision makers more accountable and adept? Yes. The path is right in front of us, hidden within the logical frameworks that leaders already use for resources like money, advertising, manufacturing systems, information systems, and product components. CHROs must redefine the mantra that HR must know the business. It is indeed important to understand business goals and create human capital strategies to reach them. However, the evolution of HR requires more. CHROs and their HR organizations must know the business tools and apply them as rigorously to talent decisions as they would to decisions about asset investments, consumer segments, inventories, supply chains, and engineering components. Seeing how the business tools apply to talent management offers untapped opportunities to redefine common talent dilemmas.

THE LESSONS OF RETOOLING HR

- Learn the business logic, not just the business.
- Find allies in functions that are outside HR, where the vital logic of the business exists.
- Seek out the risk and the inconsistencies in the mental models of leaders, because that's where improvement can make the big difference.
- Look for the pivot points where improvements have the greatest impact.
- Measure with logic first and numbers after, because it is the logic that is often more powerful.
- Build on the business models that already exist to prototype rapidly new ways to think about talent management.

REFERENCES

Boudreau, J. W. (2010). *Retooling HR: Using proven business tools to make better decisions about talent.* Boston: Harvard Business School Press.

Boudreau, J. W., & Ramstad, P. M. (2007). *Beyond HR: The new science of human capital.* Boston: Harvard Business School Press.

Cascio, W. F., & Boudreau, J. W. (2008). *Investing in people.* Upper Saddle River, NJ: Pearson.

Goldratt, E. Y. (1999). *Theory of constraints.* Great Barrington, MA: North River Press.

Lawler, E. E. III, & Boudreau, J. W. (2009). *Achieving excellence in human resources management.* Palo Alto, CA: Stanford University Press.

Reddy, R. (2001, June 13). Taming the bullwhip effect. *Intelligent Enterprise,* http://intelligent-enterprise.informationweek.com/010613/supplychain1_1.jhtm.

CHAPTER NINE

THE CHRO AS CULTURAL CHAMPION

Michael L. Davis

Many years ago when I was a compensation consultant, I asked a CEO during an introductory meeting to describe his company's culture. He looked at me with some disdain and said something to the effect of, "I don't have a lot of time for human resource people who want to talk about company culture. We are here to drive performance. End of story." It was a rocky start to the consulting engagement.

The interview was obviously memorable. This was an executive who knew what he wanted to do but didn't give a lot of thought to how he was going to engage his team and the rest of the organization toward achieving his goal. Imagine giving that kind of pep talk to a group of soon-to-be college graduates as they are thinking about which company they might join after graduation.

EMPLOYMENT VALUE PROPOSITION

The CHRO is the ultimate architect of the company's employment value proposition. For purposes of this chapter, I define *employment value proposition* (EVP) as everything employees find of value in working for their employer. The EVP includes components that are extrinsic in nature, such as the company's compensation and benefits package; employment practices such as time off for illness, vacation, holidays; or even sabbaticals. The EVP also includes components that are intrinsic in nature—for example, the work environment, the company's industry, the company's products or services, the relative success of the company in the industry or community, the work location, the company's workforce, and its approach to hiring, development, and promotion. It also includes the company's mission, core values, and culture.

As most CHROs know, it is hard to differentiate an organization in a crowded employment marketplace on extrinsic elements alone. Strong compensation and benefit programs can play an important role in creating a good employment value proposition, but to really differentiate itself, a company also needs strong intrinsic elements.

Over a long career of working in the total rewards area, it became clear to me that the winning ticket for a strong employment value proposition is twofold: (1) a strong foundation provided by competitive or better extrinsic reward elements and (2) a compelling intrinsic rewards story. In almost every case that I can think of, great companies have great intrinsic rewards stories and, in particular, great cultures.

Great company culture is the subject of this chapter.

CORE VALUES

Every company has core values. Some go to great lengths to write them down and use them in describing and running the company. Other companies are less formal; maybe the values are even unstated, but they exist nonetheless. Core values come in handy in decision making of all kinds.

A company might have a core value of being family friendly. This could manifest itself by emphasizing workplace flexibility, flexible options for paid and unpaid time away from work, or a compassionate approach to helping employees in times of family crisis. The company could openly encourage children or spouses to visit for lunch in the company cafeteria. The benefits program could include favorable pricing for the extension of benefits to other family members. Work policies can make it easy for employees to attend parent-teacher conferences. The company could have a child care center on site, allow family members to use the company fitness center, or provide medical care at the company medical clinic. Any single program or policy is not that extraordinary; it is the cumulative effect of a multifaceted approach that makes the difference. Great companies pay attention to these things, and the visible reinforcement makes a difference to employees, job candidates, and the community in general.

Another example of a core value is good corporate citizenship. This could be brought to life with a company match program on charitable contributions. The company could emphasize to its employees the value and power of community involvement and could help employees find opportunities to volunteer or join boards of local nonprofits. The company could let community groups use conference rooms or hold events on company property. It could make monetary or product contributions in times of need, such as after flooding or hurricanes. The company could pledge to improve its carbon footprint, or use less water, or strive to pollute as little as possible. The company can be a good employer to the community's citizens by being a source of good, steady jobs. The company's management can be visible in the community in many different ways. Again, any one of these actions is not all that impressive, but put a unique combination of these actions together, and they become memorable and visibly reinforce the core value.

Core values can be brought to life by building an integrated set of programs and policies that reinforce and bring value to life. Another important way to bring the core values to life is through storytelling. Whether going back historically or in the present day, telling stories of how the company walks the talk on each core value it is very powerful. In today's YouTube environment, an employee telling his or her story of how the company lives its core values can be incredibly powerful. It can be a mother telling how the company helped her during a family emergency. It can be an employee telling how the company gave him time off from work to help make and place sandbags in advance of a potential flood. It can be a work group telling of building a home through Habitat for Humanity. It can be a pilot telling a story of using a company plane to bring medical supplies to Haiti.

Core values can also be brought to life by the actions and spoken words of the company's leaders. Everyone, both inside and outside the company, watches leaders' behaviors and actions.

Think about how a large company runs its United Way campaign. You can have the campaign visibly led by a member of senior management or assign it to someone in HR. You can have leaders appropriately encouraging employees to participate, or passively pass out pledge cards. You can have leaders play a leadership role in giving, or do nothing special with this group.

Leader communication of the core values is important. Done right, there are not too many, they are memorable, and the stories keep them fresh in everyone's mind. Employees do listen to what leaders say and also discern what they do not say. As leaders travel around the company they must both live and speak the core values.

The CHRO typically is the person most responsible for keeping the core values alive; he or she makes sure that programs and policies are crafted to reinforce the values, that stories that reinforce the values are updated, and that leaders are building core values into their messages to employees and externally. Core values bring a company mission statement to life, often define physical elements of the workplace, and play a big role in shaping company culture.

WORKPLACE

A workplace can be an office building, a manufacturing plant, a retail outlet, or an airport. It can be nothing special, or it can be exceptionally special. The CHRO may not have facilities as a reporting unit, but the CHRO has a lot to say about the physical work environment. Core values and company culture might dictate a lot about the workplace. It can shape thinking about common areas and amenities. An important consideration is the front door and reception, where customers, job applicants, and recruits see the company for the first time. You want people in their first thirty seconds in the reception areas to have a positive response to something you have done to introduce the company to entering visitors.

Workplace flexibility is starting to take shape in business offices. Companies are starting to question the need for fixed offices, particularly given the time many people spend in meetings or traveling. Technology now allows staff to be as connected on vacation in Morocco as they are at work. CHROs at leading companies are questioning old workplace norms and starting the creation of twenty-first-century workplaces.

CULTURE

A recent Google search of the words *company culture* yielded many, many responses. Here are two examples:

"Organizational culture is an idea in the field of Organizational studies and management which describes the psychology, attitudes, experiences, beliefs and values (personal and cultural values) of an organization."

"Company Culture is the term given to the shared values and practices of the employees. Note that the actual culture may not match the published culture."

I like to define *company culture* as the social norms at the company, specifically as exhibited by the behavioral norms of the company's leaders.

Like core values, company culture can be documented and discussed, or it can be individually defined and undocumented. Having said that, every company has a culture. Culture can cut both ways: there can be positive aspects of the company culture and negative aspects. Not surprisingly, companies are much more inclined to talk about the positive side of company culture and remain silent on the cultural areas for improvement. The CHRO, the CEO, and the entire company senior management team are stewards of the culture, but it likely falls to the CHRO to pay the most attention to culture.

Company culture is likely to evolve over time. Certain aspects remain in the cultural core for decades. Other aspects may change as technology changes, the company's business and industry changes, or after a big acquisition occurs. Think about the profound impact that wireless Internet, personal digital assistants, and now tablet computers have had on business. You can walk down the hall and instead of seeing people greeting each other, they are all looking at their smartphones as they walk. Think about the work culture at airlines over the years or retailers, and how that has changed.

Cultures can be changed, but it can take a lot of work. A company with an insular culture can decide to become more externally connected. HR and other company leaders would need to identify specific actions that someone might do to become more externally connected. Examples might include attending trade shows, joining functional networking organizations, and creating opportunities to share information on the Internet.

Sometimes management can fool themselves into thinking that they know what the culture really is at their company. In fact, your real culture can be quite different from your stated culture. It is critically important to let your employees tell you, in their own words, how they see the company, how they describe it to friends and recruiting candidates, or how they live it day to day. This is another area where storytelling and videos can help you get at an accurate understanding of the company's culture. You don't want to be saying you are family friendly, for example, if your employees are saying they are working seventy-hour weeks. Similarly, you don't want to say you offer a flexible workplace, but then hear employees talking about the need for face time and a ten-hour day of back-to-back meetings.

Conclusion

Many duties fall uniquely to the CHRO. Although another senior executive, the senior leadership team as a whole, or even the CEO could be the culture champion, as a practical matter, it is the CHRO who probably spends the most time thinking about it and making the detailed program, policy, workplace, or communication changes necessary to keep culture fresh and on point.

Great companies are not great by accident. They are created and endure only through a lot of work and care. Mission, core values, workplace, and culture all play key roles in defining great companies.

CHAPTER TEN

WHEN CRISIS CALLS

Laurie Siegel

Tyco had been in the headlines for much of 2002—unfortunately, they were tabloid-type headlines. The large industrial conglomerate had become the latest name in a string of corporate scandals that wafted in with the new century. Other names, like Enron and WorldCom and Adelphia Communications, were already engraved in a rogue's gallery of executive malfeasance. But among the workaday public, it was the personal expenditures—like the six-thousand-dollar shower curtain in the home of then-CEO Dennis Kozlowski disclosed in the case of Tyco—that resonated with special vividness. Kozlowski and his chief financial officer, Mark Swartz, would eventually be tried, convicted, and sent to jail on larceny and misleading financial statements.

It was in the thick of this swirl that I received a phone call inquiring if I would be interested in a top HR job (yes), in the Northeast where I lived (yes), for a multi-industrial company (my background was at Honeywell—yes). Then the pieces came together: the opportunity was to lead the HR organization at Tyco International.

The decision to join a company in crisis should never be taken lightly. Many of the companies embroiled in scandal in 2002 and 2003 ended up in Chapter 11 bankruptcy. Most of my trusted mentors advised me not to take on this personal and professional risk. But as I researched Tyco, it became clear that the company's problems primarily stemmed from a leadership failure at headquarters. The business consisted of a broad portfolio of industrial enterprises that generally were profitable and managed well. It was the aberrant behavior of a handful of people at the top that drove the debacle.

Furthermore, it became clear to me that HR would play a key role in steering Tyco out of the crisis. All the tools in the HR tool kit—the fundamentals of leadership, values, governance, change management, and employee engagement—would be instrumental.

The final, and most critical, step in my due diligence was meeting the newly recruited CEO, Ed Breen. Ed also saw HR playing a central role in Tyco's turnaround. I thought that if he would leave the top post at Motorola to take on the Tyco challenge, I believed the risk was worth my while. At this point, Ed had already recruited some highly respected executives to join his management team and a lead director who brought respect, credibility, courage, and experience to a yet-to-be-formed board of directors.

Satisfied that the business was fundamentally sound, I saw Tyco as an extraordinary HR opportunity in which strategic decision making would be critical in bringing about the needed changes. And so on January 2, 2003, I became the company's senior vice president of HR.

Before I was even on the payroll, I went to work with a sense of urgency on the company's most pressing priorities:

- *Rebuilding the board of directors and senior management ranks.* Although this was an enormous challenge given the company's uncertain future and its tarnished reputation, the cachet of a turnaround and the opportunity to have a meaningful impact attracted extraordinary leaders to our company.
- *Identifying and replacing the bad actors.* Those on the new management team don't know who these bad actors are and who to trust. They have to get the facts and act quickly.
- *Revamping the pay system* so that, unlike the shortsighted outlook of the old regime, it supports a healthy, long-term-growth strategy.
- *Attracting a new corporate leadership team* to a company whose headquarters location was not yet determined. (The previous team had opulent offices in Manhattan, attended by a crew of

specialized service personnel including a personal trainer and a chef. The new team was focused on the bottom line.)

- *Reestablishing the morale and pride* in the many thousands of dedicated, hard-working, productive employees and managers around the world, who were now embarrassed to wear their Tyco T-shirts in public.
- *Shaping a stronger corporate culture* that would balance risk and opportunity, along with short-term and long-term growth, and repel behaviors that can tarnish a company's reputation.

BUILDING A NEW LEADERSHIP TEAM

For me, those early months were largely consumed in recruiting. A typical day involved seven interviews. We had obvious gaping holes that needed to be filled—information technology, communications, treasury, a corporate secretary, investor relations, executive compensation. In all, about one hundred critical corporate roles needed to be filled. There were other people changes that needed to be made even when incumbents were in place—not because the incumbents were dishonest or dishonorable in any way, but—like the personal trainer and the chef—they just didn't fit the new culture. Many people left the company with severance packages and their reputations intact.

One interesting twist to the process was that after a time, we realized that we had to make a second round of leadership changes. Some of our early executive recruits possessed the skills necessary to lead a turnaround. They could drive change with urgency and effectiveness but had management styles that didn't quite fit the more collaborative work styles that were later required.

And headquarters. Where did that finally come to be? Princeton, New Jersey. The choice logically evolved from the leadership team we were putting together, as most of us were from the tristate area (New York, New Jersey, or Connecticut). So in this bucolic, quintessential college town, we settled into a fairly basic headquarters building—nice, comfortable, but understated— emblematic, you might say, of the distance we had traveled from the Kozlowski era.

REVAMPING THE PAY SYSTEM

A new compensation system was critical. The old system was designed to encourage people to swing for the fences, placing large bets on actions that might give them instant riches. It was oriented to the short term and the potential rewards were not capped, so anyone who could find a way to blow their numbers out of the park could reap rich rewards. We wanted growth, yes, but steady, reliable growth—growth gained from sound strategy and execution that would earn the confidence of customers and investors.

Changing pay systems is really difficult. Reducing pay opportunities is brutally hard. It offers an opportunity to demonstrate conviction, drive real change, and model courage and integrity. This was a powerful chapter in our change process.

We changed the pay system in every way. We reduced pay levels. We shifted the mix to focus on long-term results. We established performance metrics to reflect the new priority on cash flow. We instituted ownership guidelines for officers and put clawbacks in place. We capped bonuses. We changed governance processes to ensure that the compensation committee and the board were ultimately accountable.

As we entered 2003, the scandal had caused our stock price to tank, and in the next several months we had to wrestle with a liquidity crisis. Thankfully, there was no Chapter 11 ordeal. But interestingly, the crisis allowed us to drive toward a vision of excellence much faster than we otherwise could have. The new pay system was part of the foundation for that vision.

ADDRESSING MORALE

Most of our 240,000 employees around the world were embarrassed and disconcerted by the scandal and shakeup. Most were also poorer, having seen their Tyco stock plunge from sixty dollars to ten dollars a share in a very short time.

Addressing the morale problem was quite an eye-opener. Employees did not take comfort in a new leadership team. To many, leadership—generically—was discredited. They had no reason to think that the "Breen team" would be any different from the previous team. We had to earn their respect through our actions, and that took time—years, in fact.

Employees have responded over time to a clear vision, candid communication, respect for and investment in employees and their development, and courage and consistency in both good and lean times. More important, employees wanted little more than to be free of distraction. Many of the businesses operated under well-respected brand names not linked in their customers' minds to Tyco. Throughout the crises, employees continued to gain satisfaction from meeting their customer needs.

ENFORCING ETHICAL CONDUCT

Tyco had an ethics code under Dennis Kozlowski. New words and a bureaucracy of compliance training would not make us a more ethical company. But an ethics code was required, and we challenged ourselves to make it meaningful. With employees scattered across the globe, it was essential to define and clarify the rules of ethical conduct. It was essential, too, in nurturing a consistent culture across the enterprise.

The new board of directors took the lead in creating what would formally become our Guide to Ethical Conduct. HR, in partnership with the legal organization and leadership across the company, had to instill the guide with meaning to employees' everyday decision making. Holding everyone, everywhere, and at every level accountable for actions consistent with the guide was absolutely critical.

The Guide to Ethical Conduct became a much-needed vehicle for creating a more unified culture at such a diverse and geographically dispersed enterprise. I've come to appreciate that each individual business—indeed, each operation and location—will have its own cultural hallmarks and its own personality. Corporate culture is therefore not really one thing but something that is manifested in layers. Certain standards of conduct, however, must be the same, no matter what the business or location, and a well-articulated code becomes a foundation for building an enterprise identity.

LESSONS LEARNED

So what sort of HR lessons might be gleaned from one company's recovery from scandal? I suggest several:

- *You can't run your company with people waiting to be fired.* This time-tested lesson to hire the people you need, and fast, proved itself again. With each critical hire, we took our transformation a giant step forward. And for those who need to be replaced, make this your first priority. On the rebuilding side, be prepared to make a second round of changes—first to get the crisis management skills necessary to mitigate the situation and then to develop the competencies and executive teamwork required to support a longer-term vision. Those emergency skills may not always be a good fit after things settle down.
- *When you want to change culture radically, change the pay systems.* Be bold, be clear, and be decisive. It will not be easy, but a crisis offers room to maneuver that you don't have in normal circumstances. Leverage that extra leeway while you can. Use the platform of pay changes to explain the new priorities and altered reality of your company. You will have everyone's attention.
- *Articulate a vision for the company that takes people beyond the crisis.* In a crisis, people yearn for something they can hold on to and convince themselves that they have a future where they are. A strong, clearly articulated vision offers more than a "we can get back to where we were" mind-set.
- *Isolate and fix core issues.* In our case, the board and senior management had to be rebuilt, ethical standards had to be reaffirmed and promulgated with strong commitment from the top, the pay system had to be revamped to support a new executive culture, and fiscal controls had to be reestablished to give us and our investors confidence that scandal would not recur. Focus on the urgent, and then move to the important.
- *Minimize distractions.* This is especially important for operations people, for the obvious reason that they are vital to the day-to-day running of the business. Crisis management can be inwardly focused and can rob operating management of their energy for serving customers. Don't let that happen.

- *Be visible and in person.* Employees need to be able to look you in the eye and shake your hand before they know they can trust you. If leadership has been discredited, an e-mail message will not turn things around.
- *Understand the art of pace.* A crisis atmosphere enables you to do some things faster and more easily than is normally possible. Changes in culture, however, still need to be nurtured over time; they can't be rushed—not, at least, in a $40 billion company with employees around the globe.
- *Don't become complacent after the crisis has passed.* The skills your organization has developed will serve you well going forward. There will likely be new, unexpected challenges for which you must be ready. Your organization has gained a newly found agility, an ability to prioritize, and a sense of purpose across your workforce. Keep those skills sharp.

Our opportunity to leverage this skill set surfaced in 2006. The business had stabilized, and the stock was reflecting a new confidence. Then the board approved a plan to split the company into three separate, independent, publicly traded corporations: Covidien Ltd. (formerly Tyco Healthcare), Tyco Electronics Ltd., and Tyco International Ltd., the last being the largest of the three, which would remain headed by Ed Breen.

Ensuring a reasonably pain-free transition for all three new entities proved to be an enormously complex HR undertaking. We were dealing with massive uncertainties in the minds of our employees while trying to avoid adverse impacts on the various businesses. We had an organization with an ability to rally and exert extraordinary effort to accomplish a mission, and this served us well in driving a focused, disciplined, and ambitious process for creating three fully functioning public companies out of one.

In July 2007, we launched three vigorous new companies— each one focused and cohesive, and with respected brands delivering quality and value to a host of customers around the world.

TYCO AND HR TODAY

Only a few vestiges of the crisis remain in our strong balance sheet today. Tyco International is a much different company than it was even two years ago. We are a market leader with leading brands in the high-growth global industries of electronic security, fire protection, and flow control.

Our HR organization has evolved from a function that primarily supported acquisition activity to an engaged, coordinated, and influential component of our enterprise leadership. We continue to recruit world-class talent to our company, but it is no longer for those seeking a turnaround experience. Today we attract people looking to join a company with a strong position in vital industries, passionate leaders, and outstanding opportunities for learning and professional development. Once again, our employees don their Tyco T-shirts with pride.

CHAPTER ELEVEN

DOING HR'S BUSINESS WITH THE GOVERNMENT

Ian Ziskin

To paraphrase John Gardner, former professor; former secretary of health, education, and welfare; and founder of Common Cause, when it comes to HR's role in doing business with the government, it's time for us to stop trying to be interesting and spend more time being interested.

In light of the evolving and ever-increasing role of government and quasi-government organizations in the HR universe, CHROs need to become more "interested" in the following:

- Shaping public policy
- Facing increased governance and regulation
- Living with customers
- Developing competence in handling government involvement and related public scrutiny
- Predicting the future of the interplay between HR and government

SHAPING PUBLIC POLICY

The CHRO role is changing dramatically as a shaper and influencer of HR-related public policy. Although many issues vary dramatically from country to country, one thing is clear: as the economy globalizes, so do HR challenges related to the workforce and workplace. Despite numerous global issues, this chapter focuses on U.S. domestic public policy with HR implications. Even within the United States, there is no shortage of public policy challenges including executive compensation; health care reform; ethics; diversity and equal employment opportunity; the environment; health and safety; pension and retirement security; workforce development and relations; labor relations; workplace flexibility; immigration; privacy; green/sustainability; and risk management, among many others.

Government oversight and enforcement are increasing, as are public scrutiny and skepticism regarding large employers. Employee commitment and engagement have been severely tested by cost-cutting, downsizing, and restructuring.

If you are looking for a silver lining, here it is. For over twenty-five years, HR professionals have been talking about becoming strategic business partners and getting a seat at the table. Not only do these issues give us a seat, we are in the hot seat. The big question is whether we are ready to step up.

The role of the CHRO in dealing with government and public policy issues is becoming increasingly important, complex, and high stakes. Accordingly, we need to rethink and reprioritize how we spend our time and become decidedly more external in our perspectives and personal leadership focus. It is time for the following shifts in our CHRO mind-set and calendars as we think about shaping public policy:

- More time with our government relations people and with federal, state, and local government officials
- More attention to external constituencies that influence government thinking and public policy
- More energy on positive, proactive solutions that are relevant to the twenty-first-century workforce and workplace, as opposed to merely trying to prevent or reshape solutions that have a potentially negative impact on the workplace
- More involvement in external public policy strategy and advocacy organizations, such as the HR Policy Association
- More emphasis on collaboration across companies, industries, and geographical boundaries to develop increasingly harmonized solutions to HR-related public policy issues that are currently in disharmony

It's time for CHROs to get involved, get informed, get in sync, make a difference, and exercise policy leadership.

Facing Increased Governance and Regulation

For years, government relations has been a crucial company function in support of strategic, operational, financial, legal, research and development, and business development initiatives. But what about HR issues? At best, our government-related issues have taken a back seat to these other priorities. At worst, we may have failed to develop sufficient internal government relations expertise within our HR functions to influence public policy. A significant proportion of corporate resources is devoted to HR-related government relations issues, but companies may be giving them too low a priority in the policy process.

This situation puts HR at a disadvantage compared with other business functions that have traditionally developed this expertise internally. It also puts us in an inferior position relative to government regulators and agencies that oversee our companies' HR processes.

Increasingly, we will find that the HR function must develop its own capabilities in government relations, including designating an HR executive at the director or perhaps vice president level with responsibility to monitor, influence, shape, and strategize around HR public policy matters. HR government relations is becoming a full-time job focused on these topics:

- Seeing around corners to anticipate and address HR public policy trends
- Understanding how the legislative and regulatory processes work and the implications that emerging government actions have on HR policies and processes
- Interfacing seamlessly with the government relations, finance, law, communications, strategy, and business development functions around public policy and risk management
- Ensuring that top corporate leaders are cognizant of HR policy issues

- Reaching across companies, industries, geographies, and constituencies to bridge differences and fashion practical agreed-on solutions

Many HR people do not have the requisite skills and experience to play an HR government relations leadership role. In the near term, we may have to reach outside the HR function for this expertise. Over the longer term, CHROs can begin to develop HR government relations professionals through rotational government relations assignments, public policy internships, and fellowships for their HR people, as well as efforts to influence university and professional association HR curricula to include government and public policy topics for up-and-coming HR professionals and students. For our best and brightest HR talent, a leadership role in HR government relations would be an important developmental assignment.

LIVING WITH OUR CUSTOMERS

Those of us who work in traditionally regulated industries such as aerospace, defense, banking, pharmaceuticals, and utilities know that our companies tend to take on certain characteristics of our customers and regulators. Symmetrical systems, policies, processes, cultures, and key people begin to blur the boundaries between regulators and the regulated. For example, within my industry of aerospace, defense, and global security, Northrop Grumman is an amalgamation of over twenty thousand programs with distinct missions and customers. Many of our employees work side-by-side with our customers, embedded in their facilities and operations. And government customers and auditors are often co-located with us in our facilities. The challenge is that sometimes our employees experience an identity crisis: they have difficulty distinguishing between the customer they serve and the company for which they work.

Dealing with heavy government regulation and oversight can sometimes masquerade as customer intimacy. But it clearly results in more scrutiny, fewer degrees of freedom, and more infrastructure required to interface with government counterparts. As we get ready for the world of increased government regulation in HR matters, so too must we put in place resources to manage that new reality. (Just ask our friends in the automotive and financial services industries.)

In today's environment of increased scrutiny and decreased trust, an irony has emerged: the closer companies get to their government customers and regulators, and vice versa, the greater the perceived need is to demonstrate an appropriate degree of distance and an arms-length relationship. This phenomenon conjures up images of two seventeen year olds at the junior prom: they want to get closer to one another, but their fears drive them to opposite sides of the dance floor.

Developing Competence in Handling Government Involvement and Related Public Scrutiny

Given the trends toward greater government regulations and oversight, increased expectations of transparency, and stronger influence by external constituent groups, CHROs and our organizations will need to become proficient in new ways:

- *Anticipating trends* regarding regulations and proposing practical solutions before impractical, inflexible, bureaucratic regulations are imposed
- *Negotiating viable solutions* that are responsive to government needs by making recommendations that will work rather than reactively fighting things that won't work
- *Putting in place a HR government relations capability* and leader to deal with the variety of demands and expectations that will be placed on companies
- *Developing HR professionals who have expertise in dealing with government regulators* and understanding the delicate balance between customer intimacy and partnership on the one hand, while on the other hand maintaining the appropriate degree of independence from and push-back on government regulations that do not make business sense
- *Building risk management capabilities in the HR function* because it will be the centerpiece of the inevitable trend toward increased government and shareholder oversight of private industry:

What could go wrong? How do we ensure it goes right? Who is accountable?

- *Leading change in how HR public policy and related risk issues are handled* at the senior leadership team level and supporting boards of directors as they debate these same issues

Predicting the Future of the Interplay Between HR and the Government Interplay

Peter Drucker said, "The best way to predict the future is to create it." Although no one really knows what's going to happen in HR-related public policy over the next few years—least of all me—it may be a useful exercise to make some educated guesses about where things might be heading and how we can work together to influence these trends toward more pragmatic and palatable outcomes.

Let's imagine how our roles and priorities will change if the following issues move from debate to inevitable reality over the next few years.

Executive Compensation

- The advisory vote on executive compensation becomes required for all publicly traded companies.
- Proxy disclosure expands from the top five named executive officers to the top twenty-five or fifty most highly compensated.
- TARP-like reporting requirements and caps are put in place for all companies that do business with the federal government.
- Bonuses, retention payments, and stock options are deemed insufficiently performance oriented, likely to promote unwanted risk, or simply too much money.
- CEO pay is capped at a fixed percentage or multiple of average employee pay or of company revenue or profit.
- Executive compensation plans become subject to external auditing requirements and standards similar to how company financials are audited.
- Compensation committees expand their purview over executive compensation to include any items affected by these potential trends.

Health Care

- Every American has health care coverage.
- Every employer must pay or play.
- Company-provided private insurance is supplemented by a public option and regional cooperatives or exchanges.
- The public option provided by the federal government looks a lot like Medicare without the age requirements.
- As the public option and exchanges become more commonplace and acceptable and as adverse selection makes private plans increasingly unaffordable, companies begin getting out of the business of providing health care for most employees except executives.
- As the health care transition evolves, companies provide vouchers or stipends for their employees to purchase their own health care coverage on the open market.
- The value of health care benefits is taxed for people who earn above a certain income, such as $200,000 a year.
- A national public health information technology initiative slowly begins to harmonize health care record keeping and patient information sharing among health care providers, but those who pay more and meet certain requirements will be fast-tracked.
- Health care reform expands access to a dysfunctional health care system without making necessary delivery reforms, and the cost of this tremendous expansion is passed on to employers, employees, and taxpayers, which provides strong incentives to limit employment growth in the United States in order to keep rising labor costs in check.

Pension and Retirement Security

- The term *retirement security* becomes an oxymoron.
- The standard retirement age for social security and related purposes increases to age sixty-seven or sixty-eight or even as high as seventy.
- Pension plans continue the shift from defined benefit to defined contribution, and then migrate from company-sponsored plans to portable plans that employees purchase on the open market, subsidized by employer contributions.

- Changes in pension legislation and design allow employees to phase their retirement so they may continue working for their current employer on a more flexible or part-time basis while beginning to draw on their pension assets.
- Due to labor shortages created by shifting workforce demographics, as well as strains on the social security system, the federal or state governments offer employers tax credits and other financial incentives to retain older workers while bolstering the enforcement of age discrimination laws.

Workforce and Workplace

- The Employee Free Choice Act eventually passes without card check (when an employee signs a certification card, it effectively counts as a vote for the union), but with provisions that call for quick elections, some restrictions on employer involvement in organizing campaigns, time limits for reaching a collective bargaining agreement, binding arbitration as a penalty for failure to reach agreement within legislated time limits, and much stiffer penalties for labor law violations (intentional or otherwise).
- As wages are restricted by global economic uncertainties and benefits and pensions migrate away from company-sponsored and government-run designs, workforce capability and workplace flexibility become the next battlegrounds on which companies differentiate themselves and compete for talent, employees make choices on where to work, and unions attempt to organize and represent workers.
- Workforce capability focuses on private partnerships between industry and government in learning and development initiatives targeted toward specific skills and technologies as a matter of national policy—such as science, engineering, technology, and health care careers.
- Workplace flexibility focuses on changes in regulations governing work hours, overtime, work schedule and work week definitions, work locations, and exempt and nonexempt determinations to better accommodate increasingly virtual work environments and support green or other environmental sustainability efforts.

This list of potential changes in HR-related public policy is just a small sample of changes that might occur over the next few years. I cannot envision what will really happen. I do know, however, that as a CHRO, I am quite excited about the challenge of improving how I do HR's business with the government. To be brutally honest, it's also scary. Let's work together to master this universe.

PART THREE

THE CHRO AS COUNSELOR/ CONFIDANT/COACH

CHAPTER TWELVE

WHO DO YOU REALLY WORK FOR?

Serving Multiple and Often Conflicting Constituencies as CHRO

David A. Pace

The ascendance to one's first assignment as CHRO is often a time of celebration. It is a role that many have been preparing for their entire career. They have held generalist roles, staff subject matter expert roles, and, in many cases, large independent business unit roles. It's an exciting time and one that generates great anticipation and excitement. At the same time, it is also an intimidating moment. You are on your own as a functional leader for the first time. It will be your strategy and your agenda, and the organization will be looking to you for leadership. Along with excitement and enthusiasm often comes intimidation because this is a critical and highly visible role to the organization.

As you settle into the role, one of your first priorities will be to decide what it is that you will do. Where will you put your focus? What are your priorities? You will hear that from many angles as the organization looks for your direction quickly, sometimes before you feel you are prepared to offer it.

Most experts will tell you that during this period, your most critical skill will be to listen. This is a time for hearing from everyone what's working well and what isn't. Where does your function perform well, and where does it need to improve? What can be done to improve the alignment of the human capital strategy with the overall business strategy? Everyone around you will no doubt have a point of view, and you should listen to them all. After all, everyone wants to please their customers and their boss, and there is no better way to do that than to hear their priorities and respond to them.

But who is your boss? Who do you really work for now? The reality is that new CHROs serve a wide variety of constituents both inside and outside the organization. Many times the goals of these constituents are in some conflict. It is important to understand who they are from the beginning. Without understanding who they are and actively managing their expectations, you face the possibility of unsatisfied customers.

Among the constituencies that you will be serving in your new assignment are these:

- The chief executive officer
- The chair of the board
- The board, and especially the members of the compensation and management development committee
- Your peers on the senior management team
- Your HR team
- The company's broad employee population
- Your company's customers
- Wall Street and your company's investors

As you consider each of these constituencies and their members, keep in mind the varying expectations that they have for you in this role. In the rest of this chapter, I explore more deeply each of these constituents, their perspectives of your role, specific challenges that you may face with each, and insights into how you might want to prepare for managing these relationships in a positive fashion.

THE CEO

In many ways, "CEO" is the obvious answer to the question, "Who do you work for?" On a day-to-day basis, this is the person who will most likely serve the traditional manager role in the supervisor-subordinate workplace relationship. The CEO will provide most of your close direction, coaching, and guidance and will in most cases be responsible for evaluating your performance in the most formal sense during end-of-year reviews.

However, even the relationship with this role becomes more complicated quickly depending on whether you were promoted internally to your position or were hired into the role from outside the organization. In either case, it is likely that the CEO was the ultimate decision maker in placing you in this role, and that decision carries an enormous degree of expected loyalty. If you have been promoted from within, you will no doubt have been forming the relationship with the CEO for some time, and this move was the logical extension of that relationship. If you were hired into the role from outside the organization, this most likely will be a newly formed relationship that dates back only as far as your first interview with the CEO.

When joining the organization as a newcomer or even if you got the assignment as a result of a change in the CEO and CHRO, the CEO will probably have many thoughts on what you should do to support his or her agenda and what needs to be done within human resources. This perspective will obviously have a great impact on what you ultimately define as your personal agenda.

Or you may in fact receive the opposite reaction: the CEO may be looking to you to define your agenda on your own. This may be because the CEO doesn't have the expertise that you bring to the role, or perhaps the CEO carries an expectation that you are the expert and will form your agenda on your own with little guidance.

This traditional role of supervisor to the CHRO will most likely be at the heart of many of the conflicts you face in defining who you really work for, but let's explore some of the others to understand why.

THE BOARD CHAIR

In some cases, the CEO and the board chair are the same person, but if they are two different individuals, you may find that you face two different sets of expectations. This is not necessarily driven by philosophical differences between the chair and the CEO, but if there are differences, this relationship can become very complex very quickly.

For instance, the chair as an independent observer of the company may see that the CEO has certain strengths that need to be leveraged in the leadership of the company, but those skills may not be on the human capital side. The CEO may be exceptionally strong in technical areas of the business or in the management of critical customer, government, or supplier relationships, but not in the identification and development of critical talent. In this case, the chair may pull you aside and say, "Look, the CEO is an excellent strategist, but he really doesn't have high enough standards for the people on the management team, and I'm looking to you as the CHRO to make sure that we are challenging standards and upgrading the overall talent of the senior team [your peers]."

The hope for you is that the chair has had a similar conversation with the CEO, but if not, you may find yourself between two of your most important customers wondering, *Who do I really work for?* Of course, the chair is only part of your challenge in managing your relationship with the company's board of directors. This leads us to your next constituent.

THE BOARD'S COMPENSATION AND MANAGEMENT DEVELOPMENT COMMITTEE

Along with the chair, one of the other high-powered constituencies that you must serve is the broader board of directors and, more specifically, the members of the compensation and management development committee. In today's corporate environments, the "comp committee" has become one of the most complex and sensitive work groups in the overall management of the company. Detailed and prescriptive rules, regulations, and reporting requirements are now the norm and must be adhered to carefully. Comp committee members are extremely sensitive in ensuring that they are in compliance lest they face unwanted shareholder challenges. Most of the time, the CEO, chair, and comp committee are aligned in their expectations for you—but not always.

In most cases, you will be responding to the committee's desire to remain in compliance with the latest shifts in Securities and Exchange Commission regulations on executive compensation, retirement programs, stock options and other equity programs, succession planning, and, now, the seismic shifts in health care. Again, in most cases, you will find alignment among the chair, the CEO, and the comp committee, but there may be conflicts here as well.

Consider what will happen if the chair of the comp committee pulls you aside during a committee meeting and says to you, "Look, the board is concerned about the overlap in salaries being paid to the chair and the CEO. We really have only one CEO, but by paying the same to both of them, it looks as if we are really paying for two. We need a recommendation from you on what we should be paying to each of them. Can you put something together and bring us a recommendation at the next board meeting?"

Now you find yourself in the middle of not only the chair and the CEO but also the comp committee, and each has a different set of expectations for what you will deliver. Suddenly you have three customers with three very different perspectives on what success looks like, and you haven't even begun to look across or down within the organization. While you will certainly have your challenges in managing up within this organization, you must also be ready to deliver horizontally to the next group that has expectations for you.

YOUR PEERS ON THE MANAGEMENT TEAM

Certainly some of your most demanding customers will be your peers on the management team. This is an area that, depending on your prior experience as a senior HR leader, you may already have experience with. As a generalist with responsibility for all aspects of human resources in a division or business unit assignment, you will likely have already served as a member of a discreet management team. In this role, you experience some of the independence that you will find in your new role as the CHRO.

As a CHRO or other senior generalist, you will often find yourself in the uncomfortable situation where you are expected to be part of the leadership team while also serving as a confidant and trusted advisor for your CEO or division president. In this situation, it is not uncommon for you to be aware of the CEO's plans to replace a struggling counterpart in another function. At the same time, that counterpart may be confiding in you about his or her situation and looking for you to help save this role. Perhaps you agree with the CEO and believe that the position needs to be upgraded and the person replaced. Be warned that your other peers may be aware of the situation and will be watching to see what you do. After all, they may be next, and they may wonder to themselves, *Is this person a team player who can be trusted—or a Rasputin whispering in the CEO's ear?*

This is an important situation to manage carefully because you will need the support of your peers to drive your agenda and have the impact your CEO expects. Satisfying only one side of this situation is not an option. Without the support of your peers over the long term, you will fail. Couple this with their own HR needs for their teams, and you have many more people with specific expectations for what success looks like from the HR team. That may be better support from their HR business partner, the need for an advocate to convince the CEO that more resources are needed in their area of responsibility, or your support for extraordinary compensation rewards that they want to deliver to their team for a project's success. Each of them wants something different.

Clearly your peers are an important customer and a group that you clearly work for, but some of your most difficult and tricky bosses come from below—those individuals who work for you.

YOUR HR TEAM

The HR team that reports to you will often be one of your most challenging constituencies. The reason is that more so than ever before, many HR executives have been trained to act as servant leaders; they view their role as clearing the way for their own teams to do the work. When you find yourself in the top chair as CHRO, the expectations of your team rise to an even higher level.

More specifically, the HR team is looking to you to step up and give them all the reasonable tools that they feel they need to do things in what they call "the right way." If you have been promoted to the CHRO role from within, there's even a chance that you may have had some of the same complaints before you took over this assignment. Providing the right level of resources is certainly part of your job. Defining what that "right" level is and convincing your team of that becomes the hard part.

Your team will tell you that they could do their job much more efficiently if they only had the right tools. As the new leader, you will want to please and inspire this customer group quickly, and there will be pressure from all corners to get them what they need. But beware: this is a slippery slope.

On the one hand, you want to continue to be viewed as a servant leader and show the team that you have impact. On the other hand, you must retain your objectivity and be able to tell the team, "We can't do that," or, "It isn't the right use of company resources at this time." Again, you're in a bind: lose the support of your team, and you can't drive your agenda; overspend and allocate a disproportionate level of resources, and you can create another set of budgetary issues with your peers.

As with your peer group of senior executives, your team will also have expectations about your ability to manage promotions or compensation on their behalf. As the senior leader of the function, they will look to you to champion them in succession or promotion discussions. You will want to set the right example for the organization even if some of your peers are making decisions that your team knows are not right. Your team will look to you as the arbiter of fairness, and if you cannot deliver against that expectation, you once again risk losing their support and commitment to your agenda.

Although your HR team is certainly another in the critical line of groups that you work for, an even larger group has big expectations for what you will deliver in your new role as CHRO.

The Company's General Population

There's little argument that one set of bosses that you must respond to is the general population of the organization. As the CHRO, you are ultimately responsible to each of them as the company's chief people officer. With this responsibility comes the role of employee advocate: the voice of the people. If you aren't the one who steps up as the conscience of the organization, who will? Now that you have the proverbial seat at the table, be prepared to see that the expectations of the employees in your organization are rising.

Like the other relationships, this is another delicate role that needs to be managed with balance and skill. In your capacity as CHRO, it's critical that you cultivate a reputation as a listener and champion of frontline employees. They will need to see you as a safe harbor—a confidential ear that represents the reasonableness of how employees are treated within the company. They will also look to you to go to bat for them when necessary. If you don't advocate on their behalf, you risk being viewed as just another member of management, and you can quickly lose the mantle of employee champion.

Now what do you do? You're the strategic business partner that you always wanted to be, but your "bosses" in the general population are looking to you as their voice. If you don't act as that voice, you could lose their support.

This relationship will test your broad communication skills. As the CHRO, you must develop this role as champion of the people, but you also must do what's right for the company. It will require you to communicate across many different forums throughout the company. Once you have an agenda, you must communicate it broadly and often. Actions that you and the company take must be framed within that agenda, and it must be clear where employee requests and expectations fall within that agenda. As always, the message must be delivered in a compassionate and understanding way.

Your biggest opportunities to develop your relationship with the general population will come during times of crisis. It is at these times that the organization is looking for leadership from the CHRO. They want to know where things stand in an honest and empathetic way. They need to be confident that even if you can't address their concerns at the time, they are being heard and understood. If you can deliver effectively at these times in these terms, you can capture the hearts and minds of your organization. If you give them a party line or a dismissive response to legitimate concerns, you will lose them and your ability to deliver your agenda. Your general population bosses are tough, but they are some of the most important that you will face.

While the bosses that I have addressed so far represent the internal constituencies that have expectations for you as the CHRO, two external constituencies also have expectations for you in your new role. They too must be responded to if you are to be successful.

YOUR COMPANY'S CUSTOMERS

Your company's executive team has a collective responsibility to answer to your customers in building a successful and sustainable business. After all, if you can't create an environment that serves your customers well, you probably won't be in business very long. So as the CHRO of your company, what is your obligation to your customers, and where is the intersection of your role with theirs?

Your obligation to customers is as great as it is to the others I have discussed so far. As CHRO, you have the responsibility to champion the organizational elements that deliver a great product or a great service to your customers. That may manifest itself in adequate staffing levels and training in a retail environment or in team structures and work flows in a manufacturing environment. In either case, as CHRO, you have to be the one who ensures that the right structure, staffing, skills, and culture are in place to deliver the company's value proposition.

This may seem obvious, but it can often put you at odds with your peers in other functions. For example, there may be times when you have to force the need for frontline pay increases or the need for additional head count in order to deliver on the promise. This may run against the grain at a time when the organization needs to reduce labor costs to hit profit targets. When it comes to human capital, you may be the only one who is in a position to champion the customer's need for service.

The customer expects you to have the right number of qualified and motivated employees doing the right work at the right time to deliver on the expectation that your marketing team has created. If they don't get the promise, they have every right to challenge you as the CHRO to know why these human capital elements have not been put in place. This is certainly outside the traditional expectation for who you work for as CHRO, but this is an important constituency if your business is to thrive in today's marketplace.

Finally, there is yet one more constituency, and they are no less legitimate than anyone else discussed thus far.

YOUR COMPANY'S SHAREHOLDERS

The final group you have to respond to are your owners. In a public company, it is not unusual to find yourself in a position where you must respond to Wall Street and your shareholders. More than ever before, activist shareholders are looking for more direct input into aspects of management that were previously in the sole domain of management and the CHRO.

As examples, shareholder resolutions on "say on pay," where shareholders are entitled to nonbinding votes on executive compensation, are more prevalent than ever before. Shareholders have also demanded that board members be declassified and required to stand for reelection as individuals. Institutional shareholders are demanding justifications for broad-based stock option programs and tighter linkages to performance. Securities and Exchange Commission reporting is more detailed than ever before, and it must be written in terms that can easily be understood and acted on by individual shareholders. Finally, the massive changes to how companies and the government will interact in the health care arena ensure that shareholder questions will only get more detailed as they seek to understand the direct impact on company financials.

In the past, your chief financial officer would probably have met with these groups and assuaged their concerns. The complexity of these arenas now means that it will be more likely that you, as CHRO, will be partnering with your CFO, if not owning some of these accountabilities outright.

Ignore these constituencies at your peril. They have more direct impact than ever before and are using this power in new and influential ways. They are definitely in the category of your boss. Just wait until you have to ask for approval for the additional allocation of shares for your option program, and you will understand quickly if you have delivered against this boss's expectations. If you haven't managed this relationship appropriately, you may find yourself redesigning your total rewards program and explaining to employees what happened to the old program that they had come to rely on.

CONCLUSION

In taking on the role of CHRO, you will no doubt work hard to ensure your success. In achieving that success, it is critical that you understand exactly what success means and to whom. There are many who will define your success. Perhaps more important, the success that they define will often be in conflict with each other's priorities. It will be your accountability to understand these conflicts, rationalize them where possible, or redefine them in a way that can be managed and communicated forthrightly to each. As you develop your transactional abilities and understand the nuances of this role, this aspect of your new job will become easier over time. Being aware of who you really work for will give you a leg up as you engage in this new and exciting role as CHRO.

Chapter Thirteen

Partnering with the CEO

Elease E. Wright

Few relationships are more important in your professional career than the one with your CEO. Unless you've grown up through the ranks with your CEO, you are inheriting preconceived notions about the role of HR in running a successful business. Your CEO's experience with other HR professionals can pave the way for establishing a good partnership from the start, or it can present you with an opportunity to demonstrate the strategic value of your presence at the table. (I'd be remiss if I did not mention that in some cases, a CEO's view of HR may be so narrow that you ultimately have to decide it's not an environment likely to make the most of your skills, experience, and engagement. It's a tough call, but sometimes even your best effort cannot influence the perception. In that case, it may be time to find a new job.)

CEOs are by nature a unique breed of leader. In my more than twenty-five years at Aetna, I have worked for five CEOs, all of whom had their own style, agenda, quirks, and attitudes about HR. With every one of them, I learned, I grew, and I survived to work with the next one. Note that I didn't say I was wildly successful with each one or that we moved mountains every time. However, with only a few exceptions, I did find a way to work effectively with each CEO through coaching, counseling, and taking calculated risks.

In this chapter, I share two basic leadership dimensions I have found critical to creating a successful partnership with CEOs and other senior executives. The first deals with the critical abilities a CHRO needs to work effectively; the second relates to the CHRO's sense of purpose. Just as one dimension may be more critical with a particular CEO, different circumstances require heightened dependency on one dimension over others. Knowing what works when is at the root of successful partnership.

CRITICAL ABILITIES

To partner effectively with a CEO, the CHRO needs many different skills. Based on my many years in this role, I've found five critical abilities that I think are relevant in most situations.

GETTING THE FUNDAMENTALS RIGHT

Today's business climate requires leaders to be successful on multiple levels simultaneously. Only by getting the fundamentals right can you earn the reputation that nets the opportunity to work on a bigger stage. And while you are operating on that bigger stage, the fundamentals must consistently and reliably function the way they are supposed to. That means the basics—payroll, administrative support, all the functions that make up HR—have to be in good working order first and always. You are accountable for having your house in order before you will be viewed as having something to contribute in a larger discussion.

This is not unique to HR. Any business leader who can't get the fundamentals right will have little, if any, voice on bigger issues. I favor a circuitous path to senior-level positions. Many roads can lead to the top HR position; it's the breadth and depth of your experience that matter most. When you can, go for meaningful cross-functional exposure. It comes in handy when you have to think on your feet. Of course, you don't have to know the fine science of every HR program, but a working knowledge of every area will serve you well.

And lest you worry that focusing on the fundamentals will tarnish your reputation as a strategic thinker, remember that on your way to the top HR role, you are building your reputation on knowing how things work, knowing what's in the best interest of the company, effectively driving change, and demonstrating your commitment to make a difference. Once you are in the top seat, the

CEO has a new set of expectations, but he or she assumes the fundamentals will remain just as strong as they were before the CEO became your primary concern. I think of this as basics before brilliance.

With the fundamentals taken care of, your skill set also needs to reflect general business acumen. We all know that the most successful profit-and-loss leaders understand the underlying drivers of market trends, profit, and how various levers will support (or obstruct) their strategy. Imagine how relevant your perspective becomes when you too are a student of your company's business. By understanding my industry, the economy, the political climate, and the regulatory arena, I can talk about our company's strategy, not HR programs, when I represent the company at an investor conference, with the media, or in a customer meeting. Just as important, speaking the language of my business colleagues allows me to do more than answer questions and respond to crises; it helps me generate new solutions they can use to succeed. A CHRO cannot fully participate in the real strategic leadership of the company without having more than a superficial grasp of the business fundamentals. In other words, the fastest way to a pigeon hole is not transcending your functional comfort zone.

Let's assume you have the functional HR fundamentals in good order and a solid grasp of the fundamentals of your business. Is that enough to be an effective strategic partner? Not yet. Once you make the move to the executive table, your CEO wants you to operate in her world. The CEO wants to know you will protect her integrity and reinforce her credibility. And most of all, she wants you to help keep her out of trouble. To be effective, you will eventually need to develop instincts for the answers to questions like these:

- What does your CEO worry about most?
- What counsel will really be in the best interests of your company?
- How can you make constructive change happen?
- How can you help your CEO stay out of trouble?

If you have a lot of access to your CEO, you may already know the answers. If not, the next section is for you. I have found a couple of ways to develop the instinct I needed to work effectively with a number of CEOs with significantly different styles.

FIGURING OUT THE ENVIRONMENT

First, you need to pay attention to the forces at play around your CEO. You may need to let go of some assumptions about the CEO's world by listening carefully to the competing interests operating at that level. Every corporate board and executive team has its own culture: study this, and you will be able to identify the issues and opportunities that your executive will care about most. You'll also want to pay attention to the informal influencers within the leadership ranks.

Second, you can identify less visible leaders with constructive agendas who could be effective allies for your CEO's agenda. These connections can be invaluable when it comes to driving difficult or significant change through your organization. You should not discount anyone because of the person's job level.

UNDERSTANDING THE PRIORITIES AND THE CURRENT CONTEXT

Everyone knows a CEO likes leaders who do what they say they're going to do. CEOs also really like leaders who stay on top of changing circumstances and adjust when, where, and how they need to. Blind execution will derail you every time if you aren't working in the context of your business environment.

Knowing what's in the best interests of your company depends on a clear understanding of its priorities. This seems straightforward, so why do so many of us know examples of great HR programs delivered at the wrong time or the wrong cost or with gaping disconnects? I had a manager once who was all set to roll with a controversial program. He had built a robust service platform, stayed within budget, and met the deadlines for introducing this groundbreaking program. The problem was that the approach had never been tested with the people who would be most affected by it. We took the time to reach out to the group. That conversation changed the rollout strategy and ultimately directly affected the success of the program. It has become standard practice to test the relevance and timeliness of everything we do at all stages of execution.

LEARN ALL THE RULES IF YOU WANT TO DRIVE CHANGE

By now you already know the formal rules that govern your business and industry. But the world of your CEO and the board of directors has a few rules that aren't written down. Fortunately some of the golden rules of childhood can help. Remember breaking something and not wanting to tell your parents about it? "Deliver bad news early and personally" was the rule in my house and it has been as well for every CEO I've known. "Play nice" was, and is, another important rule. This doesn't mean you lose your individual voice or don't stand up for yourself; it just means you should always act with integrity. When dealing with board members, you have to be perceptive and discrete. And never blindside your CEO by forgetting to give her information you are sharing with the board. This leads me to the last point: stay on top things to help your CEO.

HELP YOUR CEO STAY OUT OF TROUBLE

When I say "trouble," I'm not talking about the small percentage of headlining senior executives who commit crimes, behave unethically, or break the rules. Rather, every CEO has a blind spot. Your job is to watch his or her back, stay on top of issues, see trouble on the horizon, and, most of all, speak up even if it's difficult. Pointing out the risks and the bad ideas takes courage, particularly if no one else is speaking up. This is why you must develop the relationship before you need to deliver tough messages. In the midst of a crisis, you do not want to be offering your candid views for the first time. Your opinion can be wrong, but don't be late expressing it. Your CEO not only expects someone at your level to have the courage to speak up; she needs you to do it.

At this point, you understand the importance of nailing the fundamentals first and always, the value of developing business acumen, and a few ground rules for operating in the CEO's world.

These principles relate to your skills and experience. Let's get to a deeper level and consider who you are as an individual.

MEANINGFUL PURPOSE

A second dimension necessary to building a strong relationship deals with your own internal motivation or sense of purpose. When your purpose comes from the success of the organization, you are free to take risks, and when you take risks, win or lose, you will learn and grow.

First, your purpose has to be bigger than your own success, prestige, or position. You are prepared to move up when you believe your individual success is not nearly as important as participating in the success of your company. As altruistic as that sounds, it's tied very much to intrinsic motivation. I like rewards and compensation as much as the next person does, but I can honestly say the reason I put up with the demands and pressure of a role like this is that I can contribute to something that is bigger than me. Researchers call this a sense of purpose.

This means that sometimes a CHRO has to put his or her own interests aside for the good of the firm. Once I had to take a hit for a CEO on an issue that wasn't mine. He later said, "I know you took one for the cause." One of our board members had given me some good advice. He said sometimes you have to be willing to stand in harm's way and take the hit. It wasn't easy, and it didn't feel natural. But I did it and realized at that point how much I cared about being part of the company's success.

As I write this, the future of my industry (health insurance) is making news headlines every day. The threats to our industry are serious, real, and potentially devastating, and if one did not believe in the purpose of our business, it would be easy to jump to another company in a different industry. Although there are heroes and villains in every business, I am fortunate to be aligned with the good guys, and I believe in the basic value of what we do for people. My CEO is driven for the same reason. Despite our differences, we work well together because we share this fundamental trait.

Once you have a sense of greater purpose, your approach to taking risks changes. You no longer define them by their potential consequences to you and your career; they are defined by the consequences to the company, its employees, and others. The greatest risks I have taken so far have been very calculated. Once I was asked to take a job that nobody else wanted. My colleagues sent sympathy cards because they saw it as such a bad assignment. Despite my misgivings, I saw two possibilities with the move: I would be doing a job that needed to be done, and I might learn something. I took that job, and years later, I have no regrets. I didn't love it, but I did learn a lot, and I set myself apart as someone who was willing to be part of the team and carry the ball when and where it needed to be carried.

Finally, I've never seen learning and growth happen without taking some risks. But what about the so-called career-limiting move—that risk you took that abruptly cut off your future opportunities? If that makes you gun-shy now, consider this: What did you learn from that experience? Did it help you see your organization's priorities more clearly? Did it reflect a gap between your gut instincts or values and the culture of the organization? Did you simply make a really bad decision and could not recover from it? Whatever the outcome, I suspect you walked away with something valuable to you: insight, clarity, or experience, for example. These are all things you carry with you; they shape who you are and who you want to be. The best CEOs are the ones who want you to bring these experiences with you so that you have more than a superficial conviction about the importance of experience and character. They know that real change agents don't play it safe; they play it smart.

CONCLUSION

In this chapter, I examined two basic leadership dimensions: critical abilities and purpose. Just as one dimension may be more critical with a particular CEO, different circumstances require heightened dependency on one dimension over others. Knowing what works when is at the root of successfully partnering with your CEO.

CHAPTER FOURTEEN

FORCING EFFECTIVE RELATIONSHIPS WITH YOUR BOSS AND COLLEAGUES

Pamela O. Kimmet

Congratulations on being offered the top seat, the chance to lead the HR team and serve as your company's CHRO. Top HR leaders say that they spend nearly half of their time with senior business colleagues, serving as a strategic advisor and coach/confidant. Therefore, it is important for you to understand that your success as a CHRO will ultimately hinge on the effectiveness of the relationship you build with your new boss, the CEO, and your peers on the senior leadership team.

To get this top role, you have already demonstrated your HR expertise and business knowledge. You also understand that it will be critically important for you to run an efficient department that delivers the basic services well. But your expertise and operational leadership won't enable you to serve as a true business partner and have the impact on the success of the company that you and your HR team desire if you aren't able to cultivate a special and genuine relationship with your CEO. You need to put as much focus on building strong relationships with your boss, and also with senior peers, early in your tenure as you do on learning more about the business and formulating your HR agenda. This chapter offers a checklist of the steps for building a productive relationship with these key individuals and tips on traps to avoid.

BUILDING STRONG RELATIONSHIPS

Just because you've been named the CHRO does not mean your boss or other leaders will immediately look to confide in you and seek out your counsel on sensitive issues. You need to cultivate trust by developing rapport, build credibility by demonstrating your knowledge and business acumen, and consistently deliver results. To do this, you need to

- Get to know your boss, senior colleagues, and your team
- Establish clear expectations
- Deliver on your commitments
- Demonstrate trust
- Be open and honest, and willing to have tough conversations
- Maintain a balanced perspective
- Regularly check-in and solicit feedback

GET TO KNOW EACH OTHER

In my experience, team members who know each other and have built a genuine respect for each other produce greater results and have more fun doing it. Relationships get built through personal connection, so you have to invest the time to get to know each leader. Even if you have been with the company for some time and had the chance to work with and know many or all members of the senior team, now that you are the CHRO, your role has changed and you need to develop a deeper and different connection than you have had in the past.

The easiest way to start forging a relationship with your boss or peers is to spend time talking about the business. Your objective in these discussions is to begin to learn how your boss and colleagues think and what matters to them. Solicit each leader's perspective on what he or she sees as the business's key challenges, as well as their view of the HR function and its effectiveness. These conversations will not only help you learn more about the business, they will also assist you in developing your thoughts on how to shape your HR team's objectives and strategy.

In addition to talking about the business and HR, you should ask for advice on how each of your colleagues would like to work with you. And in talking with your peers, ask for their perspective on how they work with the CEO and each other. Make sure to also ask about what is going on in their personal lives and what hobbies and passions they have, and look for areas of mutual connection.

Getting to know your own team is another important source of information about how to build effective relationships with your new peers and boss. For starters, many of your direct reports can provide different views on how they work with these senior executives. They can outline what they think is working or not working about the approaches, and offer suggestions for improvement. If you are new to the company, your direct reports can give you insight on how your predecessor worked with the senior team, especially the CEO. Depending on the circumstances surrounding your appointment, you will want to handle these questions carefully. Talking with each member of your HR leadership team will also give you a clear picture of the key work they have under way and starts to build a relationship with each of them.

If the situation permits, spend time with your predecessor directly to learn his or her thoughts on how to work well with the CEO and other senior peers.

Establish Clear Expectations

In the early days of working together, it is especially important to have an explicit discussion with your boss about your mutual expectations of the scope of your role, your key deliverables, and the ways you would like to work together. This conversation is important, so take time to prepare your points so you are able to outline clearly what matters to you. If you have worked for the company prior to assuming the CHRO role, you will have a sense of the corporate culture relative to things like work style and communication cadence. Nevertheless, it is still important to make sure you are both aligned on how you will interact. Your appointment gives you both a special opportunity to reset past approaches and start your relationship out on the right footing. Here are some ideas of the types of points to cover:

Work Style
- Does your CEO prefer detailed briefings on issues or look for the headlines and assume you will cover the matter appropriately?

- Is a verbal update sufficient, or are PowerPoint decks required to cover issues?
- Is it acceptable to drop in on each other, or would the CEO prefer you meet at scheduled intervals unless there is an emergency?
- How much time should you regularly spend together, and in what ways (for example, field visits or one-on-one sessions)?
- Are you expected to have vetted certain issues with other colleagues before coming to the CEO with an issue, or does he or she want to be in the know first?
- Does he or she expect you to cover certain items with everyone in regular staff meetings and other topics only with the two of you?

Communication Frequency and Approach

- Does the CEO prefer face-to-face discussion, voice mail, or e-mail?
- Are certain times off-limits to connect, except in the case of an emergency?
- Should you check in with each other daily in the evenings or on weekends, even if you have no real issues to cover?
- Are you expected to always participate in staff meetings, even if you are traveling or on vacation?
- What is the norm around conversations? Is the desired approach to be direct and even confrontational if needed, or is everyone expected to talk issues through in a collegial and candid manner?
- Is there a need to modulate the style used in certain forums such as town halls and leadership meetings?

Role Definition

- What does serving as a strategic advisor mean to each of you?
- What topics do you expect to be part of?
- What does your CEO expect to regularly involve you in?
- What aspects of the HR agenda does your CEO want to be involved in?
- What things do you mutually agree will be held confidential, and what can or will be shared, and with whom?
- How do you envision handling differing views or conflicts?

DELIVER ON YOUR COMMITMENTS

Understanding what HR's key deliverables are and then ensuring that you and your team are getting them done as promised is table stakes to forging an effective relationship with all of your colleagues. In many cases when a new CHRO is appointed, something either was not working well, like a major transformational initiative in the business, or something needed to change following the appointment of a new CEO, for example. If either of these situations precipitated your appointment, it is critical that while you are assimilating to the new role, you stay focused on what needs to get done and drive action and output to avoid damaging both your team's and your own credibility. Reviewing project time lines and the status of work against the key objectives for the year is important; suggest resetting due dates or refining project scope if needed.

DEMONSTRATE TRUST

Central to any good, sustained relationship, personal or professional, is trust. Your boss and other senior colleagues need to know that information shared with you will stay with you and not be passed on to others. As a CHRO, you are privy to sensitive information from many sources. Your effectiveness will be destroyed if people believe that you will share what they have told you in confidence. People also have to believe that you would never use what they have told you against them. One slip can harm your credibility and effectiveness.

Keeping the right partitions on information can be very tricky to manage if you learn about something the CEO or a colleague needs to know. In such a case, encourage the parties with the information to bring it forward to the appropriate people directly. If you have learned about something illegal, you have a duty to bring it forward immediately and must make it clear to the person who shared this information what your course of action will be.

It is important to make it clear to your CEO that you will never violate confidences, even if he or she insists you share what someone has told you. You also need to discuss any guidelines that are important to your CEO about how information the two of you discuss can be shared, and with whom, so there is no misunderstanding. As a general rule, always assume nothing can be shared unless confirmed otherwise.

BE OPEN AND HONEST

Being open and honest in expressing your views goes hand in hand with demonstrating trust. The CEO and your colleagues need to understand that you will present information in a straightforward manner. Of course, you still need to temper how you present your points and when, depending on the issue. Sometimes this will require one-on-one sessions to have a difficult conversation. Here's where your judgment on approach and setting will be critical. Everyone needs to know that you will put issues on the table and not hold back. Making this pledge also means that you must be sure to separate your opinion and perspective from the facts, and label it as such when speaking about an issue.

Courage is also needed to raise issues that could be sensitive or invite conflict. You are not doing your job if you simply choose to remain silent on a tough issue. You always have to be willing to speak up, no matter how uncomfortable it might be for you to do so. If the CEO or your colleagues are not receptive to having difficult conversations, then you will need to have a difficult talk with your boss about the situation. You will not be able to do your job effectively and serve your team or the company appropriately if you cannot be honest and open and identify the issues that need to be discussed.

MAINTAIN A BALANCED PERSPECTIVE

A former boss once told me that my position played a special role as the organization's conscience. As an HR professional, you probably have a well-developed intuition and appropriately rely on your instincts in assessing situations. You may have come to learn that despite this skill, you must constantly challenge yourself to ensure you are not presenting only one side of an issue. It takes time and probing to be sure you have looked at something from all sides, but you have to discipline yourself to operate this way. You also have to make sure to think corporately about what makes sense when balancing the needs of the overall business and the interests of its customers, employees, shareholders, and the community.

Regularly Check In and Solicit Feedback

Taking the time to periodically ask for feedback, especially from your boss, is important. Under our performance management programs, we always cite the importance of feedback, yet at more senior levels, especially at the top of the organization, feedback is often not freely given unless you specifically seek it out. As you and your boss begin to work closely together, you will likely both identify aspects to modify. Staying true to your pledge to operate in an open and honest manner, you should be sure to let your boss or colleagues know if any issue is impeding your relationship with any of them and invite them to do the same with you. Letting issues, no matter how minor, go unaddressed can slowly derail your effectiveness and sense of connection to your fellow senior leaders. Asking for input, especially in the early months, will allow you to calibrate your own sense of the relationships. It helps to role-model the type of connection you are working to build as a coach too.

Traps to Avoid

It takes time and steady focus to become a truly effective business partner, and doing this successfully can yield meaningful dividends for you personally and, more important, for the company and its employees. Nevertheless, you have to be aware of a few traps to avoid, or your relationship will be undone.

Lose Perspective

I have seen great HR leaders get derailed by their colleagues when they stop being part of the team and try to use their relationship with the CEO to put forward their own agenda. It is important to advance programs and decisions that you believe are the right ones for the company even if everyone else in the senior ranks always agrees with what you are proposing. However, repeatedly disregarding colleagues' views and using your relationship with the CEO to get your way too often can backfire. Your peers will look for ways to level the field, your relationship with them will deteriorate, and some may even look to actively undermine you and your team. You cannot be worried about being popular to discharge your duties well. But you do need to avoid putting forth your work at the cost of others.

ADVERTISE YOUR IMPORTANCE

If you have built a strong relationship, you will likely find yourself spending significant time with the CEO and having the type of influence you desire and need to do your job effectively. Dropping comments and making special effort to let others know how much time you are spending with the CEO, or bragging about your influence, however, is a surefire recipe for destroying your relationships with your peers and possibly also your boss. An HR professor I respect a great deal once shared that in his estimation, the best HR leaders are those who "lead from behind." Your success is best spoken through the work you and your team deliver and the impact it makes on the business. Astute colleagues will see these results and will be keenly aware of the time you spend with the CEO and your influence in the organization.

FAVOR THE CEO

It takes time to build relationships, so with all of the demands on your calendar, it is easy over time to focus most of your time on interactions with your boss. Ironically, your ability to be an effective advisor to your boss requires you to have a current and balanced view of what is happening across the business. Spending time regularly with each of your fellow senior leaders gives you a broader view of what is going on in their organizations and with them personally and in their interactions with each other and with their teams. If you do not put as much consistent effort and attention into the relationships you have with your peers, you will shortchange the value you provide to your boss.

LOSE EXTERNAL FOCUS

Your effectiveness in understanding the business and providing valuable advice and counsel also depends on the currency of your functional knowledge. Often CHROs can get caught up in building effective connections with their senior colleagues at the expense of staying abreast of external best practices and trends, and think they can rely solely on their team or outside consultants for this information. This is a big mistake as this information helps you better solve problems, develop HR strategies, and manage new risks. Your fellow leaders want and need to hear what other companies are thinking about when it comes to issues such as hiring, development, and reward strategies. They need to know about how others are tackling new regulations or laws that have an impact on labor costs. Although it takes time away from the office, you should regularly participate in external professional forums and develop good relationships with peers at other companies.

CONCLUSION

You have been appointed the CHRO and earned your seat at the table. To ensure you deliver on the expectations that go along with this responsibility and serve as a true business partner requires you to build effective relationships with your new boss, the CEO, and other senior colleagues. Foundational to forging real and lasting relationships is investing the time to get to know each other personally, as well as professionally; setting shared expectations and rules of engagement for how you will work together; and displaying trust and balance in how you conduct yourself with others. The road map for doing this is straightforward, but it requires focused effort at the start and the ongoing investment of your time to bring it to reality. The impact of doing it well can produce many benefits for your company overall and also be tremendously rewarding personally as you create strong connections with your colleagues.

CHAPTER FIFTEEN

WHAT DO YOU STAND FOR?

Elizabeth "Libby" Sartain

Rising to the role of CHRO brings with it power and influence at a level that requires stewardship and a sense of duty surpassing that of other corporate C-suite executives. We are entrusted with careers and compensation, and thus workers' livelihoods. We oversee health and welfare, wellness, and retirement programs that affect the lives of our workers and their families. We make decisions about who joins, who moves forward, and who leaves our organizations. We make policy and programming decisions that guide the at-work behavior of leaders and workers and frame expectations of performance. Often we are the HR partner for the C-suite itself, which means we coach our peers on maximizing their strengths and addressing growth opportunities. We confront them with leadership and people issues in their own organizations. We are a confidante to the CEO, providing special insight into the team at the top and their business units or functions. Interaction with the board of directors on compensation, succession planning, executive performance, and the board nomination process provides opportunities to inform and influence board decisions.

At the same time, our peers in the C-suite must be able to trust us with unwavering confidence. After all, we may be the keeper of their confidences. We are key players in helping them achieve their goals and playing out their strategies. They have to know that their agenda is our agenda. They want to feel that we support their success. We have the power to say yes and at times the obligation to say no. Knowing when, why, and how to say both yes and no is what will identify you as a leader worthy of the top people role in your company.

It takes courage to face the tough issues in the corporate environment—issues like a peer who is not performing, workplace misdeeds, unethical behavior, business growth or setbacks affecting the workforce, new talent needed, mergers and acquisitions, or government intervention that is affecting the business. There are many stakeholders—people to please—in working through situations, but the CHRO cannot strive to be a people pleaser. Instead, we must focus on doing what is right for shareholders, customers, workers, and the business. In the end, it is our responsibility to do what is best overall for the business while maintaining positive relationships at all levels. That's a tall order.

HR has been described as the conscience of an organization. That may go too far, but some in our organizations view it this way. The downside is that we are expected to be the exemplar of leadership behavior. We are expected to be the champion of corporate and personal values, and that may be difficult if the values of the organization do not align with our own. There are times when the CHRO must rise above personal preferences, ambitions, or feelings for the sake of business success, but that doesn't mean compromising ethics or values. That means using our heads and our hearts and having a sense of purpose that shows in all that we do. And that means we must embrace and not misuse the power that comes with our role.

With this level of impact, we must approach our business with a sense of integrity and courage, with personal values as our guide. So before taking on a CHRO assignment we must carefully examine our own values, beliefs, and underlying assumptions about our own way of delivering results and our sense of purpose about what we do.

PERSONAL BRAND

From the moment we rise to this position from the inside or are hired from the outside, it is important to stand for something and establish a personal brand as a leader, as an HR professional, and for the HR organization. Interactions with the team at the top, the HR team, and various stakeholders, including board members, suppliers, and customers, provide important opportunities to share your point of view. This starts from the moment you are being considered for the CHRO role. Know who you are and what you stand for.

As I was being interviewed for a CHRO position, a headhunter asked me, "What are the two or three things you must do in the CHRO role, no matter where you are?" At first I thought that I might adjust what I delivered to fit the needs the new organization I would join. But I have come to realize that there are some things about my own brand of HR that I must do wherever I am. What he was really asking me was, "What is your unique brand of HR leadership? Your differentiator among your peers? What do you stand for?"

For me it is about building a best employer brand aligned with a culture that delivers the organization's brand promise to customers and establishing a talent brand that becomes a magnet for the type of talent who will propel the organization above the competition. So when seeking a new role, I looked for an organization that would allow me to do my best work in those specific ways.

WHICH BATTLES TO FIGHT

In the course of our work in the CHRO role, there are times when we have to confront a peer, boss, coworker, or board member when an organizational or leader's decision is not the right thing to do—not in keeping with organizational values or just not a wise business decision from the lens of HR. It is important to pick the right battles.

Among the several pitfalls to avoid when picking battles is to be wary of fighting battles for others. That is not our responsibility. We can help facilitate a tough discussion between peers when necessary without taking on a battle for our boss or peers. Another is not to become the official corporate scold. Rather than lecture, bring facts, analysis, and solutions. Demonstrate how the problem is affecting the business negatively, and create a vision for how the problem can be resolved in a way that is relevant and befitting the organizational culture.

There are black, white, and gray areas. Battles that must always be fought are those involving unethical or illegal behavior. But when the battle is about a business decision you don't agree with, you must state your case and defend your point of view, but carry forward if the decision is made.

It is best to avoid battles outside the HR domain. Talent management and leadership arenas are our areas, so those are where we must put a stake in the ground. So, for example, if a tyrant executive is causing problems in the workplace, that battle must be fought. Making the right decision about removing an executive, for instance, may hurt business results in the short term, but it is our responsibility to bring to light a discussion of the short-term loss versus the long-term effects that such a poor leader might have on the organization's ability to attract and retain talent. A leader who is creating a work environment that is not what the business aspires to deliver, not a good experience for those on the team, or, worse, a hostile environment for workers can hurt the organization's employment brand. A tyrannical leader can have a negative effect on the corporate reputation for the long term, especially since social media can make everything inside an organization public with the speed of a blog post, tweet, or YouTube video. The appeal must be made to the values of those making the decision. Are we going to measure up to the high bar we have set for ourselves?

As an example, my company bought a small company for its workforce—the talent and knowledge of their people we needed to shore up a new line of business. It turned out that the CEO of that company did not measure up to the leadership standards espoused by our company. But we needed his know-how, at least for the time that it took for us to get the newly acquired skills integrated into our organization. I confronted this person about his behavior and the consequences, citing specific examples. I told him that it was unlikely he could change his style, which had worked in his entrepreneurial endeavors, but that it was causing problems for the company and our workers. The high turnover in his group and the difficulty in attracting new people to the team were hurting the results of his business unit. Instead of firing him, I assigned one of my best HR leaders to his team, and I expected him to depend completely on this person when it came to the workforce. In addition, we found a lieutenant who could handle the people issues while he handled the technical and product issues. We therefore had a solution that worked for the business. It was a compromise that worked for HR and kept us closer to the values we held.

The CHRO must navigate the complexity of balancing business priorities and people priorities. I was once overruled on a policy decision that I knew would be wildly unpopular with our employees but would reduce expenses during a very tough quarter. I stated my case, but the financial decision trumped the ramifications for workers. So I went to work with my team to make the policy change as painless as possible for workers and to make sure it was communicated with transparency and compassion. As the CHRO, I announced the policy change and implemented it in the workplace as if it were my own recommendation. I took the hit for the team when worker reaction was negative. And when the media criticized the policy, it was cited as an HR policy.

Perhaps one of the thorniest situations to confront is an allegation made against a peer or a boss where the alleged behavior is unethical or illegal. The CHRO must address the situation, even at the risk of creating difficult relationships or losing a job. It might require going to the board if the CEO doesn't agree or is part of the issue. That requires real courage.

Come to the battle with solutions at the ready. We need to be able to work with the executive team through the issue to create solutions. We need to use our best and most innovative people strategies.

NEVER MAKE IT PERSONAL

The third pitfall in HR is heavily dependent on functional working relationships: never make it personal. There is an art to opposing a business cohort effectively. It cannot be about winning the battle; it has to be about the business winning against its competition. It's not a personal vendetta or an emotional argument. Battles are more easily won by the relationships built over time than by the facts of the situation. If the CHRO has proven judgment and has advised wisely, the credibility will carry a lot of weight in those tough situations.

We aren't the anointed saviors of our organizations. We alone cannot have all the answers to the complex people puzzles that each of us lives with every day. We cannot go it alone, and we better make sure that we can work as a team with all of the other C-suite executives toward the greater good. We need to get everyone involved in people issues and strategies. Look for your strongest allies to support your cause.

As the war for talent was heating up, my team faced obstacles in changing the mind-set of talent managers to embrace the importance of their role in the hiring process. We needed to move from an attitude of "that's HR's job" to "that's one of my most important roles as a manager in partnership with HR." We wanted our talent managers to be more accountable for bringing in great talent, developing their own talent inside, and selling both the organization and the work. And we wanted to end the finger pointing and form a strong partnership.

After several attempts at winning over the company, which felt like an uphill battle, I solicited the support of one of our most passionate talent managers to help us elevate the talent management programming and asked him to help carry the torch. With a respected champion on our team, we were able to change the culture around talent management.

Success in this area starts with having solid trusting relationships with experts within the organization whom you will need to work with on the tough issues. That means the general counsel when it comes to legal issues, the chief marketing officer when it comes to a brand issue, the public relations executive when it comes to a matter of the corporate reputation, and the chief financial officer when it is a financial subject. You must cultivate those relationships from the beginning.

It is best to oppose privately initially rather than to confront in an open arena. Yet sometimes the situation calls for an honest opinion during a meeting, and the CHRO must be transparent in the moment. When offering an opposing point of view, focus on the facts of the situation, the probable results, and what it will mean for the business. Consider the audience and the relationships in the room. Never make it about winners and losers. Keep it about the business result.

TAKING RISKS

When you have achieved the CHRO position, high-stakes risks come with the territory as they do with any other C-suite role. Your team is counting on you to add the benefit of your wisdom, experience, and knowledge, not to mention your values, to the corporate conversation. And there will be times when your point of view conflicts with the direction your colleagues want to go in. The risk is yours to take. That's part of your job.

Years ago I made a recommendation to include the domestic partners of our employees as eligible dependents. The executive team unequivocally shot down my idea. I could have shelved the idea but felt it was an important issue and decided to risk pushing it. I waited a few months and then convened a task force of people from various departments and with different points of view. Financial experts, lawyers, advocates for gay and lesbian issues, and those who felt making such a change was an abomination worked together to help me forge a tenable solution. After months of work, we emerged with a new recommendation: to make committed partners of the same and opposite sex eligible for benefits with strong qualification requirements. This time the recommendation was accepted. The risk, approached with due diligence rather than heroic abandon, was worth taking; the principle had been worth standing up for.

DETERMINING WHEN TO STAND UP

You're not without a road map to help guide you through the risk-taking process. To sum up this chapter, I am providing a series of five questions you can ask yourself to help you find the clarity, courage, and confidence you'll need to determine whether this is the time to step apart from the prevailing direction of your team:

• *Are you confident in the strength of your point of view?* Have all your business arguments in place, and speak about your concerns in terms that your team can relate to. When you don't have a point of view, say so. There will be times when you will be asked to weigh in on a business decision that has come up for immediate review.

If it's out of your purview, it's better to say, "I don't know enough about this issue to offer a point of view or to suggest preliminary outcomes from a talent management perspective." Having a track record of demonstrating that you know when to leave the expert decisions to others will strengthen your credibility when the time does come to speak up with authority.

- *Are you confident enough in the fabric of your company's culture and values that you can be sure you will be given a respectful hearing?* When you are the voice of opposition, it's best to have a strong, quantifiable business case to support your argument. But sometimes the decision on the table for discussion simply goes against the grain of your company's values. In these cases, it should be enough to say, "I don't feel that this action aligns with our corporate values. Am I off base with that? Help me see how it does."

- *Does your team operate within a collegial, cordial climate of mutual respect?* Do you have confidence that your fellow team members trust that you know your piece of the business? Is each member free to differ but also willing to defer to each person's individual expertise? Can you confidently ask for the additional understanding that you require in order to contribute in a meaningful way?

- *Will you be able to live with whatever the final decision is, even if it doesn't go your way?* As far as the HR function is concerned, there are two parts to any decision made at the C-suite level that will affect the people side of the business: the decision itself and how you will carry out that decision. You may not agree with the decision, but can you implement it in a way that's consistent with your values and what you stand for personally and professionally? Not all your workers will be happy with the decision. But can you implement it in such a way that they will be able to at least understand and accept it?

- *Are you clear about what your fallback options are?* There may come a time when a situation is simply untenable and you have exercised all your internal options. Do you know what your alternative game plan is? CHROs have been faced with the choice of tolerating an intolerable corporate decision or leaving the organization. At your level, if the choice is to leave, are you secure enough in your career path and professional reputation that you will know another opportunity will come your way within a reasonable amount of time?

As with most other options in our professional lives, having the confidence from knowing they're available to us should we need them keeps us centered even if we never use them.

If all the points above are in place within the culture of your colleagues in the C-suite, you will most likely be able to introduce any point of view to your team from a win-win perspective. You can assume you are already respected for your expertise and overall point of view. And since most of your points will be made through the HR lens, people will see that the point is right, and they will join you on the high road.

THE COURAGE OF THE EMPLOYEE ADVOCATE

Workers expect their organization to live up to high standards of fairness, justice, and equality. They are often disappointed. Faced with tough conditions, companies make decisions that seem right for shareholders but feel unfair to employees. We can never forget our important role as advocate for the workers. This does not mean being blind to the bottom line, but our responsibility is to represent what is fair and just for our workers in the face of difficult decisions.

You need to argue for doing the right thing for employees even when it is controversial. In some situations, doing the right thing will be very hard, and it will take every ounce of your courage.

CHAPTER SIXTEEN

GREAT LEADER OR JUST A CEO?

Insights on CEOs from the Perspective of CHROs

Patrick M. Wright, L. Kevin Cox

What makes a great CEO? Many have asked and answered this question over the years. Some have focused on the strategic insight, that is, the ability of a CEO to intuitively grasp the changing nature of competition and correspondingly reposition the firm to respond successfully. Others may focus on the charismatic leadership that engages a team and a workforce around the CEO's vision and strategy. However, seldom have researchers systematically and confidentially examined the CEO from the perspective of those who work most closely with him or her.

Recently the Center for Advanced Human Resource Studies (CAHRS) at Cornell University conducted a survey of Fortune 150 CHROs in order to understand the changing nature of this role, with an emphasis on how they work with the CEO. The survey revealed that they spend, on average, 25 percent of their time with the CEO, either individually (15 percent) or as part of the executive team (10 percent). In addition, of the time with C-suite colleagues, they spend far more time with the CEO

This research was supported by the Center for Advanced Human Resource Studies at Cornell University. The ideas expressed are solely those of the authors.

(29 percent) than any other member of the executive team (for example, chief financial officer, 16 percent; chief legal counsel, 14 percent). In addition, they spend 17 percent of their time in a role of confidant/counselor/coach to the CEO and members of the executive team. These data suggest that they are uniquely positioned to provide insights into what distinguishes a CEO who leads effectively from one who does not.

This chapter discusses how CHROs view the strengths and weaknesses of their individual CEOs from an HR perspective. Based on answers to two open-ended questions regarding their CEO's performance with regard to HR, we sought to construct a profile of what distinguishes a CEO who is a strong advocate of HR from one who is an HR disappointment.

Survey Questions Regarding the CEO

One section of the survey sought to identify the areas of strengths and weaknesses of CEOs with regard to HR. Note that the focus was not on a CEO's general strengths and weaknesses, but rather in which HR areas the CEO either exceeds or does not meet the CHRO's expectations.

The survey asked two specific open-ended questions: "In what HR areas does your CEO exceed your expectations?" and, "In what HR areas does your CEO fall short of your expectations?" It is important to note that the nature of the survey was not to assess the CEO's intelligence, strategic insight, or general business acumen. In fact, the nature of the responses suggests that many CEOs excel in their business insight while lacking in their people insight.

Before discussing these results, we note that in the pilot stage of the survey, a number of CHROs expressed reservations about whether these questions should be included. They cautioned that to reveal CEO weaknesses would not be a comfortable thing for CHROs and suggested that few would venture into such dangerous territory. Of the fifty-four respondents, forty-three provided answers, three wrote "none," two did not complete their answers, and six skipped the question. Given that 80 percent of the CHROs were willing to share the weaknesses they perceive in their CEOs, it seems these results provide one of the first deep and broad examinations of how CHROs perceive their CEOs. In addition, the nature of many of the comments suggested that these CHROs viewed this as a cathartic opportunity: a chance to share their innermost frustrations of working with their CEO.

Among the responses provided by CHROs whose CEO exceeded expectations are these:

"His understanding about the importance of a strong and positive company culture and its impact on the performance of the firm. His recognition that interpersonal skills and the ability to identify and nurture talent is among the most important qualities around senior leadership."

"My CEO is a total visionary who loves to accumulate talent and interact with talent to a degree I have never experienced. Fully empowers and trusts HR to drive his vision. Spends the time to understand what we are doing."

"Has high integrity, a very authentic leader, is extremely humble, and role-models our values. Spends quality time on talent-related issues—Has a great sense of humor even during turbulent times—He is extremely approachable."

"A great leader who connects with and likes employees. Can differentiate great talent from average talent. Generally supports the HR agenda, even when driving some tough stuff."

"He is excellent at communicating with employees at large, maintaining a culture of trust and confidence. He is highly principled and concerned about the well-being and fair treatment of associates. He has begun to understand the importance of leadership/talent development and is placing increasing emphasis on that. He is also a visible spokesperson for diversity."

"He is engaging, charismatic, and very willing to be out and 'among the people.' He develops strong relationships with his direct reports and is also a good listener."

"Performance orientation—lives it, models it, demands it. Understands well the levels in effective people management strategy. Gets the complexity and expects me to deliver on all levels—strategic, tactical, relationship driven, enabling technology and process. Very demanding, but very compassionate about the things important to human beings."

"Never forgets who he serves and that it starts with out own people. Always has time for people issues/opportunities. Funds HR initiatives when the going gets tough and never wants to make the numbers on people's backs. Anticipates very well and infuses this skill into our talent assessment and planning process."

The following comments are from CHROs whose CEO fell below expectations:

"Interactions with employees. Decisiveness, Willingness to confront poor or inappropriate behavior."

"Does not understand everything that HR can really do to help and could get a little more involved."

"Could provide more frequent performance feedback and coaching to executive team members."

"Performance differentiation."

"Sometimes I wish he would focus more on honest performance management within the executive team; he is slower to act than what is best for the company sometimes."

"Leader of the executive team and undercommitted to their effectiveness and development as individuals and as a team."

"Pulling the trigger on decisions, especially those with uncertain outcomes."

"Doesn't always deliver tough messages to direct reports."

"He is slow to address mediocre talent. He is also better at managing his staff as individuals than as a team."

"Not too interested in face-to-face communications with large groups. Does it when he has to. Struggles with differentiation or rewards to match performance at the most senior levels."

"Less aware of the need and work required to work the executive group as a team versus a collection of individuals."

"Decision making can drag longer than I think it needs to."

"Fails to value the HR function."

"Employee morale is a lower priority."

"Coaching and supporting direct reports. He doesn't appreciate the relationships among open communication, trust, and employee retention and commitment."

HR Advocates Versus HR Disappointments

Exploring the exceeds and does-not-meet-expectations answers simultaneously seems to reveal a few dimensions that truly differentiate HR advocate CEOs from HR disappointment CEOs in that these characteristics were cited as areas where some CEOs truly excelled, while others were identified as failing to live up to the expectations of CHROs. In addition, two areas emerged that were cited as particular strengths but did not seem to show up as two ends of the spectrum.

From the perspective of CHROs, CEOs hold five major responsibilities as leaders.

1. They must model leadership around talent issues by valuing and investing in the firm's talent.
2. Their focus must expand beyond just the talent, to demonstrating and modeling what it means to value the entire workforce.
3. Not surprisingly, CHROs expressed a desire to see CEOs who truly valued the work of the HR function.
4. They must be the drivers of strategic change within the firm.
5. Perhaps most important, they must be the leader of leaders who manages the team with both the rigor and empathy that they expect of others.

In addition, CHROs described CEOs in positive terms with regard to the principled nature of their leadership as well as their decisive and accountable leadership, but these areas were never mentioned in the negative. These dimensions are displayed in Figure 16.1.

Talent Champion

First, HR advocate CEOs display an appreciation for the strategic importance of talent and the recognition that they must invest

FIGURE 16.1.   HR ADVOCATE AND HR DISAPPOINTMENT CEOS

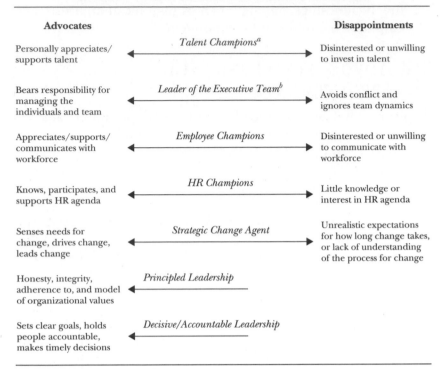

Advocates		Disappointments
Personally appreciates/ supports talent	*Talent Champions*[a]	Disinterested or unwilling to invest in talent
Bears responsibility for managing the individuals and team	*Leader of the Executive Team*[b]	Avoids conflict and ignores team dynamics
Appreciates/supports/ communicates with workforce	*Employee Champions*	Disinterested or unwilling to communicate with workforce
Knows, participates, and supports HR agenda	*HR Champions*	Little knowledge or interest in HR agenda
Senses needs for change, drives change, leads change	*Strategic Change Agent*	Unrealistic expectations for how long change takes, or lack of understanding of the process for change
Honesty, integrity, adherence to, and model of organizational values	*Principled Leadership*	
Sets clear goals, holds people accountable, makes timely decisions	*Decisive/Accountable Leadership*	

[a]Most frequently mentioned area of exceeding CHRO expectations.
[b]Most frequently mentioned area of failing to meet CHRO expectations.

their own personal time and effort in the attraction, development, and retention of talent. The HR disappointment CEOs have neither an appreciation for nor a personal commitment to talent. In fact, the most frequently cited area where CEOs seemed to exceed CHRO expectations was with regard to their focus on and support for talent. In addition, the other end of the talent focus was represented by a number of CHROs who cited a lack of appreciation for talent management as an area where the CEO did not meet their expectations.

On the positive side, CHROs wrote comments like, "Spends quality time on talent-related issues," "Loves to accumulate talent and interact with talent to a degree I have never experienced," and "Excellent skills in... the fundamentals of developing high-potential talent. Having an interest and a 'nose for external talent.' "

When asked to identify the areas where the CEO does not meet expectations, we received comments such as "talent planning," "talent development," and "appreciation of the importance of our human capital."

Dave Ulrich and the RBL Group have worked with Hewitt to develop the Best Companies for Leaders list (Hewitt Associates, 2009). One of the primary differentiators for companies that excel in leadership is that top leaders spend at least 30 percent of their time on talent issues.

The criticality of being a talent champion for effective leadership stems from the long-term orientation required to build talent. CEOs must deliver results in the short term and thus have obvious pressures to spend time with executive team members, customers, investors, and board members. Although they may truly believe in the importance of talent, the pressures unconsciously draw them away from focusing on talent. Being a talent champion requires continuous conscious commitment to investing personal time and energy, as well as company resources, toward building the future human capital of the firm—capital that may not achieve maximal impact until long after the CEO has left the organization.

LEADER OF THE EXECUTIVE TEAM

Surprisingly, one of the main differentiators between HR advocates and HR disappointments revolves around the CEO's personal responsibilities as the leader of the executive leadership team. In CHROs' eyes, effective CEOs connect with members of the team; provide clear, specific, and sometimes tough feedback to individual members; and make the hard calls in differentiating among performance levels of the various team members, especially to the point of moving out low performers. The CHROs described such CEOs in these ways: "He can differentiate great talent from average talent," "He develops strong relationships with his direct reports and is also a good listener," "Effectively deals with executive-level HR issues," and "Facilitates the effective functioning of the executive team."

While one would expect that this would be an integral competency for any executive who had moved to the CEO level, apparently many never developed this skill: "Totally conflict avoidant, very slow decision maker, especially with regard to people issues," "Doesn't always deliver tough messages to direct reports," "He can sometimes be too loyal to certain key leaders when we would probably be better off moving them out of the organization," and "[Poor at] managing conflicts among the executive team in a timely manner."

In fact, while the talent champion dimension received the most comments with regard to an area where CEOs exceed expectations, the dimension of leader of the executive team clearly garnered the most comments with regard to where the CEO disappoints.

This does not indict CEOs, only points out that they are human. Few people embrace conflict, and fewer still enjoy delivering tough messages, particularly to those with whom they may have long and deep relationships. In fact, Ed Hanway, former CEO of CIGNA, was asked where John Murabito, his CHRO, influenced him. He responded that a number of times he had hesitated to deal with a performance issue with a member of his team. He has since learned to trust John's judgment and act more quickly on those struggling in their performance.

Senior leaders who face underperformance from their direct reports often fail to do the right thing. First, they may find it easy to ignore the performance issue. In the absence of objective performance data, they can simply disregard any uneasiness with the person. A number of CHROs noted that an important aspect of their role revolves around getting CEOs to explicitly recognize team members who are underperforming, either relative to expectations or relative to the performance that would be possible with an upgrade in talent.

Second, when the objective information precludes ignoring the underperformance, CEOs may find it easier to excuse the problem. This excuse may take the form of external attributions ("It's not her fault. It's the change in accounting rules."). Or it may manifest itself as a simple justification ("He may not be perfect, but he is as good as any other chief legal counsel we could get.").

Third, they often hope that the performance problem will go away. They might have the CHRO explain to the poor performer that his or her performance has to improve. They can then hope that over the next year, those performance issues will disappear.

Finally, when ignoring, excusing, or hoping has proved futile, the CEO has to act. Failure to act has repercussions far beyond the immediate team. To ignore, excuse, or hope will be seen by the rest of the organization and interpreted as the appropriate or at least an acceptable leadership operating model. For instance, one can easily find executive leadership teams that exhibit disagreements and conflicting agendas. One company found that when surveyed, their high-potential employees expressed that one of their greatest concerns for the future of the company was the conflicting agendas of the senior leaders. A CEO who fails to rein in these conflicting agendas will not only experience dysfunctional behavior among the team members, but may soon see her talent fleeing the firm in frustration and fear.

EMPLOYEE CHAMPION

The most effective CEOs in CHROs' eyes are those who have a deep concern for employees and can effectively communicate with the larger workforce. Many CEOs disappoint CHROs by their lack of empathy, caring, or concern for employees and either their inability or unwillingness to effectively communicate with the workforce. Employee champion CEOs were described in phrases such as "very willing to be out and 'among the people,'" "excellent at communicating with employees at large," "fairness and doing the right thing on employee issues ... he is highly principled and concerned about the well-being and fair treatment of associates," and "a great leader who connects with and likes employees." When describing areas where CEOs disappoint them, CHROs wrote comments such as "interaction with employees," "employee engagement," "the relationships among open communication, trust, and employee retention and commitment," "not too interested in face-to-face communications with large groups," and, finally, "employee morale is a lower priority."

For instance, during the 1990s when Delta Airlines was implementing its disastrous Leadership 7.5 strategy (aimed at reducing cost per available seat mile to 7.5 cents from over 10 cents), CEO Ron Allen was quoted in the *Wall Street Journal* as saying, "The old

Delta is gone. Yes, there are morale problems. So be it." Within days Delta employees came to work wearing "So be it" buttons (Brannigan & Lisser, 1996).

In summary, some CEOs seem to inherently value the larger workforce and can intuitively and effectively communicate with them, while others seem unable or unwilling to forge an emotional connection with those most responsible for the production of the firm's products or the delivery of the firm's services.

HR CHAMPION

The fourth area that differentiates effective from disappointing CEOs from the standpoint of CHROs not surprisingly focuses on their appreciation of and support for the HR function and agenda. HR champion CEOs clearly see the value that the HR function can bring to the business, involve themselves in the design of the HR agenda, and provide the necessary support for its implementation. HR disappointment CEOs have little knowledge of, appreciation for, and support for HR. For instance, the CHROs wrote positive comments such as these: "Generally supports the HR agenda, even when driving some tough stuff," "He has me involved in every strategic aspect of the business, and thus I can contribute more to the company," "Fully empowers and trusts HR to drive his visions, spends time understanding what we are doing," and "Models expectations for other leaders in HR issues. Values contemporary, strategic HR." Conversely, when describing how the CEO fails to meet their expectations, CHROs wrote, for example, "understanding the underlying operations of our HR business," "valuing the HR function," and "does not understand everything that HR can really do to help and could get a little more involved," It is important to note the self-interested nature of these respondents. Clearly the CHRO has a vested interest in a CEO who values what he or she does and delivers to the firm. In addition, in some cases, the lack of valuing the function may in fact be a lack of valuing the individual who leads the function. Thus, responses on the negative end of this spectrum may reflect as much about the respondent as it does about the CEO. However, this dimension certainly says something about the relationship between the CEO and the HR function.

STRATEGIC CHANGE AGENT

Another dimension that saw CHROs describe on both the positive and negative sides of the continuum had to do with the ability of the CEO to drive strategic change. On the positive end of the spectrum were comments such as "driving organization change," "change management," and "solid support for driving change" that described the CEO's general orientation toward effective implementation. In addition, comments such as "external market awareness, extremely intuitive on market developments," and "the can-do attitude in the face of difficult market conditions" seem to describe the CEO's competency at identifying the need for change and exuding a confidence about the firm's ability to manage change.

A number of CHROs described disappointing CEOs as seeming to have unrealistic expectations about what it takes to implement programs. In most cases, this appears as impatience or unrealistic expectations about how long it takes to drive change in the firm. Comments such as the following evidence this concern: "Underestimates change management required for transformational initiatives," "No real sense of cost/investment to implement global programs ... decisions can be made one day with the expectations they can be rolled out broadly in a matter of days," and "can be impatient on process ... because he gets it, he thinks others do too, yet some don't." However, sometimes the focus is on failing to get the structure and people lined up in a way to make the change happen. For instance, one CHRO wrote that the CEO was "not execution oriented," and another that "getting all the layers between me and the HR frontline to react similarly—change occurs too slow."

PRINCIPLED LEADERSHIP

A number of CHROs described their CEOs as exceeding their expectations in terms that either explicitly or implicitly praised their principled leadership and personal integrity. For instance, participants described their CEO in these ways: "He is as genuine as the day is long—not an ounce of pretentiousness in him, thus, he can be trusted," "Has high integrity, a very authentic leader, is extremely humble, and role-models our values," and "Strong sense of values and respect for the best aspects of corporate culture." In addition, this principle- or values-based leadership affects the decisions such that these CEOs emphasize fairness in dealing with employees and caring and compassion for employees as a whole as well as individuals. This factor shows up only as a positive; no CHROs reported that CEOs disappoint on the dimension of principled leadership.

DECISIVE AND ACCOUNTABLE LEADERSHIP

While somewhat related to the leadership of the executive team, a number of comments emerged with regard to how CEOs effectively communicate expectations, hold people accountable for results, and act decisively. CHROs made comments like these: "Sets clear goals, keeps team focused on priorities and the prize," "Business strategy balance sheet management," and "Ability to confront and demand real accountability." This is seen as an ability to hold people accountable while still caring about them, as evidenced by the following comment: "Very demanding, but compassionate about the things important to human beings." Like principled leadership, this showed up only as a positive factor.

CONCLUSION

This chapter does not indict CEOs as being less-than-effective leaders of their firms. In fact, many of the CHROs presented glowing descriptions of their CEOs and discussed their weaknesses more from a developmental than a disappointment perspective. In addition, the nature of the questions focused narrowly on CEOs' strengths and weaknesses with regard to HR areas, ignoring the strategic, financial, and business acumen that may be significantly more critical to their effective performance.

These results from the Cornell/CAHRS Survey of CHROs provide insights into how CHROs view their CEOs' relative strengths and weaknesses with regard to the HR agenda. CHROs clearly do not idolize the CEO as a perfect leader who has no faults, but rather described aspects of CEO behavior that can be dysfunctional and even detrimental to the firm's performance. This can be the springboard from which to examine CEOs when trying to decide whether to take a particular CHRO job or from trying to develop qualities that a CEO is weak on for a CHRO already in the job.

REFERENCES

Brannigan, M., & Lisser, E. (1996, June 20). Ground control: Cost cutting at Delta raises stock price but lowers the service. *Wall Street Journal*, p. A1.

Hewitt Associates. (2009). Top companies for leaders 2009: Research highlights from North America. https://rblip.s3.amazonaws.com/Articles/TCFL-%20Research%20Highlights.pdf.

PART FOUR

THE CHRO AS LIAISON TO THE BOARD OF DIRECTORS

Chapter Seventeen

Working with the Board of Directors

Bill Rosner

Working effectively with a board of directors is probably not something for which you've been well prepared. Even if you've made presentations or had some limited interactions with board members, it's not the same as supporting their decision-making processes. And once you become engaged in their decision processes, you can have a powerful impact, positive or negative. The consequences to your career can be tremendous.

In this chapter, I offer some perspective and preparation on these important responsibilities in a CHRO's role. This will be done primarily through the lens of my work with the personnel and compensation committee over the course of a thirteen-year tenure as CHRO in a major financial services firm under two CEOs. What you may find most valuable are the learnings from my missteps and recoveries. May you learn from my mistakes but also realize, and even embrace, that you will make your share as well. You will not please every stakeholder, and you will still be doing an effective job. This is the nature of the CHRO as well as the other C-suite positions.

IT WAS THE BEST OF TIMES, IT WAS THE WORST OF TIMES (CURRENT ENVIRONMENT)

Working with the board's personnel and compensation committee is challenging most of the time but is exponentially more difficult when the nature of the economy, regulatory environment, or the company's results are plus or minus two standard deviations from the norm. This is true even on the plus side when your company has knocked the ball out of the park and management believes their compensation should follow the same trajectory.

But here my intent is just to highlight the readily apparent. The recent economic and political environment seems unparalleled in my thirty-five-year career. A full discussion of this exceptional period is not my goal or consistent with my expertise. You've probably read more on this topic than you'd like already. Nevertheless, the implications of a major recession, unprecedented government involvement in executive compensation and risk management, greater shareholder activism, and ever-increasing regulatory scrutiny are enormous.

Guidance from various agencies, regulators, and legislation does not always appear to be consistent, yet it is still necessary to comply with the requirements of the various constituencies. These conditions have increased the complexity and difficulty of a director's role and therefore have done the same for those in management supporting their governance responsibilities. As painful as it may be, I still believe valuable learnings can come from this period. However, for me personally, it also makes me conclude that my transition from the CHRO role was well timed!

I will not attempt to focus on the ramifications of these turbulent times, but examine more broadly the issues and practices of board governance. I focus on working with the personnel and compensation committee and the implications for the CHRO role. Toward this end, I'll discuss some of the fundamentals of this process, related disclosure, various roles, and experiential learnings.

Let's Start at the Very Beginning . . . (Personnel and Compensation Committee Charter)

The personnel and compensation committee charter serves as the foundational document defining the committee's roles and responsibilities and management's role relative to this board committee. The charter defines functional coverage such as executive compensation. Contrary to popular belief, however, this is not the sole focus of this committee. Typically the charter includes oversight responsibility for succession planning and executive development, diversity, benefits, HR compliance and risk management, employee engagement, and nonexecutive compensation.

I have gotten feedback from directors on this point, that is, their desire for balance and not focusing exclusively on executive compensation. Furthermore, they don't want to discuss executive compensation only in the November through February time frame when the pressure is on. They also want to consider the topic more strategically when cooler heads prevail. In addition, they want the CHRO to structure more time for review in other functional areas to ensure that management is fulfilling its responsibilities in the key HR result areas: capability building, organization climate, productivity, and employee service.

Review of the committee charter should be done at least annually. In my experience, the charter does indeed require modifications most years driven by director input or regulatory changes. The charter usually defines a process in which the committee members provide feedback on the operation of the committee, which is invaluable and has caused important changes in the timing of discussions and decision making. Specifically, the issues and recommendations are discussed completely in one meeting, and the decision making and voting on a particular issue is held at a subsequent meeting.

WITH A LITTLE HELP FROM MY FRIENDS (PERSONNEL AND COMPENSATION COMMITTEE MEMBERS)

Examining the charter and the associated processes is important, but understanding the directors' backgrounds, experiences, and perspectives is critical. Factors such as the sector from which they came (corporate, government, academia, military, or something else), the industry in which they served, the role they had at their company, whether they are retired or currently employed, and whether they have experience with compensation programs similar to yours all have significant implications for the CHRO. If the director comes from a publicly traded firm, you'd be wise to closely examine his or her latest proxy in order to understand the perspective she or he will be bringing to the discussion. In another case, I certainly needed to put in additional time communicating with and understanding the perspective of a director who came from a joint venture structure that didn't use publicly traded equity in its compensation programs.

Making assumptions about how individual directors view the role of certain compensation vehicles (for example, base pay, cash bonus, options, or restricted stock) is also dangerous. All directors have their own experiences and perspectives, and the CHRO needs to embrace those and bridge the gap to the existing companies' industry, competition, and strategic plan. Having these different perspectives can be valuable and complementary, but it does take time and effort to establish a common framework and even common language. A well-organized orientation for new committee members plays an important role toward this end, but ongoing discussions regarding the changing environment and company circumstances are still essential.

Of course, you'll have similar challenges with the directors you face with your other senior clients. You'll need to understand their preferences for taking on information: written or verbal, how far in advance, and whether they want individual premeetings, for example. You'll need to have enough conversations to determine what worked for the director in the past, to understand this person's perspective, and how to make the best use of his or her time.

In summary, from a competency perspective, you'll need to stretch your abilities in listening, patience, audience sensitivity, and understanding others to achieve the full value from your directors. This will allow an effective working relationship that will well serve both management's interests and the directors' governance responsibilities.

LET THE SUNSHINE IN (CRITICALITY OF DISCLOSURE)

It wasn't very long into my relationship with the directors on the personnel and compensation committee that it was made very clear to me how critical disclosure is in its various forms. If an otherwise valid decision regarding the compensation program cannot be effectively communicated to external stakeholders with its associated rationale, then you will face cleaning up the mis- understanding after the fact, which can be damaging. It can unnecessarily place directors in time-consuming and contentious situations. At the least, poor disclosure can hide the light of strong governance under the proverbial bushel.

In more than one committee meeting, the discussion was dom- inated by exactly how the disclosure of a particular decision would appear and when. Generalities were not sufficient. If I didn't come with clear answers on these specifics and the related implications, I was appropriately sent back to the drawing board (or taken behind the woodshed—take your pick).

Some of the larger disclosure items like the compensation discussion and analysis (CD&A) within the proxy take a great deal of work and present some dilemmas. There is a desire for the document to contain explanation and rationale while still valuing simplicity and brevity. The Securities and Exchange Commission (SEC) requirements are expressed in over four hundred pages, and that can drive a very legalistic and compliant approach while overlooking the basic tenets of transparency, clearly representing the directors, the decision-making process, and speaking directly to priority issues.

Although I don't suggest our CD&A was perfect, I believe we did overcome some of these issues. For instance, through networking and reviewing multiple approaches, we successfully worked with our directors to develop an original table that out-lined the committee's decisions made just for that performance year. The SEC-required Summary Compensation Table provides useful information, but due to its utilization of Financial Account-ing Standards Board expensing standards, it does not segregate the impact of the most recent decisions. We also fully explained some unique features of our program, addressed the rationale for our performance metrics, and directly addressed issues that had recently received a great deal of attention in Congress.

Nothing of this significance is accomplished alone. It is critical to establish a cross-functional team that contains the appropriate expertise, communicates effectively, and works in a highly coordi-nated fashion. Beyond the compensation staff, we were fortunate to have skilled professionals from the finance and legal depart-ments, including the corporate secretary, who pulled together and developed a CD&A that effectively represented our P&C commit-tee. When CD&As are dominated by the legal department, they can read like incomprehensible legal documents; if dominated by finance, they can read like statistics and formulas. Thus, the goal is to combine the strengths and perspectives across functions to create a document that communicates clearly and transparently.

Who's on First? (Roles and Responsibilities)

Most of the time you really do need to figure out what Abbott and Costello were talking about. It is important for there to be consistent understanding on the role of management, the com-pensation committee, and the full board. There has to be clarity on review versus approval issues. Generally the committee doesn't want, or need, to approve a great many items since it can divert their attention from the most critical issues. Limited delegation of authority to management can be worked out on routine issues, such as benefit plan amendments after an acquisition. These actions can then be reviewed with the committee periodically.

Another question that can arise is whether the directors are on management's turf. In my experience, this potential concern remedies itself fairly quickly. The directors are, or were, members of management elsewhere and usually have a strong sensitivity to this issue. Directors often check themselves when getting in too deeply on management-level decision making. If not, this question of role clarification generally can be raised without rebuke.

Naturally conflicts can also arise between the compensation committee and other members of the board. The CHRO implications here are to ensure that the committee members are well prepared to convey the decision rationale to the full board. In some cases, the CHRO should reach out to noncommittee directors for more in-depth discussions. This, of course, should be done in coordination with the compensation committee chair.

The role that the committee chair plays is also critical to understand. I was fortunate to serve under two strong committee chairs in my tenure as CHRO, but each approached the role somewhat differently, and that had various implications. You might want to consider some questions in this regard:

- What is the function of premeetings with the chair?
- How directive versus facilitative is the chair relative to committee members?
- How much are committee members relying on the chair for guidance?
- What are the relationships and communication norms between the chair, committee members, and the CEO?
- What function does advanced meeting material play?
- Are you communicating to five or six committee members directly or through the committee chair?

Role alignment within the committee may be an issue, and here the CHRO can often use the CEO, the board's executive compensation consultant, or the committee's self-evaluation process to facilitate a resolution.

The role of the executive compensation consultant to the committee presents another set of issues for the CHRO. In some ways, you are both adversaries and partners. To deal with this duality, you must identify the common ground on an issue but also understand that at times, you will agree to disagree. Management will continue to use other consultants, and it's important to define the role of these consultants versus the role of the committee's advisor. Often it is a matter of management's consultant providing survey information and analysis. This should be reviewed and reconciled with the board's consultant in advance to avoid battling consultants on stage in front of the committee.

It's important to develop open communications with the committee's consultant. There can't be any surprises on either side. The CHRO and the board's consultant both have insight that's important to share with each other based on their relationships with their primary clients, the CEO and the directors, respectively.

Finding and maintaining a quality compensation consultant for the committee also requires acknowledgment of potential conflicts of interest. If your company has all their benefits administration and actuarial work done with firm X, any compensation consultant from firm X will be disqualified as a consultant for your directors. Firm X could, however, continue to serve managements' survey and analysis needs.

You can readily see the dilemma for the consulting firms. Although these board assignments are prestigious, they often pale in their impact to the consulting firm's bottom line relative to the other product lines. This can all add up to restricting the supply of quality consultants for the board.

I CAN'T GET NO SATISFACTION (DIRECTOR EXPECTATIONS)

Understanding the pressures and conflicts inherent in the director's role as a committee member can only contribute to the CHRO's effectiveness. At the fundamental level, the directors' role is to ensure effective corporate governance. However, the CHRO needs to appreciate the various stakeholders to which the directors are, or are perceived to be, accountable: state and federal government, numerous regulatory agencies, institutional shareholders, retail shareholders, shareholder service organizations, customers, labor unions, the full board, management, and the broader base of employees, to name a few. The impact of public opinion, the media, and how the directors factor this into their decision making is also a consideration for the CHRO. All of these stakeholders have different expectations and requirements for the directors, who often require direct support from the CHRO to respond effectively.

Often it feels as if there are too many cooks in the kitchen. I'm afraid the directors' ability to please everyone is no better than the CHRO's ability to please one and all. Certainly effective disclosure is a critical contribution. However, in some cases, written disclosure in its various forms will be insufficient. More CHROs are taking part in the CEO and CFO discussions with shareholders and regulators and explaining the pay-for-performance linkages of executive compensation plans and how these plans are consistent with good risk management practice. The new CD&A format is clearly value-added, but it's not the whole story. For example, do shareholders and other interested parties really appreciate the consequences of performance through well-designed equity-based plans on an executive's W-2 or net worth? Let me assure you that the executive does. That's not always clear in the summary compensation table.

Man in the Mirror (Learning from Experience)

I hope this chapter will allow you to learn from some of my mistakes as well as the occasional success. Learning from all my mistakes would take the whole book, and I have only a chapter.

In one case, the committee requested a change in the calendar for year-end decisions on bonuses and long-term grants to allow them to be done on the same date. Certainly this integrated decision making was a reasonable and logical request. The issue was that it would change the grant date for our options and stock awards from late January, two days after earnings were released, to mid-February, when the board met for bonus decisions. We had strong legal and regulatory advice that the original date was a particularly desirable one for pricing options since it was two days after a full disclosure of earnings so that the market price was likely to fully reflect comprehensive material information about the company. Pricing in mid-February could open up second-guessing from shareholders and others around how information was handled during that two- to three-week period. If significant events were to occur, was the announcement of good news delayed, or was bad news accelerated to affect the strike price? Was good news during that period seen as immaterial and bad news as exaggerated?

My initial reaction was to see the issue as black and white and recommend that we not make this change for the reasons cited. I comforted myself that possibly the directors didn't fully understand the issue. Big mistake! Whenever you hear yourself saying, "They don't understand," you probably need to rethink your options. You are probably thinking about the issue too narrowly. Certainly I was.

Eventually I discussed the apparent dilemma with the CEO, and he felt we could manage the risk. I reached out for more advice from counsel and agreed that we could accommodate this change and significantly mitigate our risk through advance disclosure in the preceding year's CD&A. We worked this resolution through the directors, and all's well that ends well. Actually, not really. The way I handled this issue allowed a perception of inflexibility or nonresponsiveness to grow. The mistake was not reaching out earlier for other perspectives on the issue. Mistakes will still be made, but don't make them in isolation.

In a more successful case where things were done right the first time, we effectively engaged a cross-functional team that led to the withdrawal of a shareholder proposal whose principles we felt we had already embraced and implemented. The original proposal related to the pay-for-performance attributes of one of our long-term incentive plans. In essence, the recommendations for specific metrics and measuring these relative to an appropriate peer group were all in place. The inclusion of this proposal could certainly give the impression that we were at significant variance from these recommendations.

Initially we had difficulty setting up time with the shareholder group to discuss their proposal. We were able to get through to them with one of our senior relationship managers. Meanwhile a team that included me, our compensation director, the corporate secretary, and senior counsel developed our rationale and approach to the discussion. The combination of HR's compensation expertise with the legal function's in-depth understanding of regulation, disclosure, negotiation, and strong written communication skills proved a formidable team. After a visit from our compensation director and corporate secretary and an exchange of written communications clarifying each party's position, the proposal was withdrawn just prior to the deadline.

This was far better than trying to get a "no" recommendation from a shareholder service organization on the proposal, since even though it was largely redundant, it would be difficult for them to vote no on a basic pay-for-performance proposal.

In our interaction with the shareholder group, we focused intently on understanding their objective and perspectives. By doing so, we were able to demonstrate our commonalities and show our practices to be consistent with their principles. They were also able to express their views on our written disclosures. They pointed out a few opportunities for us to clarify points they felt didn't fully represent our positive practices.

The learnings here related to constructing a team with the necessary combination of expertise, including a senior customer relationship manager. In addition, our team's collective listening skills and openness diffused a potentially contentious situation.

You Can't Always Get What You Want (CHRO Role)

As the song goes, you can't always get what you want; however, in the CHRO role, you just might find that you get what you need. The CHRO role often feels like a no-win situation. In other cases, your work is sufficiently behind the scenes that your good work can go unrecognized. That's okay; referees and umpires doing a good job are also relatively invisible, but their contribution to the game is critical. If you want to be the superstar getting all the attention, this is not the job for you.

I finish this chapter with a few more observations on the CHRO role as it relates to working with the board of directors. Managerial courage is clearly a critical competency. In one case, just prior to our board committee meeting, I discovered an error one of our consultants had made. I had to disclose that fully to the directors and make a recommendation that was contrary to the one in the premeeting material. This certainly was not comfortable and didn't put us in the best light, but it was the right thing to do for both management and the shareholders. In general, to be an effective shareholder advocate, managerial courage must be present. As you attempt to play that advocacy role, you may put yourself on the opposite side of issues from your management clients, the executive compensation consultant, or the directors themselves. In these cases, strong communication of your rationale is important, but even more critical is an understanding of the other party's perspective, which may allow you to craft an appropriate compromise.

Clear, aligned communication with the directors is also essential. You must avoid communication triangles. When the CEO is speaking directly to the committee chair and you're getting the feedback second-hand, you need to check and clarify the messages to avoid any surprises or misunderstandings. A follow-up call with directors after committee meetings is also a good idea. Like most other human interactions, what you're sending isn't always what they're receiving.

Finally, walking the fine line in the use of data or information with the directors to drive decisions is important. The issue here is that you need competitive data to structure decision making, but you can't become a slave to the data. There are compensation structures and plans that can be created, that when data from your company and the competition are inserted, you basically get an $A + B = C$ outcome. In my experience, directors don't want to be spoon-fed in this fashion. They appreciate structure and rationality, but there can be too much structure and not enough room made for their judgment. The issues are complex, and the directors possess considerable experience and expertise that should be brought to bear on most decisions. The committee needs to examine all relevant facts and circumstances and not just follow blind benchmarking.

My intent in this chapter has been to offer a glimpse behind the curtain of working with the board. Although there is no substitute for experience, I hope I've been able to provide some perspective that will better prepare you for the CHRO role.

CHAPTER EIGHTEEN

CHROs AND BOARDS
A Missing Link
Edward E. Lawler III

The relationship between corporate boards and CHROs is often so distant as to be of little practical significance from a board and organizational effectiveness perspective. There are a number of reasons for this and some ways to improve the relationship between CHROs and boards. However, before considering them, we need to look at the nature of this relationship.

CHRO's Role with the Board

The role of CHROs is complex and multifaceted, as the other chapters in this book point out. Because of this, there are definite limits to the amount of time that CHROs can spend dealing with the board and board-related issues. This may be one of the reasons, but perhaps not the most important one, that CHROs report spending only 10 percent of their time in dealing with corporate board issues (Wright, 2010). In any case, given this small amount of time, it's hard to imagine CHROs having a major impact on board decision making in many areas.

Relatively few CHROs are on their company's board or, for that matter, any other board. About 10 percent of the boards of large U.S. corporations report that they have a former or current CHRO as a member (Lawler, 2009). When combined with other HR experts who can serve on boards—for example, consultants and university professors—only about 20 percent of the boards in

TABLE 18.1. SENIOR EXECUTIVES' ATTENDANCE AT BOARD MEETINGS
(IN PERCENTAGES)

Executive	Board Meeting Attendance					
	Never	Rarely	Sometimes	Often	Always	On Board
Chief counsel	1	3	4	7	85	3
Business unit heads	0	4	22	43	31	0
Head of HR	6	19	35	22	19	1
CFO	0	0	1	8	91	7
CIO	8	28	40	15	9	0
Head of marketing	10	29	37	15	9	0
Other executives	0	10	51	28	11	1

the United States have someone on them who can be classified as a human capital expert. Thus, not only are HR executives usually not on boards, other individuals with HR expertise are not likely to be on boards either.

The low level of HR expertise on boards means that for good HR advice, boards would have to rely on nonboard members invited to the meetings. This raises the question of whether the head of HR is typically invited to attend board meetings. Table 18.1 presents data from a survey of corporate boards that addresses this question (Lawler & Finegold, 2006). The table shows that the head of HR always attends board meetings in only 19 percent of the corporations studied and often attends board meetings in an additional 22 percent of corporations. This is more than most of the other functional heads in these corporations but significantly less than CFOs, who in 91 percent of the companies are always in attendance at board meetings.

HR SUPPORT FOR BOARDS

CHRO attendance at board meetings and support for board activities are positively related to a number of board effectiveness measures (Lawler & Boudreau, 2006). Particularly notable are board activities that involve the compensation and executive succession decisions the board plays a role in, such as assessing the performance of senior executives and the CEO's performance evaluation. Thus, the relatively infrequent presence of CHROs at board meetings is in fact a potentially significant factor in reducing the overall effectiveness of corporate boards.

CHROs can provide expertise to corporate boards in a number of areas and help them with their decision making and ongoing operation. Table 18.2 shows how frequently senior HR executives report that their board calls on them for support. The areas where help is requested can roughly be categorized into dealing with either the operation of the board with respect to talent management issues (such as compensation) or with organizational strategy, effectiveness, and change issues. Not surprisingly, there is a big difference between the amount of support they provide in these two areas, with talent issues being the highest.

TABLE 18.2. AMOUNT OF SUPPORT HR PROVIDES TO THE BOARD

Amount of Support HR Provides to the Board					
Areas of Support	Little or No Extent	Some Extent	Moderate Extent	Great Extent	Very Great Extent	Mean
Executive compensation	4	5	7	32	52	**4.2**
Board compensation	18	17	7	25	33	**3.4**
Developing board effectiveness and corporate governance	33	20	21	17	8	**2.5**
Addressing strategic readiness	19	24	22	25	9	**2.8**
Executive succession	4	14	18	29	34	**3.8**
Change consulting	24	22	35	13	6	**2.6**
Risk assessment	27	28	29	12	3	**2.4**
Information about the condition and capability of the workforce	10	10	37	27	15	**3.3**

The highest-rated single issue is executive compensation, followed by executive succession. Board compensation also receives a high rating, which is not surprising given the importance of compensation to the board members and the expertise and knowledge that HR executives have in this area. Perhaps the best way of characterizing the kind of help that the CHRO usually provides to the board is that it is human capital management consulting. When it comes to what might be called strategic partner help, that is, addressing strategy and organizational effectiveness issues, much less help is provided (Conger, Lawler, & Finegold, 2001). Somewhat surprisingly, the same is true when it comes to helping develop the board as an effective unit and with respect to corporate governance. The HR functions in some corporations have organization development capabilities and process consulting capabilities that potentially could help the board develop its decision-making processes and make better use of its time. But these apparently are not frequently used by boards to improve their effectiveness.

HR provides relatively little support in such key business strategy areas as assessing strategic readiness, change management, and—a particularly critical issue in the last decade—risk assessment. One area where it does provide a moderate amount of information that potentially could play a major role in influencing the board's strategic decision making is the condition and capability of the workforce. This of course is a topic that is in the traditional scope and is potentially very much related to the business strategy decisions that boards make. How relevant workforce capability is when it comes to strategy depends on the nature of the business the organization is in and how it seeks to gain a competitive advantage (Conger, 2009).

One piece of evidence showing that boards don't take human capital as seriously as financial capital when it comes to decision making concerns their committee structures. Most boards do not have a human capital committee that focuses on talent management (Conger, 2009). They often have a committee that's called a human resource committee, but its major, almost exclusive, focus is on executive compensation and executive succession. It is rarely a true overseer of the human capital of the organization—one that gathers data on the condition of the human capital, monitors it, and determines whether the human capital policies and practices of the organization are well aligned with the business strategy.

It may be a bit too negative, but a reasonable conclusion based on my studies of boards in the United States is that boards do not place great importance on the condition of the workforce and the availability of talent when they make strategy decisions. If they did, there would be a much greater presence of the CHRO in board meetings, and boards themselves would have more HR executives, or at least HR experts, on them.

Perhaps the best way to characterize the relationship between CHROs and boards is that as representatives of HR, they are likely to be business partners, not strategic partners. They are business partners in the sense that they help their board deal with the HR issues the board has to deal concerning both board members and key executives—typically compensation and succession issues. They fall short as strategic partners because of their relatively low input into issues like strategic readiness, developing and improving the board's effectiveness, and corporate governance practices. It seems that when the issue is not clearly a traditional HR issue, the board is not particularly inclined to ask for help from HR or get input from an HR expert because no one in the boardroom recognizes the relevance of HR knowledge to these issues.

WHAT THE ROLE OF THE CHRO SHOULD BE

A strong case can be made that CHROs should be at most, if not all, board meetings. Just like CFOs, CHROs are responsible for one of the most important assets that corporations have. The importance of financial capital is reflected by the fact that in 91 percent of U.S. companies, the CFO is always at board meetings. The degree to which companies give only lip-service to the importance of human capital is reflected by a fact that in only 19 percent of companies is the CHRO present at all board meetings.

In addition to having the CHRO attend meetings, organizations should have an independent (outside) board member who is an expert in HR. Given the emphasis on independent board members, it is quite understandable, and in fact appropriate, that while the CHRO should attend board meetings, he or she need not be on the board. However, this doesn't mean there shouldn't be an HR expert on the board. To the contrary, an HR expert should be on the board to provide informed judgments on issues involving human capital and organizational effectiveness.

The presence of the CHRO in the boardroom and the presence on the board of an HR expert should create a situation in which the board takes a strategic look at human capital and HR issues. Their presence, combined with the right expertise in the HR organization, should in fact create a more effective board. It particularly should open the door to HR as a true partner in developing and implementing the business strategy of an organization.

Data suggest that HR is only infrequently a full partner in developing the business strategy of an organization; in most cases, it has an input role but not a partnership role (Lawler & Boudreau, 2009). In order to successfully fill the role of strategic partner, the CHRO needs a considerable amount of HR data and well-established decision-making frameworks. An interesting model here is the chief financial officer. CFOs come to boards and set the table for discussions concerning operations and business strategies by bringing financial metrics and well established decision-making frameworks like return on investment (Boudreau & Ramstad, 2007). CHROs need to come to board meetings with human capital metrics and decision models that guide business decisions based on organization capabilities and the availability of human capital. In other words, human capital management needs to be elevated not just in the attention it gets, but in its use of metrics and analytics. Unless this happens, it's unlikely that CHROs will ever be effective at setting the table for discussions about business strategy and organizational effectiveness.

MAKING IT HAPPEN

What needs to happen for CHROs to become true strategic partners with the board? One way to answer that question is to look briefly at what currently prevents it from happening. At or near the top of the list is the fact that CHROs rarely have any training in dealing with boards. Since they aren't on outside boards, they don't have the experience of seeing what happens with the boards of other companies. Since they aren't on their own company's board, they miss that opportunity to learn as well. And finally, because they don't attend board meetings, they often don't even have the chance to observe how boards deal with issues, make decisions, and operate.

Some of the things that CHROs need to know in order to work effectively with a board can be learned in the classroom and by being on boards other than those of large corporations. This leads to the suggestion that CHROs join the boards of nonprofits and smaller companies. In addition, CHROs should consider taking one of the numerous educational programs directed at educating board members.

To be credible and effective board members, CHROs need to know the language and decision models of finance and accounting and demonstrate an understanding of the business and the business strategy. Much of this can be learned before HR executives become the CHRO, and increasingly having this expertise should be a condition for appointment as CHRO. Appointing someone whose business experience is only in HR to the CHRO role almost predetermines that the individual will not be a true strategic partner with the board.

Another barrier to being a strategic partner is that CHROs are not meeting the information needs of their boards with respect to talent management. When board members were asked in our annual CEO survey of board members about the information they get and what they want to get, some interesting failures appeared. As can be seen in Table 18.3, over a third of the board members don't get, but would like to get, some basic data on the condition of the human capital in their organizations. CHROs must provide this information. Providing it may not make them strategic partners, but it can be a step toward making the CHRO a source of useful metrics.

Yet another challenge for CHROs is the tendency of board members to think they or others on the board are experts in HR. When asked whom they rely on for HR expertise, board members often say the CEOs of other companies who are on their board. But a great deal of research on evidence-based management shows that most executives do not know a great deal about human capital management. Clearly more managers' knowing and accepting

TABLE 18.3.   HR INFORMATION GIVEN TO THE BOARD

Information Given to the Board				
	Get and Should	Get but Shouldn't	Don't Get but Should	Don't Get and Shouldn't
Succession planning data for most management positions	73.1	0	24.4	2.6
Succession planning data for key technical positions	46.8	1.3	32.5	19.5
Metrics on turnover	59.0	3.8	33.3	3.8
Metrics on recruiting success	49.4	5.2	36.4	9.1
Attitude survey data	51.9	1.3	42.9	3.9

this would make it easier for CHROs to be influential in the boardroom.

There are some things that CHROs can do to get other executives to recognize their misguided sense of competency when it comes to talent management. The use of sophisticated analytics and the right metrics can help CHROs demonstrate that there is more to human capital management than applying gut feels. Part of the credibility of areas like marketing and finance comes from their analytical approaches and the fact that they make it clear to other executives that there is an expertise here that is not just common sense. HR needs to take a similar approach.

Finally, the way the HR function itself is structured can also have an important influence on the degree to which the CHRO plays a strategic role with the board. Research shows that having corporate staff groups with strategic HR expertise is significantly related to the degree to which the board looks to HR for strategic help (Lawler & Boudreau, 2006). Corporate staff groups are needed that can do the kind of analytical work that ties organizational effectiveness to organization design and HR policies and practices. Similarly, HR staff expertise in human capital development, labor economics, talent supply, and the cost of talent procurement and development are important determinants of how much boards look to the CHRO for input on strategic decision making.

Time for a Change

It is time for CHROs to change their role with respect to boards. They need to go beyond simply providing input to the board with respect to compensation and succession decisions and enter into a strategic support and advice relationship with the board. Human capital management and business strategy decisions are too important to be left to board members who lack expertise and data on talent management and organizational effectiveness.

Today the typical CHRO has occasional access to the corporate boardroom but is not a valued board support person in the way the CFO is. This clearly needs to change if the CHRO is going to be a strategic business partner. It also needs to change if organizations are to manage their human capital in a way that optimizes the performance of the organization.

Strategic business decisions need to be made by informed boards that understand how human capital and organization design issues affect the performance of organizations. Boards need to be taught how to think about, analyze, and manage the human capital and human capital systems of their organizations. Getting this done requires the presence of HR experts, both on boards and in the boardroom as supporters of the board. It also requires a committee of the board that looks at HR and organizational issues in more depth. The CHRO's role in this should be to support both the human capital committee of the board and the board itself with data, decision models, and strategic analyses of the organization's human capital and how human capital influences organizational performance. Finally, in order to become true strategic partners, CHROs need to develop expertise in how boards operate, as well as in the business issues boards face.

References

Boudreau, J. W., & Ramstad, P. M. (2007). *Beyond HR: The new science of human capital*. Boston: Harvard Business School Press.

Conger, J. A. (2009). *Boardroom realities: Building leaders across your board*. San Francisco: Jossey-Bass.

Conger, J. A., Lawler, E. E., & Finegold, D. (2001). *Corporate boards: New strategies for adding value at the top*. San Francisco: Jossey-Bass.

Lawler, E. E. III. (2009). Boards as overseers of human capital. *Directors and Boards, 33*(3), 56–59.

Lawler, E. E. III, & Boudreau, J. W. (2006). HR support for corporate boards. *Human Resource Planning, 29*(1), 15–24.

Lawler, E. E. III, & Boudreau, J. W. (2009). *Achieving excellence in human resources management: An assessment of human resource functions.* Palo Alto, CA: Stanford University Press.

Lawler, E. E., & Finegold, D. A. (2006). Who's in the boardroom and does it matter? The impact of having non-director executives attend board meetings. *Organizational Dynamics, 35*(1), 106–115.

Wright, P. (2010). Strategies and challenges of the chief human resource officer: Results of the First Annual Cornell/CAHRS Survey of CHRO's. *CAHRS working paper.* www.ilr.cornell.edu/cahrs/workingpapers.

CHAPTER NINETEEN

THE ROLE OF THE CHRO IN MANAGING EXECUTIVE COMPENSATION

Charles G. Tharp

Working with the senior management team and the compensation committee of the board of directors on matters relating to executive compensation has become an increasingly important and time-consuming aspect of the CHRO role. Unlike other areas of human resources, executive compensation is a topic that very few HR professionals are exposed to prior to assuming the top HR position. Annually, the HR Policy Association (HRPA), the organization of the top 280 HR leaders in the country, conducts a survey of the HRPA directors to identify the top priorities they face. Over recent years, executive compensation has consistently ranked among the top five topics; however, for 2009, executive compensation was ranked as the top priority, tied for first place with the perennial top priority of leadership development. In view of the compensation debate that has been generated by the financial crisis and the corresponding increased global focus on executive compensation, there is no doubt that executive compensation will continue to be a top, if not the top, priority facing CHROs in the years to come. Unfortunately, too few new CHROs are fully prepared to take on this challenge.

Executive compensation requires the CHRO to work closely with the compensation committee of the board of directors in setting compensation for the company's executive officers. Dealing with executive compensation tests the CHRO's ability to address the interests of a variety of internal and external constituents, manage the corporate governance process, and deal with the myriad requirements imposed by the stock exchanges, the Securities and Exchange Commission (SEC), state law, and the interests of shareholders and other external stakeholders. This complexity and scope of executive compensation makes it both a challenge for the new CHRO as well as a unique developmental opportunity.

THREE BASIC QUESTIONS ON EXECUTIVE COMPENSATION

The CHRO must help the company answer three basic questions of executive compensation design:

- *Versus whom?*—defining the competitive market for executive talent and the relevant peer group companies for both pay and performance comparisons
- *In what form?*—developing a mix of compensation that is competitive, aligns the interests of senior management with shareholders, provides a clear pay-for-performance linkage, and is both efficient from a financial accounting and expense perspective and tax effective for both the company and the executive
- *For what?*—identifying the key performance and market measures that produce sustainable creation of shareholder value while not encouraging excessively risky behavior

VERSUS WHOM?

Increasingly attention is focused on the selection of market comparisons used to determine executive compensation and assess performance. Under SEC rules governing the disclosure of executive compensation in the compensation discussion and analysis (CD&A) section of the proxy, companies are required to disclose the peer group companies used for determining market rates of compensation. The identification of industry competitors, competitors for talent, and companies of similar size and stature that represent investment alternatives for shareholders is a key decision for the compensation committee as it develops a frame of setting executive pay. The CHRO must play an active role in helping to identify and define key competitors and ensure that the company's level and form of pay are consistent with the targeted competitive objective. Defining the relevant competitive comparisons ("versus whom") is a key building block of the executive compensation program and a key responsibility of the CHRO.

In What Form?

Determining the mix of pay provided to executives is the second building block in developing the overall executive compensation program. An assessment must be conducted of not only competitive practices but also the extent to which compensation is aligned with the long-term creation of sustained shareholder value. Furthermore, the mix of pay must be balanced toward long-term incentives, with corresponding clawback and share ownership provisions to guard against motivating excessively risky behavior that might jeopardize the value of the company. The general trend is to place a greater portion of executive compensation on the long-term elements of pay and require that executives establish a significant ownership position in the company so as to align the interests of management with those of shareholders. This focus on long-term incentives, however, must be balanced with the need to provide near-term incentives to achieve line-of-sight goals and key corporate objectives.

The mix of pay will also have implications for reported earnings and corporate tax. Generally the expense for compensation is spread over the period for which services are rendered (generally the vesting period for the award), and the expense assigned to a particular form of compensation will vary depending on the form of the award. The expense of stock-based awards is generally fixed based on the grant date value, while cash-based awards will vary based on the actual payouts the executive receives. Similarly, the timing and amount of executive compensation that may be deducted by the company is dependent on satisfying various provisions of the tax code (for example, the limitation on the deductibility of non-performance-based compensation as defined under section 162m of the Internal Revenue Code). A working knowledge of the rules regarding the timing and amount of deductibility and the requirements for the postponement of taxation to the executive is important if the CHRO is to help the company design an efficient and effective mix of total rewards.

In addition to tax and expense considerations, the CHRO must be sensitive to shareholder and policymaker reactions to certain types of compensation. As outlined below, various flash points in the mix of pay trigger negative shareholder, media, and activist reaction. The CHRO must help the company be aware of the pros and cons of the various elements of the pay package and structure a total reward package that minimizes negative reactions. The CHRO should realize that executive compensation is a powerful internal form of communication to employees and thereby should ensure that the executive pay program is not inconsistent with the broader pay culture of the company.

FOR WHAT?

A key decision in the design of executive compensation is the establishment of performance criteria for both annual and long-term incentives. Working closely with the chief financial officer, the head of strategic planning, and the senior risk management officer, the CHRO is responsible for developing the performance objectives. In determining incentive metrics, consideration should be given to both the level of performance and the quality of performance, how the annual performance objectives relate to the longer-term creation of value, and whether to reward absolute performance or performance relative to the peer group companies. The CHRO must have a sound understanding of the business, the corporate strategy, and the competitive environment in order to provide advice and counsel on the design of performance criteria for incentive awards.

While executive compensation is potentially a powerful tool to focus the senior management team on near-term operational goals and the creation of longer-term increases in shareholder value, it is also a key form of communication within the company and to external stakeholders. Increasingly executive compensation has become a lightning rod for shareholder activists, organized labor, politicians, the media, and the general population. The role of the CHRO is to help the organization bridge these various interests while reinforcing the pay-for-performance philosophy and communicating executive pay in a manner that is understandable and transparent.

Flash Points

As a result of the increased disclosure requirements and the insatiable interest of the media in all matters relating to executive pay, it is critical that the CHRO understand the flash points that may expose his or her company to negative shareholder reaction and may provide fodder for political initiatives aimed at constraining and reforming executive compensation. Among the flash points that draw the attention of activists and critics are these:

- Perquisites, particularly personal use of corporate aircraft
- Supplemental executive retirement programs that provide additional benefits to executives at a time when many companies are abandoning broad-based employee pension programs
- Multiyear bonus guarantees
- Gross-ups on perquisites and golden parachute payments
- Severance, especially severance programs that provide multiyear severance payments and acceleration of long-term incentive awards in the face of termination resulting from what is deemed to be a poor performance by the departing executive

The CHRO should lead a discussion of the trade-offs between the benefits of providing various forms of compensation and the potential that perquisites and other disfavored pay practices may draw criticism. The CHRO is often put in the uncomfortable position of advocating the reduction or elimination of highly valued perquisites in an effort to avoid criticism that diverts attention away from the key message of a performance-based pay model and the alignment of executive pay with the creation of sustainable shareholder value. Given that compensation is a very personal issue to most executives, eliminating certain benefits may be highly unpopular and test the CHRO's courage of his or her convictions. If the CHRO has a high need to be liked and is not comfortable with conflict, the management of executive compensation will be a very unpleasant part of the top HR role.

CREDIBILITY WITH THE COMPENSATION COMMITTEE

An important aspect of the CHRO role is building credibility with the board's compensation committee. Since the CHRO works for the CEO, and in view of the fact that the CHRO is a participant in the executive compensation programs for which he or she is responsible for designing and presenting for committee approval, it is natural that the CHRO may be viewed as less than totally objective on matters concerning executive compensation. In addition, it is an emerging best practice that compensation committees engage an independent executive compensation consultant to advise them on the pay of the senior leadership team and thereby potentially introduce a source of conflict between the recommendations of management and the advice received from the independent consultant.

It is critical that the CHRO establish an open and fact-based approach to dealing with the committee on compensation issues. The CHRO is expected to have his or her own reasoned point of view regarding compensation and have the courage to disagree with management should their views of the appropriate level and form of pay differ. If the CHRO is viewed as merely carrying the water for management regarding pay, he or she will be marginalized in the eyes of the committee. Failing to build credibility with the committee runs the risk that the role of the external consultant will increase and may result in pay programs that are not properly aligned with the company's business strategy and the overall leadership development and succession plans.

A key objective of a new CHRO should be to work closely with the chair of the compensation committee to establish a good working relationship that will allow a free exchange of ideas and thereby contribute to the overall effectiveness of the executive compensation programs and practices. The building blocks for developing a credible and effective working relationship with the committee rest on the accuracy of the information provided by the CHRO, the objectivity demonstrated on key compensation issues, and the willingness to listen to and weigh the input provided by the committee.

To build the appropriate level of credibility requires that the CHRO keep abreast of emerging trends and best practices in the area of executive compensation and be sensitive to the way in which key external audiences will perceive various elements of executive compensation. Alerting the committee to the potential pros and cons of the recommendations presented will allow the committee to make an informed decision and position the CHRO as a trusted advisor. Downplaying potential negatives of the recommendations or failing to present a balanced review of the pros and cons of various proposed actions will greatly reduce the ability of the CHRO to work effectively with the committee.

Coming Up to Speed on Executive Pay

A challenge for the new CHRO is to quickly come up to speed on the company's executive compensation programs and practices and develop a broad understanding of current issues and emerging trends in the design of executive pay. The following ten tips for a developmental game plan should help a new CHRO build a solid base of expertise in executive compensation and help increase the level of comfort in dealing with the compensation committee and other key stakeholders:

1. *Read your company's CD&A.* The CD&A is one of the most comprehensive descriptions of the company's executive compensation programs. It will also give a flavor for how the company and the committee communicate the company's pay programs and practices to shareholders.
2. *Read the CD&A of the companies represented by the committee chair and the members of the compensation committee.* Understanding

the programs and practices of the companies represented by the committee members will provide a perspective on their approaches to pay and their frame of reference for viewing your company's programs.

3. *Read the minutes of prior years' compensation committee meetings.* Your company's compensation programs have evolved over the years, and studying the historical decisions of the committee will help you understand what has been reviewed and approved or rejected. Knowledge of past proposals and the reaction of the committee to changes in the compensation programs will be invaluable as you set the agenda for continued refinement of the company's executive compensation strategy.

4. *Learn from the experience of the internal cross-functional team that manages executive pay.* The development, management, and reporting of executive compensation require a close working relationship with the compensation department, legal, public relations, the corporate secretary, finance, and tax. The CHRO would benefit from hearing firsthand the views of each of these players and soliciting ideas as to how the executive compensation programs and practices can be enhanced.

5. *Conduct an in-depth review of each element of the executive compensation program.* Learn from the compensation team the specific details of each component of executive compensation focusing on the purpose of each element of pay, history of payouts, cost, administration, and the feedback from employees and shareholders on the current pay program.

6. *Meet with the chair of the compensation committee.* Get to know how the chair likes to work with the CHRO, how he or she prefers to see material, if there is specific premeeting information the chair likes to review, the role that he or she wants the CHRO to play in committee meetings, and the overall views of what is working well or not so well in the current pay program.

7. *Meet with the company's external compensation consultant.* Given that compensation committees are increasingly engaging an independent compensation consultant or legal advisor to serve the committee, it would be helpful to meet with the consultant to get his or her perspective on the company's compensation programs and the specific hot buttons or issues on the committee's agenda. Since the consultant is often

prohibited from working for both the committee and management, it is important to first get the chair's permission to meet with the consultant.

8. *Meet with leading executive compensation consultants to broaden your understanding of best practices.* Consulting firms are generally willing to meet with a new CHRO to discuss the firm's view on executive pay, current best practices, and emerging trends. Hearing the views of various executive compensation consultants will provide a broader frame of reference for reviewing the company's approach to executive pay and assessing the recommendations of the committee's consultant. The new CHRO should also sign up for newsletters from the major executive compensation consulting firms to stay abreast of new developments, legislative changes, and emerging best practices.

9. *Join professional organizations where executive compensation is discussed from the perspective of the CHRO.* There is a willingness of fellow CHROs to share their experience and perspective on executive compensation with their peers and to foster a sharing of best practices. Many of the compensation issues facing companies are not unique to a specific industry, and there is an opportunity to learn from others who have dealt with similar issues to those your company is facing. There are several organizations the CHRO should consider joining, and the most beneficial may be the HR Policy Association, the Center on Executive Compensation, and Cornell's Center for Advanced HR Studies.

10. *Consider hiring a personal coach.* The new CHRO may benefit from having a personal coach to accelerate his or her coming up to speed on executive compensation. Having access to an expert who is not trying to sell consulting services and with whom one can feel comfortable asking questions may be beneficial over a period of three to six months as the CHRO becomes comfortable in the executive compensation aspects of the new role.

CONCLUSION

Success in the CHRO role is increasingly dependent on effectively handling the complex area of executive compensation. The multidisciplinary, multistakeholder nature of executive compensation provides the CHRO with the opportunity to help drive the long-term success of the company through the proper design and communication of the executive incentive systems. Alternatively, I have seen examples of executive compensation that created inappropriate incentives that harmed the company's image and failed to support long-term value creation. The importance of the CHRO's ability to develop effective compensation programs has increased and will continue to be one of the most important aspects of the CHRO role.

CHAPTER TWENTY

How to Be a High-Performing CHRO in the Executive Compensation Arena

Ursula O. Fairbairn

Compensation, including executive compensation, is among the most important functional areas for a CHRO to tackle and demonstrate proficiency in. Compensation has always been important but in this environment, it is a nonnegotiable requirement of the job for these reasons:

- Compensation motivates behavior and business results.
- Good compensation practices are an important element of good governance and corporate reputation.
- Bad compensation practices are lightning rods for negative outcomes.

Executive compensation has become a topic of great interest for external critics. Their discussions and actions, driven initially by examples of egregious pay policies and actions and then fueled by economic crisis, are resulting in additional regulation and legislation, extensive news coverage, shareholder voting recommendations, and congressional hearings. This activity is providing a spotlight on company compensation committee decisions and decreasing flexibility for these decisions. CHROs need to stay on top of these issues and anticipate the effects on their company.

It is not unusual for a new CHRO to have relatively little executive compensation experience and little exposure to the board of directors. However, as CHRO, you need to become the leader in these crucial areas.

This chapter does not purport to be a proponent of specific executive compensation techniques. Rather it tries to transcend that content to propose principles and actions that make you, as a CHRO, successful no matter what compensation forms or techniques are used or what executive compensation designs are needed.

I write from the perspective of having been CHRO for two very successful companies for over seventeen years, having served on the corporate boards of nine companies, having served as a compensation committee member at each of them, and having been compensation committee chair at four of them. That means I have had responsibility for about 150 committee meetings as CHRO and been a participant in an additional 350 committee meetings as a board member. I also coach CHROs, especially new ones, as they develop their compensation experience.

That doesn't mean I know it all. It does mean I've seen a lot, made some mistakes, and learned a lot about how to be successful in this balancing act between the CHRO and compensation committee. My counsel here is straightforward. My advice is logical, and at times very simple, but you may never have seen it all together.

The topics of executive compensation and the CHRO's relationship to the board compensation committee are incredibly important because compensation is a strong motivational tool; CEOs, named executive officers (NEOs), and management teams are motivated by rewards. Also, compensation, if not done properly, can be a lightning rod for negative outcomes, both internal and external. Therefore, company and CEO credibility, as well as your own, hinge on good compensation work and good relationships with the board of directors' compensation committee.

If you are not successful in this area of a CHRO's responsibility, you will personally damage the CEO and company, as well as the board dynamic. And you will not be seen as an outstanding CHRO (or you will be seen as an average CHRO at best).

The following sections address nine major questions on this major topic that CHROs frequently asked:

1. What are the key elements of CHRO success in compensation?
2. Who is your boss in this topic?
3. How do you work with the compensation committee's consultant?
4. What does a board member expect from the CHRO?
5. What does a compensation committee chair expect from the CHRO?
6. What are the important compensation committee (and board) functions you need to focus on?
7. How does the CHRO prepare for excellent compensation committee meetings?
8. What are the other to-do's set?
9. What are the no-no's?

WHAT ARE THE KEY ELEMENTS OF CHRO SUCCESS IN COMPENSATION?

You must learn the executive compensation content—both your company program's content at a detailed level and external best practices and issues. You can use others to help you learn, such as your company's executive compensation function, your compensation consultants (both the company's and the board's), compensation and governance newsletters, compensation and governance conferences, and other CHRO colleagues.

If your succession process to becoming CHRO permits, sit in the compensation committee for three meetings with your soon-to-be predecessor to gain perspective and knowledge that will help you get off to a quick start.

It is important to understand you can't learn this once and then assume the learning is over. And you can't delegate this responsibility; everyone needs to know you understand it thoroughly. This topic is constantly evolving because of regulatory changes, changing external critics' viewpoints, changing best practices, and changing company needs.

WHO IS YOUR BOSS IN THIS TOPIC?

Although you report to the CEO, you report equally to the board of directors, a proxy for the shareholders or owners of the company. Your work product and behaviors must reflect that relationship to them.

Although you have a corporate reporting relationship to the CEO, work hard not to become the CEO's tool to accomplish what is not in the shareholders' best interest. This often requires additional thoughtfulness, credibility, and courage. It is something every CHRO must be mindful of at all times.

HOW DO YOU WORK WITH THE COMPENSATION COMMITTEE'S CONSULTANT?

The compensation consultant should be selected and hired by the compensation committee and report to the committee. In today's world, the compensation consultant must be independent; this person should perform no other work for the company of any kind (even if that work is done by a different part of the consultant's company). This is all about the perception of biased alignment with management. A compensation committee consultant selection should be based on experience, company needs, and chemistry with the committee, CEO, and HR management. This focus on independent compensation consultants results in more competition for the best consultants and their potentially being overscheduled, as well as an increasing number of "beauty contests" (parading multiple consultants before the CEO and board) to select a truly independent consultant.

Here are a few of the increasing number of models of how to work with the board's compensation consultant:

- The committee consultant provides his or her data and acts totally independent of management and their consultant.
- The committee consultant uses management's compensation consultant data, supplemented with his or her own data, and provides analyses.
- The committee consultant does all work on the CEO's and NEO's direct reports and comments on rest.

- The committee consultant is independent. Management has its own consultant, but at times the committee can authorize its consultant to work on a project with management (requires preauthorization).

In this relationship, the committee chair should review and approve all committee consultant invoices prior to payment and then pass them on to management for payment.

WHAT DOES A BOARD MEMBER EXPECT FROM THE CHRO?

As a board member, I want to support actions that help the CEO and company achieve its corporate goals on behalf of the shareholder. The CHRO can make that decision support process easier or more difficult. Also, board members don't want to be embarrassed by the compensation actions and decisions; your role as a CHRO is to prevent embarrassment by providing good information and good recommendations. Data provided to the committee need to be accurate, complete, simple, and legally compliant.

A board member wants the CHRO to think ahead about several issues:

- How will we disclose this decision, and what's the disclosure impact?
- What precedents are we setting?
- What behaviors are we motivating?
- What are future pros and cons?

Board and compensation committee members want to receive committee materials with adequate time to prepare (at least five workdays in advance). For a new compensation committee member, a CHRO may want to provide an initial briefing book (thorough but manageable in size) and conduct a one-on-one orientation as well as consider a call before the first committee meeting to ensure he or she is knowledgeable and will be comfortable in the first meeting.

On difficult issues, a CHRO should not only provide excellent material at one meeting, but schedule the issue discussion for several meetings so committee members really understand it and are ready to vote. "Multiple bites at the apple" is the best approach. Examples of such issues are new compensation plans, new compensation goals, and new policies.

WHAT DOES A COMPENSATION COMMITTEE CHAIR EXPECT FROM THE CHRO?

A compensation committee chair expects the same as board members, but even more so, given his or her role: honesty and integrity; absolute accuracy of data and recommendations and all elements in mailings; full information (not selective) including external data and viewpoints; and no surprises—early alerts on issues.

WHAT ARE THE IMPORTANT COMPENSATION COMMITTEE AND BOARD FUNCTIONS YOU NEED TO FOCUS ON?

CHROs have many compensation issues and transactions they bring before the committee. Major ones include the award cycle, new plan designs and approvals, the proxy (especially the compensation committee report), executive data, major new hire compensation package approvals, talent assessments, construction and monitoring of the annual compensation committee calendar, the annual compensation committee assessment, and external compensation and proxy trends.

Some of the current tough compensation topics are lightning rod issues such as stock ownership goals, change in control provisions, severance plans and eligibility, perks, gross-ups, internal pay equity, say-on-pay, and clawback. Each company's compensation committee needs to discuss these topics thoroughly, using CHRO and compensation consultant data, to determine what is best for that company. Other difficult discussions include complex situational issues such as appropriate benchmarking methodology; the role of nonqualified stock options (NQSQs); underwater NQSOs; sustained pay for performance versus pay for failure; where bonuses are paid if goals are not met and, if not, how to retain talent; and what the company does if a company has successive zero bonus payouts. In addition, the continued complexity of events has caused a focus on what risk-taking compensation plans incent and further disclosure requirements on the topic of risk.

HOW DOES THE CHRO PREPARE FOR EXCELLENT COMPENSATION COMMITTEES?

Most high-performing compensation committees build into their processes a pre–compensation committee telephone call among the compensation chair, CHRO, the committee's compensation consultant, and the company's internal executive compensation executive in order to review committee materials before they are mailed to the rest of the committee. Best practice is that the CEO has reviewed committee materials prior to this call so the CHRO knows his or her position before discussions with compensation chair. There is also a prereview by the compensation committee's consultant. Again, the compensation chair should have at least five workdays to review material prior to the call because of other responsibilities and priorities. The content of all agenda items should be reviewed on this call.

For major issues such as the annual cycle and new plans, consider doing the call at the chair's location to ensure greatest clarity and understanding.

Ensure as CHRO that you have personally reviewed, understand, and are accountable for all committee mailings. During this review of mailing materials, look at the final review of the material as a committee member would, not as CHRO.

WHAT ARE THE OTHER TO-DO'S?

Ensure your CEO knows the issues and know how he or she thinks about them. Use the committee compensation consultant to explain issues, but take your own independent position based on what is right. Own all aspects of the committee, including content, recommendations, and data. Have duplicate books in case a committee member forgets his or her copy (it happens regularly). Focus on the details down to administrative items like pads, pencils, and coffee because it all reflects on you and your preparation.

WHAT ARE THE NO-NO'S?

Don't stack the deck, make sure you are balanced and accurate, and don't jeopardize your credibility: it's hard to gain, easy to lose, and very hard to regain. Don't be the CEO's "flak." Compensation committee members will make judgments about you if you don't take balanced, fact-based positions.

Finally, if you are a CHRO and not attending the compensation committee, ask yourself why. If you are not, you should discuss this with the CEO because he or she is not getting full value from you. Make sure you have value to provide.

CONCLUSION

These are the major points to remember as CHRO when you manage the executive compensation function and balance the requirements of your company, the CEO and management, the compensation committee (and board), and shareholders.

- Learn compensation details thoroughly (internal and external)—plans, programs, results, issues.
- Everyone needs to know you know this information cold.
- Gain and maintain credibility with the compensation committee. Credibility is precious: it is hard to gain, easy to lose, and very hard to regain.
- Compensation expertise is a mandatory for a CHRO; it's not a discretionary topic.

Once you know this area, it's a very interesting subject, not something to be afraid of. Jump in with enthusiasm!

PART FIVE

THE CHRO AS LEADER OF THE HR FUNCTION

CHAPTER TWENTY-ONE

MAKING A DIFFERENCE IN THE FIRST 100 DAYS

Ken Carrig

In today's competitive business environment and volatile economic climate, market forces such as technology, acquisitions, downsizing, bankruptcy, and globalization require HR leaders to have the requisite knowledge needed to keep pace with the business and to partner in navigating through uncharted waters. So critical is this need for leadership and business savvy that many companies have started to look to experts outside HR to fill the CHRO role. A recent survey reported that 25 percent of CHROs have no HR background. The need for business and operational knowledge is so paramount that they are willing to trade off HR expertise, as if it's an either-or proposition. Ultimately what they are looking for is both, but this trend highlights the premium placed on business knowledge and the need for HR to help the business meet its strategic objectives and operational goals through human capital strategy. This trend should serve as an admonition to all HR leaders and practitioners to get on board. For HR leadership to survive at all, we need to be entrenched in the business. This is no longer the differentiator it may have been in times past, but rather an imperative for HR to have a strategic impact on the business. Steve Burke, chief operating officer of Comcast Corporation, urges "HR to redefine itself and become more aggressive and progressive—be a proactive agent of change, partnering with operational leaders and 'getting into the nitty-gritty of the business.'"

Given this, what does today's successful CHRO look like? The most successful CHROs are those who are able to make a strategic contribution to the company by leveraging human capital to achieve profitability. They establish credibility and as a result are involved in business decisions that are important to the company's bottom line. These executives

- Are trusted advisors to the CEO and top management team. They need to be credible and have values that align with the organization. They need to cultivate peer relationships with business unit line executives and the top leadership team.
- Possess business knowledge and savvy. They must understand the business strategy and be able to develop HR strategy and practices that will drive business performance.
- Are HR experts with a track record of building world-class HR teams that can advance best HR practices such as performance-connected, state-of-the-art compensation and rewards programs. Their background includes

  - Fifteen to twenty years of experience
  - Time spent at an HR best practice company
  - Top generalist experience
  - Relevant industry experience

- Understand organizational culture and the role it plays in supporting or hindering business strategy. They know how to build workplace practices that shape the environment in a way that reflects the company vision and ensure that culture isn't working against them, but can adapt to changing conditions when needed. Organizational practices, systems, processes, and people all play a role in shaping culture and have an impact on both individual and organizational performance.

In short, the CHRO needs to be smart, have business savvy and multiple company experiences, and be adept at navigating in complex organizations. The CHRO needs to be able to authentically connect with everyone from the front line to the board of directors. The balance of this chapter represents the experience that I have had in serving as CHRO for three organizations. As with most other executive positions, you have one opportunity to establish your credibility in an organization, with the first 100 days being the most critical to your success.

LEVERAGING THE FIRST 100 DAYS: THREE KEYS TO SUCCESS

Although there is no shortage of sound advice on how to navigate through the first 100 days in any new leadership role, a good place to start is to be clear on why you were brought into the new role and what you've been chartered to do. The approach will be different depending on the health and circumstances of the organization. If you've been brought in to quickly turn things around in a company that's teetering on the brink of bankruptcy, you will need to be directive and urgent in your execution of change. Conversely, if you have joined an organization that acknowledges transformation as critical to staying competitive but wants to go about the transformation in a way that preserves its culture, you will need to be more collaborative and iterative in making changes.

Getting to know the business is the starting place. It is critical to understand the business model and be well-versed on business issues. Out of this will flow the beginnings of credibility and trust. By getting to know the business and building credibility and trust, you are creating an environment that will be receptive to your agenda. And remember that change isn't solely driven by positional power. Although leadership is key, as Peter Drucker aptly stated, "Culture eats strategy for breakfast." Understanding the culture, its nuances, and how it can hamper or support change will go a long way to making your first 100 days successful.

This section focuses on three critical essentials that form the underpinnings of future success for the CHRO and serves as a springboard to transform the organization through transforming HR. These three essentials—knowing the business, building credibility and trust, and setting your agenda—are all interdependent (Figure 21.1). Within the first 100 days, each subsequent element builds from the one it follows. But it is also important to note that these essentials transcend the first 100 days. The CHRO must remain connected to the business, continue to establish credibility and trust, and reshape the agenda based on business imperatives.

FIGURE 21.1.   THREE KEYS TO SUCCESS

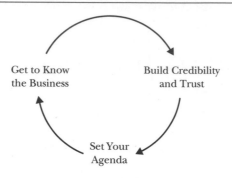

GET TO KNOW THE BUSINESS

You'll need to become conversant on the business to the point where you can contribute to discussions about how to maximize the organization's competitiveness and how to drive profit.

What It Means to Know the Business

This means knowing both your industry and your company. You'll need to know the business model and how money is made. Start by finding answers to the following questions:

- What are your products and services?
- Who are your competitors?
- What is your company's competitive position in the marketplace?
- What is its market brand?
- What are the competitive threats?
- What is the mission of your company?
- What are its short-term goals and long-term strategy?
- Are there regulatory requirements that shape the industry?
- What are the top challenges facing the company today?
- What are the cultural elements that are most important to the company (the sacred cows)?
- What do employees say about the company?

You'll need to gain a firm grasp of the financials and be able to read the balance sheet and cash flow statements, including understanding the company's financial performance, key financial indicators, and benchmarks used. Review the profit-and-loss statements and understand how various departments contribute to the bottom line, including your own HR department. To that end, understanding how HR is viewed in the organization and the role it plays will give you insight on what needs to change or be better leveraged.

You'll also need to get out of your office and into the trenches and take time to listen to employees. Visit as many locations and departments as possible to do your primary research on the company. You'll get a sense of employees' engagement and learn firsthand where there are disconnects, breakdowns, and everyday frustrations that are standing in the way of what the company is trying to achieve. The resulting analysis will help you measure employees' engagement and help you develop your road map for enabling the company to achieve its goals. It will also give you insight into the culture. Knowing which cultural elements should be preserved and what should be shaped differently are important considerations.

A unique hallmark of the Comcast culture is that everyone feels as if they are part of a big family. At ninety years old, Ralph Roberts is still actively engaged in the company he founded in Tupelo, Mississippi, in 1963. His son, Brian, fifty years old, is now chairman and CEO, so it was especially important for me to spend time with both of them to learn the culture and what they valued. The culture at Comcast is something that sets it apart from other organizations and is critical to sustain. Ralph Roberts has this to say about the company:

> When you join Comcast, you become a member of our extended family. While the family has grown dramatically, we work hard to maintain the culture we have created. Our values are based on the highest standards of honesty, fairness, and integrity. Our enthusiasm and passion for our business...keeps the company strong...enabling our employees to grow and develop their careers.

Why Knowing the Business Is So Important

Knowing the business is important for several reasons. First is to be seen as credible. Regardless of your HR background and past achievements, you'll need to demonstrate knowledge of the business. This is requisite to your ability to diagnose and problem-solve. You'll need to know how current HR practices and programs affect organizational performance and how you can shape them and the culture in the future to contribute to the company's success. Being conversant is paramount to your success and ability to move the workforce in the right direction and will help establish your role as peer to the CFO and operations leads. It will be what gets you involved in decision making at the front end of discussions rather than being in the position of reacting to or implementing decisions others have already made.

During my first couple of months at Comcast, I visited each of the twenty-one field regions, meeting with both leadership and frontline employees. During these visits, ten focus groups were conducted so I was able to engage directly with frontline supervisors and listen to their issues and concerns. Accompanying several technicians on truck rolls riding alongside them helped me understand the role of the frontline employees. We went into customer homes, and I observed as they installed or serviced our products and interacted with our customers. I spent four days in different call centers, talking with frontline customer service representatives and listening to them interact with customers. All of this gave me a firsthand understanding of our operation and the critical roles in our service delivery model. It provided knowledge from multiple perspectives, including the customer. This knowledge served to inform our HR strategy going forward, but also went a long way to building relationships across the organization and seeing opportunities to make some quick wins along the way.

BUILD CREDIBILITY AND TRUST

If the three essentials being discussed here are the underpinnings of future success, then this particular essential is the linchpin. Knowing the business is a precursor, because without that, your credibility can go only so far. Credibility is the ability to inspire belief and trust. The following four key components outline how to go about establishing it:

- *Build effective relationships.* This is imperative to building trust. As CHRO, your initial focus should be to build relationships with peers and stakeholders outside HR. By focusing on people and issues outside your function, you send a strong message about HR's role in furthering the business. This means meeting with the board of directors, chief financial officer, key executives, customers, and frontline employees. Spending time with Ralph Roberts, Brian Roberts, and Steve Burke, Comcast's chief operating officer and cable president, was invaluable. At SYSCO, I was part of a corporate executive team that built relations with investment analysts. If your organization has a large frontline workforce, as at Comcast and SYSCO, you'll want to spend a lot of time with these employees and their supervisors so you can gain a firsthand understanding of the issues and challenges they face and to get a sense on their level of engagement.

- *Listen and ask questions.* This cannot be overstated. Listening to both people and the culture are paramount (remember that culture shapes strategy and will help or hinder your efforts). Without listening, you won't be able to understand. Without understanding, you won't be able to diagnose and contribute solutions. You won't, in short, have any credibility.
- *Have candid conversations.* This is also crucial to relationship and trust building. Engaging in candid, frank conversations and creating a safe environment for others to do so will lead to faster understanding and resolution of issues. But it's not merely done for expedience. It allows for more in-depth problem solving and shows a common motivation of putting company issues first and ahead of individual or departmental agendas.
- *Create quick wins.* Identify a few things in the business that you can fix right away, and act on them. Quick wins on noncontroversial issues will help define you as an engaged, results-oriented, responsive leader.

This approach worked well during the initial phases of HR transformation at Comcast. Comcast University was the first area within HR to undergo change as we moved to standardize and centralize the function in a still entrepreneurial and heavily decentralized company. It was also the largest HR population to be affected. Given the magnitude of this change to our business, we knew it was critical to have strong change management around this transition. To build buy-in and trust, we involved critical HR and business leaders throughout the process. We went to each of our key locations and mapped out a detailed plan, discussing the change with regional business and HR leadership, as well as our executive team. Along the way, we provided them with ongoing updates and created opportunities for them to give us their thoughts. This approach helped establish the trust and credibility needed to move forward with the transformation and ultimately freed up managers to deliver more consistent training to equip our employees to deliver a consistently superior customer experience.

The four building blocks will go a long way in establishing your credibility and reputation as a leader. As we learned, mere credentials alone will not grant you trust. Trust is earned, not granted, and comes from following through and delivering on commitments. To do that in a quality way, you'll first need to understand the business and then listen for understanding as part of building effective relationships. Effective listening and understanding will foster candor and allow you to demonstrate your ability to deliver on some quick wins. You've now set the stage and paved the way for setting your agenda as CHRO.

SET YOUR AGENDA

Once you've gotten a grasp on the business, have a good read on the culture, and have established credibility, you'll be well positioned to lay out your strategy. At this point, your peers and direct reports will be expecting to hear your vision and direction and learn what it means to them. To get this right, you'll need to consider a few key things:

- *The right team.* You will have been assessing your team along the way to determine if you have the right people in the right roles. Knowing which roles will be critical to your success will inform your selection, as well as knowing who has the requisite expertise, credibility, and commitment. It is important to remember that your team's credibility is as important as your own. After ninety days at Comcast, we established a senior HR leadership team to help determine the best way to organize and which roles would be broadened or improved. From there, we framed the strategy for the future HR organization. We reorganized leadership, placing top talent in key roles, leveraging both internal and external candidates. For example, we built out the talent function by bundling talent acquisition, talent management, and diversity under an incumbent leader. We brought together performance management and organizational analytics under the leadership of an individual brought in from a consulting firm.

- *A three-perspective portfolio.* Putting your knowledge of the business into the framework of a balanced portfolio of your company's major constituents—employees, customers, and sharcholders—will help you stay focused on the things that matter most. Your comprehension of business issues and workforce challenges will shape how you can leverage HR practices and programs to create value, drive business results, and ultimately affect all three stakeholder groups. During my initial time at Comcast, we recognized that one of the critical links to this three-part equation was the frontline supervisor. In addition to focus group findings, we identified three levers to focus on: redefining the role of the supervisor to allow more time for coaching, redefining the learning process to create real-time learning modules, and redefining the employee-supervisor relationship to drive employee engagement. In short, we learned that if we focused on the role of the frontline supervisor, we could have a positive impact on both customers and shareholders and ultimately improve the bottom line.

- *Strategize around a burning platform.* Now you're positioned to create your strategy, and focus on one or two dominant themes that will have the most impact on business objectives and where there is the greatest urgency. At Comcast, a primary focus is on building employee capability and commitment as a means to improving the customer experience. This critical company objective of focusing on the customer experience has now become HR's main focus. A new human capital scorecard was created to measure the key indicators shown in Figure 21.2 and to establish the new HR brand. In addition, an organizational structure was identified to optimize HR, bring us closer to the customer, and drive efficiency. Three critical roles were identified to ensure the right focus and expertise where needed:

- *HR business leaders:* Focus on strategy connected to the end-to-end employee life cycle.

FIGURE 21.2.   KEY HR INDICATORS

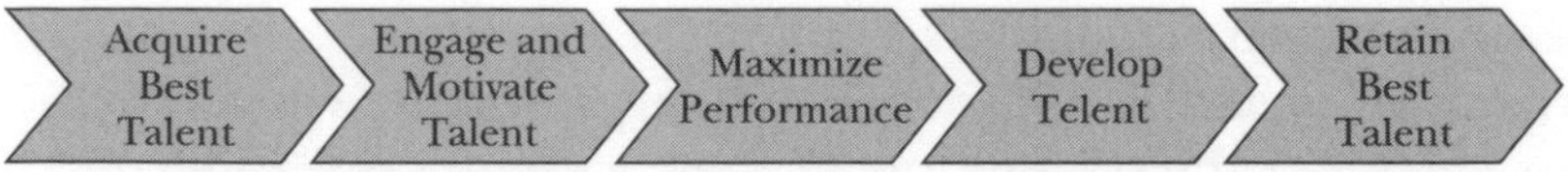

- *Centers of expertise:* Focus on HR operations, the programmatic arm of HR.
- *Shared services:* Focus on the administration and transactional execution of day-to-day activities.

This combination of organizational structure and strategy ensures HR is aligned with the business and is positioned well to help meet organizational objectives.

THE ROAD MAP FOR GETTING THERE: KEY ACTIONS AND TIME LINE

The first 100 days can be broken down into phases that align with the three core essentials. There are also specific actions to be taken within each phase to ensure your success. Table 21.1 depicts the phases and the main objectives of each, along with the approximate timing within the first 100 days. Note that the initial stage begins well before day 1. The Appendix at the end of

TABLE 21.1.   THE ROAD MAP

30 Days Out	Days 1–45	Days 46–90	Days 91–100	The Next
Phase One: Preparation	*Phase Two: Assessment*	*Phase Three: Implementation*	*Phase Four: Evaluate*	*100 Days*
Get to know the business	Listen	Set your agenda	Present findings	Continue to refine your agenda
Get to know the culture	Build credibility and trust	Obtain buy-in	Review plans	Implement transformation initiatives
	Assess HR	Keep building on quick wins	Obtain feedback	

this chapter contains a checklist with detailed actions to be taken. Although it is not a comprehensive list, it highlights key steps for the CHRO in his or her first 100 days.

HELPFUL TIPS AND MISTAKES TO AVOID

Understanding common pitfalls and knowing what mistakes to avoid are also important considerations. A critical misstep in the first few months could prove detrimental to future success. The following list captures some of the common derailers and highlights some key success factors discussed in this chapter:

Tips	Derailers
Actively listen; understand your role.	Trying to fix everything at once
Keep it simple; stick to key imperatives that create value.	Underestimating and not engaging the culture; not learning the business
Take control of the agenda.	Neglecting to enlist key stakeholders: all levels, all functions
Do the unexpected, and build on quick wins.	
Rely on your senior leadership team to help form and drive change.	Making change for change's sake
Be patient and flexible; understand the culture and its willingness and capacity to embrace change.	Citing how you did things at your former company

CLOSING

Once you've completed your first 100 days, your foundation will be built, and you can continue to refine your agenda and build on your momentum. Continue to listen and deliver consistent and strong results. You have only one shot to get this role right. Remember that you'll be under just as much scrutiny if you were promoted into the role from within as opposed to coming in from the outside. The foundation for success must be established within the first 100 days. If done right, you can make a difference by knowing the business, understanding its challenges, and transform the organization by transforming HR.

Carrying this same approach over into the next 100 days will help further your agenda as you continue to make progress, monitor issues, and adjust your plan as needed. In the end, you'll want to focus on building a high-performance HR team that blends well with other business teams. If you create a collaborative culture where the team wins, then everybody wins.

APPENDIX: THE 100-DAY CHECKLIST

PHASE ONE: PREPARATION

Focus on getting to know the business.

- ☐ *Leverage and fine-tune your strengths.* Play into strengths that landed you in the role, such as business acumen, functional expertise, or operational execution.
- ☐ *Mitigate any weaknesses.* Use your strengths to compensate for any lack of cross-functional or operational experience or industry experience.
- ☐ *Ensure fit in both role and the company.* Know the culture, leadership, and history. Determining this at the start will be less painful and more productive than discovering it down the line.
- ☐ *Become a student of your new business or industry.* Get to know the business, financials, and the role your organization wants you to play.

PHASE TWO: ASSESSMENT OF THE ORGANIZATION AND YOUR TEAM

Focus on building credibility and trust.

- ☐ *Identify key stakeholders.* Begin to build relationships with key people across all levels of the organization and in every direction—up, down, across—and with those external to the organization. Include peers, internal allies, and direct and indirect reports.

- ☐ *Manage your setup needs.* Ensure readiness at the office. Conduct an initial assessment of the HR function's capabilities, strengths, and weaknesses.
- ☐ *Work the line.* Begin to engage with the culture. Focus on critical areas such as sales, marketing, and customer operations. Meet teams at their work location.
- ☐ *Conduct key meetings and telephone calls.* Meet with key teams, leaders, peers, and others, and focus these meetings on the state of the business.
- ☐ *Ask, listen, and observe.* Spend most of your time in initial meetings listening. Refrain from sharing details of how things were done at your previous employer.
- ☐ *Set the stage for your action plan.* Begin socializing your point of view with the CEO and key leaders and with direct reports.
- ☐ *Assess the HR function.* Understand how the function is viewed from multiple perspectives. Get to know the history of the function and the CHRO role. Meet with both HR leaders and line leaders.
- ☐ *Establish top-level HR governance.* Establish a working leadership team and core communications vehicles. Set the stage for an action plan with a schedule of meetings and calls for direct reports, core teams, and greater HR community.
- ☐ *Quick wins.* Identify a few things that you can do immediately, and act on them.

PHASE THREE: IMPLEMENTATION

Focus on setting your agenda.

- ☐ *Conduct an HR effectiveness survey or interviews.* Get leadership perspectives on how well HR supports leaders and key initiatives; understand key issues and needs.
- ☐ *Get buy-in for key issues and opportunities.* Ensure strong two-way communications and involvement.
- ☐ *Quick wins.* Continue to identify a few things that you can do immediately, and act on them.
- ☐ *Develop milestones to drive performance.* Define how success will be measured and access/communicate along the way.

At Comcast, this was done by building out three key levers in the HR delivery model:

- *HR business leaders:* Focus on strategy connected to the end-to-end employee life cycle.
- *Centers of expertise:* Focus on HR operations, the programmatic arm of HR.
- *Shared services:* Focus on administration and transactional execution of day-to-day activities.

Next came the design of HR success measures, centered on five key dimensions:

- Acquiring the best talent
- Engaging and motivating talent
- Maximizing performance
- Developing talent
- Retaining the best talent

PHASE FOUR: EVALUATE AND REVISIT YOUR AGENDA AND REFINE AS NEEDED

☐ Formally present your findings and observations to the executive team and HR.
☐ Review plans for how HR will transform to support business goals.
☐ Announce key people changes.
☐ Obtain feedback, and solicit buy-in.

CHAPTER TWENTY-TWO

DELIVERING RESULTS WITH A GLOBAL HR TEAM

Hugh Mitchell

Human resource leaders know that their firm's long-term competitiveness is closely tied to their ability to nurture human capital. However, as businesses become more global, managing the workforce becomes increasingly complex.

Managers must cope with skill pools stretching across ever-increasing numbers of cultures, countries, and languages. HR practices and tools can become fragmented as different parts of a growing organization go their different ways or as the company makes acquisitions. HR managers face intense competition for talent, especially in emerging markets where companies hope to ride the wave of future growth.

Yet many multinational companies continue to manage their human capital in a fragmented fashion. The HR function remains closely tied to individual countries or business units, which limits the ability of HR to play a strategic role on a global scale—a missed opportunity.

At Shell we've spent the past decade making the transition from a decentralized, sometimes unwieldy HR function to one that is linked up globally. We've done that by creating a consistent, long-term people strategy and building the skills and capabilities of our HR professionals. We've put into place a global system of standards and tools that helps us manage our three-thousand-person function in a uniform way across more than one hundred countries. Other companies have been on similar paths, but only a few have done it on the same vast scale. It's been quite a journey, with many daunting challenges, and it isn't over yet. But we are now beginning to reap the benefits of our hard work.

ENERGY CHALLENGES

Today the competitive strength of companies relies more than ever before on their ability to attract and retain talented, motivated knowledge workers—people with advanced degrees or special know-how—and a good deal of choice in where and how they work. That means companies must get the people part right in order to deliver good business results. Indeed, studies by the Corporate Executive Board (2007) and others provide evidence that effective HR functions contribute to the bottom line.

That's particularly true in the oil and gas industry. We face huge technical challenges meeting the world's growing energy needs, while at the same time reducing the environmental impact of energy production and use. As easy-to-access oil and gas grows scarcer, energy companies are pushing the frontiers of what is technically possible. They are pursuing sustainable biofuels and other alternatives, as well as extracting oil and natural gas from hard-to-reach places, such as the icy ocean depths. It takes creative scientists and engineers to unlock new sources of energy and experienced project managers to build the massive infrastructure needed to produce it on a large scale. In fact, today one of the most constrained resources for a company like Shell is human capital.

Moreover, being a big global business brings special challenges. Shell operates in more than one hundred countries and has approximately 100,000 employees worldwide. As a company, we must leverage the advantage of global scale and at the same time operate as an effective and credible local player in countries in all regions of the world.

That requires developing local staff with world-class capabilities and experience. In particular, globally experienced managers with intimate local knowledge are critical to operating successfully in individual countries with unique cultures and well-established, savvy local competitors. In fact, international oil companies often gain access to countries rich in natural resources based on their ability to boost the skills of local staff.

Shell also has a long history of developing people through international experience. We have an active program of sending professionals on foreign assignments to broaden their perspective and give them new challenges. Executives have typically had several foreign postings by the time they reach top jobs at Shell. On average, Shell has about seventy-five hundred expatriates—roughly twice as many as the other major international oil and gas companies.

In this complex operating environment, a globally linked-up HR function can yield significant efficiency benefits. In particular, it can help eliminate duplicate roles and activities across countries. In addition, it offers the chance to automate routine activities across the function—but only if computer systems, standards, and procedures are globally uniform.

BUILDING FUNCTIONAL CAPABILITY

To enhance overall performance in a global company, the HR function must help drive implementation of the firm's overall strategy. That means effectively managing the talent pool at a global scale to produce the desired business results. We found that one of the key elements of success is spelling out a clear, detailed set of skills and competences that HR professionals need to do their jobs effectively.

In the late 1990s, Shell had dozens of HR competence models operating across the globe. There were no standard job profiles of typical roles. Multiple information technology platforms were unable to communicate with each other, and no information was available using a Web-based portal. This mirrored the situation in the broader enterprise at the time. Through most of its history, Shell had been a decentralized business with strong country organizations. In the 1990s, it was shifting to a regional organizational model. The lack of interconnection among HR professionals all over Shell hindered the ability to raise skill levels across the function. For some colleagues outside of Shell's traditional bases in the United Kingdom and the Netherlands, it was a roadblock to building global careers through experience in a variety of countries and regions.

Today there's a single HR competence framework across Shell and its subsidiaries. It covers twenty-six competences, from labor law to organization design, and five proficiency levels. It's Web-based and can be accessed anywhere in the world. Whether an employee is in Laos, Canada, or New Zealand, he or she can tap into the system, look at the competence framework, identify his or her skills gaps, and find training to fill them.

This approach facilitates a broad, uniform network of HR professionals able to share best practices. It's linked to skill-building courses that allow HR professionals to up their game. It also allows a high-quality global response by the function's leaders to common shortcomings. For instance, one of the biggest knowledge gaps we identified among senior HR professionals was a lack of clear understanding of business objectives and priorities. That made it difficult for them to provide strategic counsel to business leaders. To address this gap, we created two one-week training programs in partnership with business schools INSEAD and IMD in Europe and Cornell University in the United States.

The program helps HR professionals understand their roles when they sit at the table with other business leaders to trouble-shoot critical problems or make important strategic decisions. It teaches them how business strategy is created, how to understand customer or stakeholder analysis and marketing plans, and how to link the people agenda to them. With these tools, HR professionals can ensure that business strategies take into account the skills that employees will need in order to make the strategies work and to flag shortcomings to be filled through training or hiring.

The competence framework is also linked to a career trajectory through what we call the experience navigator. It makes clear the types of experiences that are necessary to advance in the HR function at Shell. That can include jobs of increasing responsibility, those with regional or global aspects, or even a foreign posting. At any time, up to 5 percent of all senior HR leaders in the company could be in an expatriate position.

CONSISTENT STRATEGY

Due to Shell's history as a decentralized organization, there were numerous HR visions, missions, and strategies in the past. They were often created by global lines of business seeking to increase employee engagement by expressing business-specific intent and values. In 2005, Shell took a significant step toward a more centralized structure. Its two founding companies, Shell Transport and Trading and Royal Dutch, merged to become Royal Dutch Shell plc, with a single board of directors and a single chief executive. With unification came a sharper articulation of purpose and strategy. We retired the many existing statements of values and strategy and aligned the whole company under a common business strategy of "more upstream, profitable downstream." The strategy was supported by a common set of people values encouraging all employees, no matter their business unit, to behave in ways that benefit the entire enterprise.

Under the new structure, the HR function quickly established four key strategic areas that underpinned the company's overall strategy: talent, leadership and professionalism, improving performance, and systems and processes. These strategic imperatives have remained constant and provide a common framework for developing short- and medium-term plans, appraising the performance of teams and individuals, and creating a common language to connect HR to the business. The power of this framework is less in the strategic choices themselves than in their consistency and uniform application. "Joined-up HR" became the catchphrase to express this new approach.

Managing a Global Function

To effectively run a global function, the HR management team needs a clear line of sight from the top to the bottom of the organization. It's surprising how few companies are structured that way. Often the HR function mirrors the structure of the company, with HR professionals dedicated to individual business units and little or no connection among various subsidiaries.

Until a few years ago, that was also the case at Shell. Shell's HR structure was built around more than fifteen business units, with the CEO of each business unit accountable for HR in his or her organization. Decisions about policy and direction affecting the entire Shell group of companies were discussed and decided by an HR council of fifteen members. It was a decision-making model that produced strong consensus but often lacked speed.

The 2005 merger of Shell Transport and Trading and Royal Dutch provided the opportunity to create a single global HR function. Today all three thousand HR professionals report to the HR director. Top decisions are made by the director and the HR Executive, a ten-person group of the function's top leaders. This produced clear accountability and improved functional management based on a global HR plan and priorities. It facilitated adoption of uniform approaches to many common HR challenges, from change management to employee performance reviews. It also allowed centralized management of important skill pools, rather than function- or business-based management.

For instance, the top two hundred leaders at Shell, regardless of the specific business in which they work, are managed by the eight-member executive committee, the company's top operational decision-making body. Nothing happens to those top leaders or their jobs without the executive committee's review and approval. The committee decides on assignments, career progression, performance appraisal, and all elements of pay and incentives for each member of this global senior cadre. In individual businesses and corporate functions, leadership teams exercise similar tight ownership of their senior ranks.

Core technical skill pools at Shell are also managed on a global basis, since special knowledge and experience are so critical to unlocking the world's hard-to-reach energy resources and addressing environmental concerns. Dedicated HR talent managers work with global business leaders to assess requirements and ensure that the appropriate technical professionals can be deployed where the businesses need them. They also monitor the career progression and development of younger professionals, as well as the recruiting of new talent in the locations where the business is likely to need them in the future. Again, corporate functions such as legal and communications use a similar skill pool management approach.

Having a global HR function has also made it possible to develop more efficient ways of operating. They include automating many routine HR functions and promoting self-service for employees. For issues that still require a human hand, a network of HR service centers in Poland, the Philippines, and Malaysia handles employee queries worldwide.

In 2002 we began implementing the Shell People System, a uniform, SAP-based global information platform designed to gather in one location important details about all Shell employees and to provide the platform for automating many employee transactions. Before Shell People existed, we knew only approximately how many people worked for Shell globally and what jobs they were doing. It was an important step that built a foundation to support many subsequent improvements in the way Shell manages its workforce.

Implementing Shell People meant overcoming a host of challenges. Since information technology was central to what we were trying to do, there was an extra layer of complexity. We rolled it out country by country. Each time, there were heated debates about what elements from the existing country's system to keep and what to standardize—although we learned to manage those issues, and the process became smoother over time. But we underestimated some of the hurdles we had to overcome. For instance, we hadn't realized just how much training would be needed to get everyone up to speed on the new system. In addition, we misjudged how much effort it would take to transfer data from the existing systems to the new one, often manually.

By 2004, employees were able to perform simple functions online, such as requesting vacation time or filling out performance appraisal forms. An upgrade in late 2008 added more functions, such as providing Web forms for HR transactions. The system now enables us to manage important HR functions globally, notably our global reward system covering performance pay and stock awards.

Encouraging Self-Service

The simplest operations, such as accessing information about pay, constitute the majority of HR interactions with employees. We've made steady progress in automating these processes and giving employees the tools to manage them individually. In 2006 about 5 percent of HR interactions with employees were handled using our online self-service system. Our aim is to reach about 40 percent, which we believe represents best practice for a company like ours outside the IT industry.

That automation is reducing the number of operations handled by HR case workers, allowing them to concentrate on complex situations where special expertise is needed. In 2006 about 75 percent of all HR interactions with employees were handled by case workers. Our goal is to get to about 25 percent.

The global people information system also provides the HR leadership team with an important management tool. It provides a detailed overview of the company's entire skill pool and allows managers to monitor and manage progress toward key HR objectives. For example, the leadership team can track movement toward Shell's goal of having more women in senior management roles. The numbers showed steady progress; however, they also revealed a serious gap in the pipeline of possible female candidates for senior jobs in the future. As one HR leader put it, "Outside the top executive offices, the waiting room was empty."

To respond, the HR team implemented policies to help women juggle job and family, the core issue influencing our ability to retain women in midcareer. Measures included more flexible work hours, job sharing, and part-time work. We also stepped up recruiting experienced women to help fill the gap. These steps allowed us to continue our record of year-on-year increases in the number of women in our most senior ranks.

The system also permits us to monitor other aspects of the workforce, such as whether the progression at Shell of those who join us midcareer matches the development of long-time employees, or whether young people identified as having high potential actually progress as quickly in their careers as we anticipated.

Another important efficiency gain came through a more centralized approach to providing individual support to employees when they need it. We gradually shifted some of our HR support staff from our country and business organizations to global shared service centers. In contrast to many other companies that have outsourced such operations, we decided to keep it in-house as a means of maximizing the value we get from our service centers and of ensuring service quality. Each center covers multiple countries and businesses, reducing duplication in the organization. So far we have reduced the number of HR case workers by 25 percent and significantly lowered the cost of providing HR services to employees. We think further gains are possible as we fine-tune the system.

Next Steps

We are just taking the next important step for the HR function at Shell as part of the company's overall restructuring at the end of 2010. In the new structure, there will be a clearer distinction between roles focused on strategic business issues and those focused on delivering HR services on the ground. This should clarify who has prime accountability for what, both within the HR function and for our colleagues in the rest of the company.

People in strategic roles will be closely tied to businesses such as chemicals or oil and gas exploration. They will participate in business leadership teams, helping to set strategic direction. They will also focus on areas that are important for business success, such as talent identification and development, employee learning, and performance management. Meanwhile, service delivery roles, as well as employee and industrial relations, will be tied to country organizations. They will participate in local leadership teams. In addition, they will focus on local HR policy, as well as on local implementation of global HR processes.

The key words in this change are *primary* and *interdependent*. These two parts of the organization, which we call HR in the Business and HR in Countries, will be interdependent, relying on each other to function effectively. However, the new structure also makes it clear who has primary responsibility for each initiative. We think this new organizational approach will take us to the next level of HR performance in terms of helping the broader enterprise achieve important strategic goals.

Creating an efficient, linked-up global HR function in a multinational company is a major undertaking. The ingredients for success are a simple set of global HR priorities linked to the company's business strategy and plans; a global infrastructure of HR standards, tools, systems, definitions, and competences; a single HR organizational model with similar roles in businesses and functions; and a cadre of well-trained, motivated HR professionals.

At Shell we have been working toward that goal for a decade. And we are starting to achieve it.

REFERENCE

Corporate Executive Board. Corporate Leadership Council. (2007). *Building next-generation HR-line partnerships*. Washington, DC: Author.

CHAPTER TWENTY-THREE

EXPERIENCES AS A NEW CHRO IN A NEW INDUSTRY

Mirian M. Graddick-Weir

It's difficult enough to join a new company as a CHRO and rapidly build relationships, learn to navigate the culture, develop an HR agenda aligned with the business goals, and deliver results. The transition to a new industry adds yet another dimension of challenge and complexity. Part of making that transition a success depends heavily on asking the right questions and doing the appropriate amount of due diligence prior to accepting an offer. The first part of this chapter focuses on these important challenges. Once you have joined your new company, you should then follow a set of specific strategies to increase your ability to be effective and successful. The insights I share are based on my own experiences and those of many other colleagues who have made this same journey, albeit some more successfully than others.

To begin, let me share a short summary of my background. I spent almost twenty-five years in the telecommunications industry at AT&T. I was in the CHRO role at AT&T for the last five years of my tenure and had the opportunity to transition from one CEO to another during that time. While the majority of my positions were in human resources (both HR business partner roles and center of excellence roles), I did have the opportunity to support a large line organization in our consumer sales and services group for several years. I also held the role of chief of staff to one of our vice chairs. During my tenure at AT&T, I supported several major organizational restructurings, including spin-off, divestitures, major acquisitions, and significant downsizings.

I joined Merck (a pharmaceutical company) in September 2006 as the CHRO. In early 2009 Merck announced a major merger with Schering-Plough that formally closed in November of that year. Much of the work in HR during the past year, and over the next several years, will be the successful integration of the two companies.

As you think about making a transition to a new company and a new industry, I believe there are several important questions to seriously consider during the due diligence phase of your interviews.

Tips on Due Diligence Before Deciding to Move

Do You Have a Passion for the Mission of the Company?

It's often energizing being on a steep learning curve and developing a good understanding of the business. Channeling that energy into effective strategies and actions is critical for success in the new role. An important question to answer is whether you fundamentally get charged up about the industry you are considering or whether you simply like the people and the job. In the first case, you are much more likely to have a natural curiosity and excitement about truly learning the business. In my case, joining a company whose primary mission is to help patients around the world with their medical needs was very inspiring. I couldn't wait to understand the drug development and manufacturing processes, how sales reps both anticipate and meet customer needs, and learn about growth opportunities in various emerging markets.

Is the Culture Compatible with Your Own Style and Values?

This is an area where I would not cut corners when it comes to doing in-depth due diligence. Most people being considered for these roles have proven they are bright and have the right functional and leadership capabilities required for success. Yet they sometimes fail or aren't happy because of incompatibility with the culture. Companies often hire from the outside because they desire strong change agents to drive transformational change. Yet CHROs often find it almost impossible to get things done because of the culture. It is critical to talk with as many people as possible at all levels about the culture and to ask about specific cultural attributes such as these:

- Bias for action versus bureaucratic and slow to make decisions
- Top-down command-and-control versus consensus or empowerment oriented
- Relationship and loyalty based versus performance based
- Internally versus externally focused
- Open and candid versus passive-aggressive

A useful exercise is to list the cultural attributes that are most important to you and try to assess where people you talk to would place the company along a continuum. Part of my ability to successfully move from a company like AT&T to a company like Merck is that the cultures are much more compatible than they are different. This has allowed me to more easily leverage lessons I have learned, especially in the face of various challenges. The key is to identify an environment that is most compatible with your personal leadership style and values and where you will have the greatest probability of success. Otherwise you will end up enormously frustrated, unhappy, or, worse, unsuccessful.

It's also important to understand the company's track record of success in hiring executives from the outside. A revolving door of executives might suggest, from a culture perspective, that the organization tends to reject people who come in with innovative ideas and new ways of doing things. My experience has been that if senior line leaders have not historically done a good job sponsoring major change initiatives within their respective organizations (and they are allowed to opt out without a good business rationale), this should be regarded as a major warning sign. It will likely be very difficult to implement change in that type of environment.

DO YOU UNDERSTAND THE CHALLENGES FACING THE COMPANY AND THE INDUSTRY?

Part of your due diligence should involve understanding the short- and long-term challenges facing the industry. It's important to have a realistic view of today's business challenges and the opportunities over the horizon. This will give you an idea of the kinds of issues you will face from an HR perspective and allow you to make an assessment as to whether you can leverage your experience and add immediate value. Merger and acquisition experience, for example, will be very useful if the company is planning acquisitions as part of its strategy or if the industry is ripe for additional consolidation.

It's equally important to ask your potential colleagues during the interview process what they perceive to be the internal enablers and barriers to successfully executing a strategy and the role of HR in achieving the business priorities. If you get very different responses from people, this can be another warning sign that the senior team may not be aligned around the HR agenda. It simply won't be sufficient to have the CEO's support for change if the major division or business unit heads don't share the same goals.

MY TRANSITION EXPERIENCE

My transition to Merck was challenging yet smoother than I had expected. This was in large part due to the similarities in cultures and business challenges between Merck and AT&T. Both companies have long histories and were the undisputed leader of their respective industries in performance and reputation. However, both companies had begun to face significant competitive threats and other business challenges that required a significant transformation of their business models and culture to ensure continued success.

Examples of positive similarities between the two cultures include very strong values and ethics that permeated the environment and extremely smart people who are dedicated and committed to the mission of the company. Shared cultural challenges include being more heavily relationship oriented (as opposed to results oriented), more focused on historical practices rather than external best practices, and a need to become more focused on external customers. The cultures clearly had significant strengths, yet they also posed challenges for any senior leader coming in from the outside with a transformational change agenda.

The advantage I found of working in one company for a long time is that I had a support base and, more important, knew where the difficulties were. The obvious disadvantage is that I didn't always recognize the need for change. As a newcomer, quickly acquiring relationships and learning where the potholes and pitfalls exist is crucial for success. This is why it's so important to build new relationships quickly and leverage those relationships as you execute your change agenda.

TIPS FOR SUCCESS IN A NEW JOB

Seven strategies have helped me and other CHROs transition successfully into a new company or industry. This list, not an exhaustive one, focuses on the strategies that have had the greatest impact during my career.

GET OUT AND LEARN THE BUSINESS

As a newcomer to the industry, one of the quickest ways to begin adding value is to get out and learn all aspects of the business. Visit the operations, travel with sales reps, and get to know what customers expect and value. Conduct focus groups with employees in different divisions and regions so you can identify the hot spots with respect to the HR capability gaps or gaps in alignment between the business strategy and various HR policies and practices. As an example, an initial observation in my new role at Merck was that the CEO and the senior team wanted to foster greater collaboration across divisions given the strong business interdependencies. There was also a heavy emphasis on the importance of key leader behaviors such as collaboration, championing change, and becoming more customer focused. Yet the annual incentive plan placed more of an emphasis on rewarding individual unit competitiveness rather than encouraging and rewarding divisions to work more collaboratively. To better align the incentive system with the business strategy, we modified the incentive plan so that for the top two hundred leaders, 70 percent of their annual incentive plan was tied to company performance. This reinforced the need for leaders to make decisions that were in the best interest of the company. We also incorporated the leadership behaviors that senior management wanted to be displayed into the incentive plan in a more visible manner.

BUILD STRONG RELATIONSHIPS WITH COLLEAGUES

Presumably you have bonded with the CEO since he or she made the ultimate decision to hire you. Equally important is to build trust and credibility with your colleagues. This won't happen overnight; however, it should be a high priority when deciding how to prioritize your time initially. You will need them on your side to sponsor major change initiatives and potentially convince them that you need to upgrade the talent in HR. This could even mean upgrading their own HR business partner. I have seen many CHROs derail because they focused primarily on supporting the CEO and did not take sufficient time to build support among their peers. Having established a trusted relationship with your colleagues also positions you to be a much more effective advisor and coach to the CEO. This means spending time with your line colleagues and their respective leadership teams to build partnerships and deepen your knowledge of the business.

BUILD A STRONG AND COHESIVE HR TEAM

Quickly assessing the talent in HR should also be a high priority. It's important to understand whether you have the depth of expertise in your centers of excellence and that the HR business partners have a strong seat at the table and are truly adding value to the business. Equally important is to ensure you have a team that works effectively together and collaborates in a way that strengthens your ability to execute with excellence.

All too often the HR business partners are deeply aligned with their line leader, which is essential, but to the point where they don't work well with other parts of HR. In some cases, this contributes to undermining the entire HR function by HR colleagues who are critical of their peers and the function rather than demonstrating leadership by constructively solving problems. Worse yet, they can often become impediments to driving change, especially if their line leaders are resisting change as well. If these individuals continue to demonstrate a refusal to change once you have made your expectations clear, you should replace them. It's impossible to be a truly world-class function if you are relying on individuals who won't collaborate and can't effectively balance their division priorities with corporate priorities.

Probably one of my most significant challenges as a leader of a global support function is the need to constantly balance meeting client needs and business priorities and making time to upgrade HR talent and transform the function. Tipping the scale too dramatically in one direction or the other can have a deleterious impact on the credibility of the function.

Leverage Quick Wins

While many of us are brought in to lead major transformational change to support the business priorities, it's important to be prudent about the scope and magnitude of what you decide to take on as your first priority. Remember that you have a huge task of building trust and credibility. Taking on a large-scale project where the degree of difficulty to implement is extremely high is probably not a good idea. I would be cautious about taking on large outsourcing projects, major system conversions, or initiatives that involve payroll given the high risk associated with not implementing these projects well. Furthermore, projects like these require enormous sponsorship within the line organizations, and that takes time to establish. Instead, find quick wins where you can build credibility for the function and solve urgent business priorities. Line leaders will be much more supportive when you begin to tackle the more difficult, challenging, and controversial projects down the road. Modifying the incentive system was an example of a quick win.

Develop Trusted Critics for Feedback

Joining a new company can be like starting a new high school in your senior year. Relationships are already well established, and there are lots of unwritten rules on how you actually get things done. It becomes even more challenging if you have joined a passive-aggressive culture or one where people are too polite to disagree or challenge you publicly.

It's always good to seek out people who are well networked and key influencers. Ask them for feedback frequently as you begin to learn the organization and take action. Make sure these people are willing to tell you the brutal truth, not just the positive feedback we all enjoy hearing. Having your pulse on the organization and how people are responding to your personal leadership style is extremely important. These individuals can also help you navigate the culture and can advise you on strategies to build sponsorship for your HR agenda.

Several individuals at Merck were very gracious about telling me where I lacked sponsorship for a change initiative (particularly since people there were sometimes overly polite) or ways I might be more effective at influencing others (particularly with the region heads outside the United States).

EFFECTIVELY BALANCE COMPETING PRIORITIES

One of the most challenging aspects of the CHRO role is the ability to balance competing priorities and multiple stakeholders. In addition to building strong relationships and credibility with our colleagues, you also have to earn the trust and respect of the board of directors. A key aspect of our role is to support the compensation and benefits committee, and this requires time and attention to detail, with little margin for error.

Most CHROs are also challenged with having to transform their organizations and upgrade the talent. This requires assessing the state of your HR function and its people and setting an HR agenda aligned with the business. Finally, getting out and learning the broader leadership team in the global organization to assess the talent capabilities and gaps is also important. Calendar management is critical to ensure that you allocate your time in a way that allows you to balance all aspects of the role yet create opportunities to engage with others at many levels so that you stay in touch with the pulse of the organization. The plan described in the next section helped me focus and allocate my time effectively during my first ninety days at Merck.

Build a First Ninety-Day Plan

Several people suggested that I build a first ninety-day plan on stepping into my new role. Although I initially resisted the idea, I finally put one together partly because I thought it would be a useful way to ensure that the CEO and I were on the same page regarding initial expectations, priorities, and how I should spend my time.

Given the challenge of managing competing stakeholders, outlining a ninety-day plan helps you manage your time appropriately and remain focused. It's too easy to get pulled into less important issues because almost every group has an HR issue they want fixed and they all want time with the new CHRO. Also, there is often a "crisis" a day in HR so it is easy to get distracted.

My ninety-day plan was simple and focused on these elements: (1) accelerating knowledge of the industry and the business, (2) building relationships and partnerships with my peers and a few other key line leaders, (3) doing a preliminary baseline assessment of the state of the HR function and the talent, and (4) getting to know the compensation and benefits committee chair and understanding his expectations. Everyone may have a slightly different list; however, putting it on paper and using it to clarify expectations between you and the CEO can be enormously helpful.

Conclusion

There is nothing more challenging—and rewarding—than joining a new company and a new industry as a CHRO. It's a high-risk, high-reward endeavor. Employees at all levels in the organization will have very high expectations since they hired an outsider who also has to learn the industry. But the rewards in terms of professional growth, job satisfaction, and impact are great. I hope this chapter has provided some useful information for those who decide to make this exciting career transition.

CHAPTER TWENTY-FOUR

DESIGNING AN INTEGRATED HR FUNCTION

What the CHRO Needs to Know

*Amy Kates, John W. Boudreau,
Jay Galbraith*

One of the most important decisions a CHRO makes is how to design the HR function. The design of the organization—structure, power, roles, decision processes, reward systems, and staffing profiles—sets the framework for what work gets done, how well the work is executed, and the satisfaction for both clients and HR staff of working in the function.

As strategies change, organization designs change (Galbraith, 1995). Leaders are always adjusting the shape of their organizations in response to their specific context. However, two broad trends, across industries, are influencing how HR leaders are configuring their functions. The first trend is an emphasis on gaining synergies from the business portfolio, which requires a more globally integrated HR function. The second is a rising expectation that the function can provide higher-order decision support, along with flawless execution of processes and transactions. HR leaders are finding that the widely used business partner/center of excellence structure is inadequate to respond to these trends. After discussing these factors, we provide some observations regarding how CHROs are responding in the design of their HR functions.

FACTORS FORCING CHANGES IN THE DESIGN OF THE HR FUNCTION

CHANGING BUSINESS MODELS

Today's corporate business models are modern implementations of some old concepts such as matrix and synergy. Previously companies preferred to implement autonomous profit center models. If the company sold business-to-business, it used autonomous business units. If it sold business-to-consumer, it used regions and countries as profit centers. These models continue to exist, but increasingly companies are returning to matrix designs. Still other companies, particularly in the West, are learning to master synergies in order to offer solutions and leverage intellectual property.

Many companies are rediscovering the performance benefits of the matrix organization. They have replaced the myth that "matrix doesn't work" with the question, "How do I make a matrix work?" The recessions of 2001 and 2009 have shown the defects of the autonomous profit-and-loss (P+L) model. Whether business units or countries, the autonomous P+L model leads to duplication and silos, which lock up talent. The benefits of strong functions are that they reduce duplication and share talent across P+Ls. Companies that have performed well in the recessions are those that have mastered the function-profit center matrix. Their profit centers have delivered new products and services, while their functions have reduced costs and shared talent. The benefit of the matrix is good business performance and functional excellence.

Once a company has mastered the two-dimensional matrix of functions and P+Ls, it encounters a higher performance bar. Nestlé and Philips are now implementing three-dimensional matrix designs consisting of countries, business units, and functions. The graduates of the 3D matrix can then try organizations like Procter & Gamble's Four Pillar structure by adding a customer dimension. IBM has gone even further in creating multidimensional designs, to include customer segments, channels, and solutions, along with functions, geographies, and product sets. Indeed these companies are seeing advantages by getting good performance on all dimensions. However, the good performance comes at a price: increased organizational complexity. Most managers have not previously experienced this level of complexity. In response, many HR departments are increasing their competence levels in organization design and development. They are helping management design and manage in this new multidimensional matrix environment.

The other trend is to introduce synergies across businesses. Western companies are experiencing competitive threats from companies in emerging markets. These emerging market companies are introducing lower-cost products for their own countries that are being embraced by developed countries as well. So as products commoditize, Western companies are combining products into customized solutions and leveraging intellectual property across business units. IBM is the best example of a solutions provider, while Disney provides the model for leverage. If the portfolios of business units for these two companies were examined, we would call them conglomerates. Yet both are able to combine disparate businesses to create value for customers and shareholders.

The IBM portfolio consists of semiconductor components, hardware products, software products, high-technology services, business consulting, information technology solutions, and financial services. Clearly IBM's portfolio qualifies it as a conglomerate. Yet all of these products and services are combined into solutions under the Smart Planet initiative. The products and services are combined into smart traffic systems for the city of London, smart electric grids for the island of Malta, and smart food chains from "farm to fork" for Norway. Just as the products and services must work together in a smart solution, so must IBM's business units work together to create the solutions. How do they do it? First, they have units for customer segments. These units have the responsibility to combine products and services and customize them for their customer segment or industry. Second, IBM has designed a system of human capital that creates a collaborative environment. People are both selected and self-select; they are promoted, rewarded, and developed in programs that foster synergies across businesses (Boudreau, 2010). The HR department is a key player in creating the solutions capability.

Disney is the champion of the intellectual property leverage model. Starting with Disney characters such as Mickey Mouse, Snow White, and Pinocchio, the company has learned to use all of its businesses to offer products based on these characters. The most recent success story using this model is Hannah Montana. Starting as a half-hour program on the Disney Channel, Hannah Montana's popularity spread to novelettes and magazines through Disney Publishing and albums and songs through Disney Music and iTunes. Disney Consumer Products has licensed Hannah Montana to all types of apparel and teen product manufacturers. In the 2007 Christmas season, Hannah Montana was the largest-selling product line at Macy's. These successes have been followed by a full-length film for theaters and DVDs, a year-long concert tour, and an ice show. Disney Stores will feature Hannah Montana promotions designed to sell books, albums, merchandise, DVDs, concert tickets, and other Hannah Montana memorabilia. Disney is currently planning an interactive theme park attraction at Disney World. Indeed a business unit at Disney would be under pressure to show why it is not profiting from the popularity of Hannah Montana.

How does Disney successfully execute cross-business unit synergies when synergy has proved to be so elusive elsewhere? The answer is that the company has designed an organization specifically to create synergy across all of its businesses. Originally there was a synergy group run by a vice president who reported directly to the CEO. After a while, it was disbanded, and responsibility was moved to the business group level in a marketing and synergy department. Each business unit is expected to produce business ideas that are profitable and can be leveraged by other Disney businesses. These ideas are gathered, funded, and reviewed in the annual planning process. The plans are presented to the top one hundred executives in a gathering of the "Cast of 100." Everyone is supposed to know what is going on in all of the businesses. The HR practices are to build and reinforce the synergy capability. People are selected and removed based on their ability to generate and implement ideas that can be leveraged. The compensation system rewards these people as well. The high potentials go through a two-week Synergy Boot Camp. So the strategy, structure, processes, and HR human capital system are all aligned around creating value through synergy.

Fashion houses like Armani and Ralph Lauren also use the leverage model. Apparel maker VF Corporation and shoe retailer Collective Brands are perfecting their versions of the model. Intel and Qualcomm both strategically leverage their microprocessor architectures to deliver superior organizational and economic performance. Whether it is characters, brands, design capabilities, or technologies, all of these companies are learning to leverage their intellectual property across their business units.

Today's business models require an HR function able to build the collaboration that supports the matrix and synergy-driven organizations through the capabilities of organization design and human capital creation.

REQUIREMENTS FOR HIGHER-ORDER DECISION SUPPORT

The outward manifestations of HR's response to these business model changes are structural designs that affect where work is done and how the roles of HR leaders are combined. However, these structural design elements need to place decisions and decision support where they are most vital. The design needs to ensure high-quality talent and human capital decisions wherever they are made (Boudreau & Ramstad, 2007).

Vital talent decisions are usually not made solely by HR professionals. Decisions about talent deployment, talent implications of mergers and acquisitions, talent reductions and additions, and so on are often made by line leaders outside the HR function. One reason for frustration with current HR designs is that the best decision framework, or the most informed and qualified HR expert, may not be in place when vital decisions are made. While HR processes, HR costs, and the roles of HR leaders get a great deal of attention in HR design, creating the right decision support for line managers is often at the heart of the problems they are solving.

For example, a core premise of an effective decision science in areas such as finance, marketing, and operations is to provide frameworks that are consistent whether decisions are made at corporate, unit, or functional levels. Examples include net present value, customer segmentation, and logistical optimization. Business units do not reinvent net present value or logistics optimization to suit their particular preferences.

An important future goal of HR organization designs is to maximize the quality of decisions, not just HR practices or costs. HR leaders often wrestle with competing frameworks for common problems such as performance evaluation, optimized talent acquisition systems, measuring and evaluating incentive compensation systems, and identifying and deploying talent across the organization. Traditional HR designs, relying solely on strictly delineated roles such as business partner, centers of excellence, and operations leaders, often produce divergent frameworks across business units or functions that may have little resemblance to each other.

IBM, for example, realized in 2003 that its system for identifying and deploying global talent needed a common decision framework, which in this case meant a better common language for discussing talent. Decisions about talent deployments often happened only when IBM's HR or business leaders happened to know each other and could translate the capabilities resident in one unit against the needs of another unit. The solution required a common language for employee capabilities, consisting of about three hundred role descriptions. The supporting HR design elements included building a small team of language governance leaders, who double-hatted in high-level HR functional roles as well as support for key business units and functions (Boudreau, 2010).

HR functional design is often driven by questions of cost and process, but the core dilemmas usually are more fundamental questions about the talent decision frameworks that will be used and the type and quality of the decision support the design will create. In this example from IBM, HR was not creating a new program or service; it was creating a decision framework all managers and HR professionals could use.

How CHROs Are Responding

The business partner/center of excellence model, which became popular in the 1990s, features three components. Business partners (BPs) are aligned to the major operating units of the firm in a hierarchy of generalist support from midlevel managers to senior leaders. BPs manage the HR relationship, serve as the main point of contact for their clients, and diagnose and provide solutions across a broad spectrum of client needs. The centers of excellence (CoEs) are typically small groups that develop enterprise policies and programs and provide support to the BPs in the form of tools, advice, and highly specialized expertise. The third element of the model is a shared service, either in-house or outsourced, to process transactions and address individual employee questions and needs. Enterprise resource planning systems provide a platform for manager and employee self-service and data management in the function.

Many HR leaders have fully implemented this model with sound processes, clarity around roles and responsibilities, and talented staff. Nevertheless, many are frustrated by a number of flaws inherent in this model:

- Resources are not flexible. They are locked up in the business units or geographies. Everyone is busy, but HR leadership is not clear if everyone is doing the highest-impact work. Rather than facilitating the matrix or synergy business model, HR exacerbates the fragmentation of the business by aligning to the business units.
- HR planning is often a roll-up of activities and projects from the business units or geographies rather than a top-down set of priorities. As a result, all work is deemed equally important. Lower-level HR staff are overwhelmed and always feel there is a shortage of resources. Often the clients are happy with their business partner because their needs are on the HR agenda, but they wonder what the rest of the HR budget is being spent on.
- Resources are allocated by number of employees or current revenue, not differentiated by business unit need. Start-ups, innovations, and emerging markets are underattended.
- There is frustration between the business partners and the CoEs. It is unclear who works for whom, and there can be an "us" and "them" friction between the center and the field. Frustrated by slow response time from the center, the BPs recreate talent models and programs, diverging in the language

and frameworks used across business units. Information is hoarded, and the opportunity to have an impact on high-value decisions is lost.

As businesses try to get more out of their portfolios, the CHRO is under pressure to create a function that can help to integrate the business units. As a result, the HR function needs to be ahead of the business in this regard. Along with IT, finance, marketing, supply chain, and other functions, HR needs to foster commonality where variability in work, process, or policy only adds cost and creates conflict. The BP/CoE model presumes that HR mirrors the business in order to create alignment. However, this tends to create a support function that mirrors the fragmentation of the business rather than serve as the glue that helps connect the operating units closer together.

CHROs are responding by converting the traditional hierarchies of generalists into deployment teams, managing the intake process and limiting who contracts for work, and using rotations and dual hat positions to link the HR leadership team more tightly together. Each is discussed below.

Deployment Teams Rather Than Generalists

In the typical BP/CoE model, generalists are renamed business partners and told to focus on strategic high-value work. They are promised that all transactional and low-value work will migrate to shared services or self-service. Unfortunately, no matter how robust the shared service center is, there remains an entire body of work that doesn't go away—projects, process execution, high value transactions—and that neither the newly rebranded business partners nor the experts in the CoEs see any longer as falling within their role.

This work, the ownership of which is the source of much friction in HR organizations today, needs a new role for execution. We see this new role variously called operational executors, deployment teams, delivery teams, field services, or solutions centers (Kates, 2009). Creating this capability without adding head count requires a change in the BP structure.

CHROs are creating a thin layer of strategic business partners aligned to top business executives. Rather than a hierarchy of generalists underneath these business partners, however, the new models have teams of specialists—talent, organization development, compensation, learning, employee relations—who can be deployed against business needs as they arise and across business unit boundaries.

These deployment teams are not a pool. They most often spend the majority of their time working together supporting the same operating unit. This allows the staff on the teams to maintain knowledge and relationships with the business and HR colleagues. The big idea, however, is that while they may work with and be managed by an HR business partner, they do not belong solely to one operating unit. Rather, conceptually they are the "property" of the HR function and can be redeployed as the need arises. For example, they can be marshaled to assist with an acquisition, rollout of a new program, or the opening of a new facility.

In addition to flexibility, the deployment teams allow individuals and the function to build specialist depth. For example, a team member may support the HR work of the R&D function for 80 percent of her time. However, she also wears a second hat as a member of the extended talent development CoE. She would participate in the talent team's key meetings, training, and learning opportunities and become highly competent using the company's talent tools and methodology. Her talent role will be activated when she serves as the point person for the annual talent review process in R&D. She may also support the talent review process for another function. Furthermore, when there is an acquisition during the year in one of the business units, she assists on a project basis with completing talent assessments quickly.

These specialist roles rotate so that the team members experience a series of deep learning and application working across a variety of business situations and with expert colleagues from the CoEs. Rather than a model that perpetuates a cadre of low-skill generalists that serve midlevel managers and execute perhaps less than critical work, this more focused career path provides variety, depth, and exposure to senior members of the HR team while ensuring that the most important priorities of the function are met.

INTAKE PROCESS

In order to ensure that the deployment team members are focused on the right work, the intake process must be redefined so that only the true business partners and the CoE leaders can contract with the line managers for work. Therefore, generalists can no longer agree to facilitate meetings or conduct 360-degree assessments or source training solutions for employee populations that may not fit into the strategic human capital plan.

Of course, deployment team members continue to interact with employees and answer questions, and they may even serve a point person for midlevel managers. The difference in this model is that the deployment team members cannot commit the resources of the HR organization. The benefit of limiting the intake process to a higher level is that it focuses resources on the highest priorities and forces the HR leadership team to work together to set, monitor, and adjust the plan and manage the resources of the organization holistically.

INTEGRATION OF THE HR LEADERSHIP TEAM

A highly integrated HR function, just like any business unit, requires a high-performing leadership team. The team must see its role not as a collection of functional experts or representatives of a business unit but as an enterprise leadership team. Metrics and rewards have to be set to ensure interdependence. The definition of success for one must be dependent on success for all. In addition to rewards, the team needs a vigorous planning and priority-setting process. They need to know the skills resident in the HR organization in order to make smart decisions about allocating resources. CHROs are finding that a powerful way to integrate the HR team is through rotations between BP and CoE roles. This helps to break down we-versus-they perspectives and build a more general management perspective. For small HR teams or those where forcing an enterprise view is critical, some CHROs have found that dual-hat roles are effective. Members of the HR leadership team each serve as a BP for a business unit or function as well as leading a CoE team. Broadening positions in this way also helps to elevate the performance of the next level of HR staff. Leaders with such a wide span of control are unlikely to micromanage.

CONCLUSION

Organization design has become an important part of the HR service offering to the business. The CHRO has an opportunity, with the design of the HR function, to demonstrate the power of alignment among strategy, structure, process, rewards, and talent to support business models that require highly integrated decision making across organizational boundaries.

REFERENCES

Boudreau, J. W. (2010). *IBM's global workforce initiative.* Washington, DC: Society for Human Resource Management.

Boudreau, J., & Ramstad, P. M. (2007). *Beyond HR: The new science of human capital.* Boston: Harvard Business School Press.

Galbraith, J. (1995). *Designing organizations: An executive briefing on strategy, structure, and process.* San Francisco: Jossey-Bass.

Kates, A. (2009). (Re)Designing the HR organization. *People and Strategy Journal, 29*(2), 22–30.

CHAPTER TWENTY-FIVE

HR FOR IMPACT

Sandy Ogg

HR's roots are as an administrative function previously known as "personnel." The function has been going through a radical transformation in many companies as HR leaders have worked to create modern HR functions to support the growing need for HR services. This has led to HR transformation approaches that have included outsourcing, centers of expertise, and business partners. We are now entering the next phase as HR moves from partnering in support of the business to leading on business imperatives such as talent, organization readiness, and leadership development. We must now deliver HR for impact. In this chapter I describe our HR story at Unilever over the past six years, focusing on areas where HR played the most significant role.

UNILEVER, 2005–2008: HR TO SUPPORT RESTRUCTURING

In September 2004, Unilever issued its first profit warning in the company's proud seventy-five-year history. It was time for change. In early 2005, we embarked on arguably the most ambitious change agenda we had ever attempted.

NEW ORGANIZATION

A new organization was the first step in this process. We needed to find a way to move from a multilocal multinational to a truly global organization. The success model of the past was more than eighty independent, decentralized "full-kit" operating companies around the world that had served the company well but were now out of steam. As global competitors brought their scale to bear and local competitors could move faster and cheaper, we found ourselves stuck in the middle. In addition, our global matrix had become unworkably complex: two hundred operating units and more than twenty categories in the matrix with too much governance. A decision was made to dramatically simplify the matrix and work toward a matrix that was twenty geographical clusters (we call them multicountry organizations) and ten global categories, a much more manageable proposition. Figure 25.1 shows the chart that was used to explain to employees and investors how the new Unilever organization would be transformed and the rationales behind these changes. "One Unilever" was the name given to the transformation process from a decentralized to a more centralized structure.

NEW OPERATING FRAMEWORK

Holding this global matrix together was the desire to continue to have the benefits of the intimacy of the local businesses and

FIGURE 25.1. TOWARD A SIMPLER ORGANIZATION, 2005

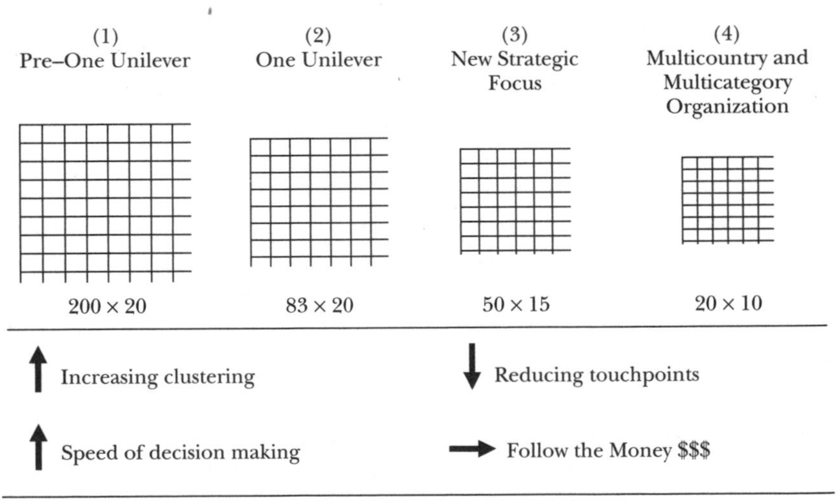

(1)	(2)	(3)	(4)
Pre–One Unilever	One Unilever	New Strategic Focus	Multicountry and Multicategory Organization
200×20	83×20	50×15	20×10

↑ Increasing clustering   ↓ Reducing touchpoints

↑ Speed of decision making   → Follow the Money $$$

add to it the benefits of our global scale (decentralized but interdependent). In order to make this happen we needed to disaggregate the "full kit" local organizations and create an interdependent operating framework. The metaphor we used was to move from "running the 400 meters" to "running the 4 × 100 relay." We decided to leave brand building, marketing, and sales and distribution in the full authority of the local general manager; pull the supply chain to regional control; and take brand development, R&D, HR, and finance global. We then introduced a clear operating framework clarifying what decisions were to be made and by whom. This was a major undertaking because of our decentralized and independent culture. This meant we needed to change behaviors in order to make this undertaking work.

New Behaviors

We have all confronted organization changes; some work and some do not. It was helpful that we clarified the new operating framework, but if we did not support it with new behaviors, our chances of success were low. So we decided to be quite specific about the changes in leadership behavior that would be necessary to make the changes happen:

- From local to global mind-set
- From excuses to real accountability
- From an internal to external orientation
- From debate to action
- From independent to team alignment
- Focus on building superior talent

We called this our new Standards of Leadership (Figure 25.2), and we embedded this into our performance management process and tools and used it as a major input to our selection process for the leaders who would have the key jobs in the new organization.

New Leaders

It was clear that simplifying the organization would significantly reduce the number of senior management positions. In fact, we

FIGURE 25.2. THE SIX STANDARDS OF LEADERSHIP

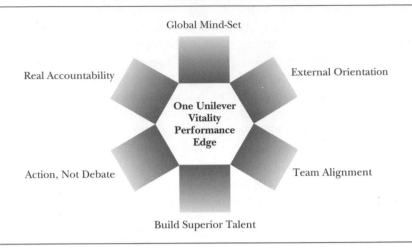

ended up reducing our top one thousand jobs by more than 50 percent. I personally handled most of the seventy-three changes at the very top. These were proud leaders with generally more than twenty years with a company they loved. Many of them were not happy. These conversations were not always pleasant but were necessary. Once we got these top roles configured properly and staffed with people who wanted to make the needed changes, we started to make progress.

This was our most potent lever in the early stages of this change process, and it was critical to start at the very top with the most leveraged roles and people.

HR TRANSFORMATION

In support of this dramatic simplification, we also need to simplify and improve the HR organization. This was asking a great deal of the HR team since we were fully engaged with the other changes, and the organization needed our support. Given the history of independent and decentralized operations, it is not surprising that HR suffered from the same issues. There were 400 different HR software applications, 350 different leadership training programs, 80 different approaches to reward, and too many people doing transactional work by hand all over the world. This led to an HR organization that was too heavy and uncoordinated to keep pace with the demands of the new Unilever that was emerging.

In 2005, along with the business, we embarked on a comprehensive HR transformation program that would lead us to outsource our core thirteen HR transactional processes, overhaul our data quality and install one instance of PeopleSoft, create four core centers of expertise, and move from HR generalists by market and category to a globally integrated business partner organization. This was all held together by our own version of the HR operating framework.

This was hard, painful work. These are the lessons we have learned:

- *Data quality, data quality, data quality.* We learned that we needed to have a rock-solid data foundation. This was something very basic, but it was also something that could not be ignored. Data accuracy, data quality, and data reliability formed the integrity of the HR service operating system. Without them, it would be pure garbage in and garbage out. Our service provider would not be able to support the HR service operating system on our behalf if accurate and reliable basic people data were not there. We spent month after month just to go through the data-cleaning exercises.
- *Don't sign up for a business case you cannot deliver.* This was as much a business project as it was an HR project. There had to be a good financial business case behind it. Just one pointer to share: if I had to do this again, I would not be persuaded by the finance team to go for DCF (discounted cash flow) yield. I would go for exit savings instead. The key learning here is that as in all other large-scale projects of this size, it will take some time for the HR service providers and the retained HR teams to learn how to deliver business results. A business case built on a straight-line DCF yield basis may not fully capture the true synergistic patterns of how the benefits from the HR transformation will eventually pan out.
- *Get personally involved with each business leader until the go-live date.* The Unilever HR outsourcing effort was across multiple businesses and geographies. I led myself to believe that once a business leader or a country leader had signed up on the HR

case, he or she would stay committed until the end. In the majority of instances, they do. But when the first signs of trouble hit, if you as CHRO are not on the ground with your team, it could easily spin the other way before you realize it. In reflection, I wished I had been there to personally meet with each of these business leaders. You have to make this a personal connection between the CHRO and the business leader all the way until the go-live date.

• *Set the right expectations with HR team from the beginning.* Managing a HR transformation that is peppered with enough challenges and complexity is exciting and will get the HR adrenaline pumping. These are all good. We need the energy, the enthusiasm, and the commitment. However, in the heat of these excitements, it is important to be level-headed. Therefore, set the right expectations with the HR team from the beginning. Keep your promises modest and pragmatic. Then aim to deliver on them, one by one. Don't overpromise. The bigger payoffs will come once the outsourcing momentum enters the mature stage. But you need to get past the teething pains first. Be realistic that things can get worse before they get better. You need to hold yourselves together and work toward getting better. Eventually it will.

• *Keep some operational HR staff on the ground.* It is easy to imagine that you could release the operational HR people because the outsourcing partner will pick up the operational administrative work from day 1 on going live. You thought you could release your HR operational staff from that date. Such considerations could already be factored into the business case considerations. The fact is far from the truth (sometimes), as I learned. My strong advice is to retain some of your operational HR staff because there will be HR transactional work that you will not be able to outsource or your outsourcing partners may not be able to take this work over for various reasons. Work still needs to get done. So put attention on getting a grip on reality after going live and combing out what the retained HR operational work needs to get done. These could well be different aspects of HR operational work, but they still to be attended by your own crew.

These were important lessons for us indeed. By then we were a battle-hardened HR team ready to face the challenges that were about to come.

By the end of 2008, we had implemented most of the changes outlined above, and our business performance and resulting share price had improved by more than 50 percent. But we still had work to do to improve our competitiveness as an organization. Our market shares had stabilized but were still declining slightly, and our employee engagement (although still pretty high) had been flat for five years. There was still work to do.

The CEO who led this effort had engineered the most comprehensive and fundamental transformation in recent decades. He had changed nearly every aspect of the business except its character and values. At the end of 2008, he stepped down, leaving the reins for a new leader to take the organization to the next level.

UNILEVER 2009–2010: HR TO SUPPORT A GROWTH VISION

A NEW CEO

The board of directors had the wisdom and courage to run a thorough process of CEO succession. Although the organization had several outstanding internal candidates, the board of directors selected the first externally appointed CEO in the long history of the company. In January 2009, the new CEO took over and immediately began to energize the organization. He declared to the market that he would stop giving guidance, and he then refocused the organization on volume growth (key for a consumer goods business) to turn around market shares and cash. He also began to immediately craft a bold growth vision for the organization.

THE COMPASS

During 2009 the economic recession was in full bloom. Markets were declining, and unemployment was rising. Fortunately the CEO had the foresight to quickly focus the organization on consumer and volume growth. This allowed us to actually grow during these difficult times. It created the space for us to cocreate with our top thirty leaders from around the world a bold new vision for the organization: to double our business while reducing environmental impact. This was packaged in a one-page document we call the Compass. We wanted to stay away from calling it a mission or a vision or a strategy, although it is visionary, it is strategic, and we need missionaries to make it happen. We wanted something more practical—a "magnetic north" to rally the organization.

INSTANT THUNDER

We decided to roll out the Compass in a compressed time frame, letting it roll like thunder quickly across the organization. The impact was big. We got a 10 percentage point improvement in employee engagement in our people survey following the rollout—the first time our engagement scores had moved in more than five years.

ORGANIZATION READINESS

On the heels of the Compass rollout we began to create specific business strategies for each market and category. As I sat through each business strategy discussion, one thought kept running though my mind: *Where are the people and capabilities going to come from to make all these bold plans come to life?* As a result, we kicked off a process specifically to assess our readiness in each market and in each category to achieve our bold vision.

We decided to define our organization readiness (Figure 23.3):

- *Talent:* Do we have the people, the head count, and the talent management process to match our growth ambition?
- *Organization:* Do we have the organization to make us consumer- and customer-centric?
- *Skills:* Do we have the right skills to deliver on our performance plans?
- *Culture:* Do we have the culture to match our performance ambition?

We worked systematically through each of our twenty geographies and ten categories to identify the readiness gaps and a plan to close those gaps. This is owned by the business team in each instance and led by the HR team locally. We have since been able

Figure 25.3. Talent and Organization Readiness Framework, 2010

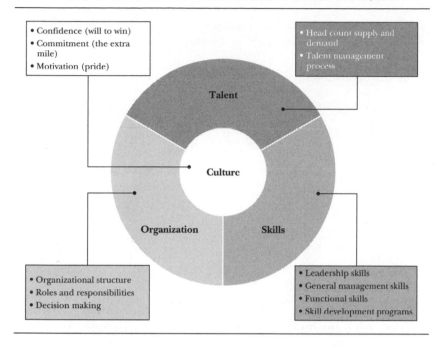

- Confidence (will to win)
- Commitment (the extra mile)
- Motivation (pride)

- Head count supply and demand
- Talent management process

Talent

Culture

Organization

Skills

- Organizational structure
- Roles and responsibilities
- Decision making

- Leadership skills
- General management skills
- Functional skills
- Skill development programs

to look at the opportunities to scale the effort as we looked across the businesses for common issues and best practices. In addition we built a repeatable mode that we are using to do skill building for HR teams around the globe.

We can now clearly see how we need to retool our talent machine to meet these new requirements. We can also prioritize our skill- and capability-building efforts to meet these specific needs. This improves not only our efficiency but also our effectiveness. Finally, we are clear about the interventions required to make the culture changes required to support the business strategies defined to achieve our growth ambition.

A Performance Culture

Since changing our culture was identified as a major issue across the business, we decided we need to sharpen our accountability and performance. We have taken a pragmatic approach to culture change by focusing on performance culture. Our approach is to

FIGURE 25.4. THE UNILEVER ANNUAL CYCLE OF PERFORMANCE MANAGEMENT, 2010

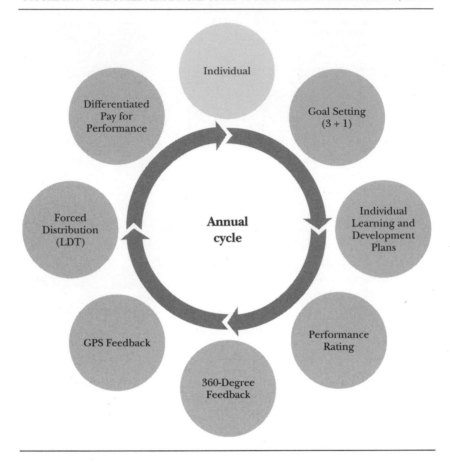

look at our annual cycle of performance management and use our suite of performance management tools and to see each step in the process as a leadership moment (Figure 25.4).

Starting with the individual employee, the performance management tools that support our annual performance cycle are as follows:

- *Goal setting (3+1)*. We have labeled the goal-setting process in Unilever as "3+1" because it refers to the "3" business goals and "1" developmental goals that each employee will set at the beginning of the year, which will drive his or her work agenda and delivery.

- *Individual learning and development plans.* We emphasize that each employee will take his or her own respective development program seriously, as defined by the "plus 1" in goal setting.
- *Performance rating.* All employees will be assessed on how they have performed against their 3+1 goals at the end of the year. A performance rating (1 to 5) will be assigned based on what they have achieved relative to their peer group.
- *360-degree feedback.* This refers to the leadership behavioral ratings that leaders receive using 360-degree feedback. Such feedback may be performed annually as a mechanism to support the development of a leader's leadership behavior and styles.
- *GPS feedback.* This Global People Survey (GPS) is usually conducted on a biennial basis covering all employees in Unilever. From time to time, we also call for a smaller-scale pulse survey of similar format but applying to specific target groups of employees. Results are normally collected and published on companywide basis, as well as by each operating unit or department.
- *Forced distribution (LDT).* This is a relative ranking process where each employee is ranked against his or her respective peer group, looking over a three-year horizon, on two dimensions, leadership behavior and performance delivery, using a nine-square matrix known as the leadership differentiation tool (LDT).
- *Differentiated pay for performance.* Underpinning a strong performance culture is the tight link between annual bonus awards with performance ratings and long-term incentives to relative rankings.

HR for Impact

It is clear that our HR team is now an experienced group of professionals. We have served the business through two important phases of major change: restructuring and growth. Although the growth journey is only eighteen months old at this writing, it is clear that we have a major impact on that agenda.

During the restructuring phase, our team developed a sharp set of skills in doing everything I would call organizational effectiveness. We counted everything in the organization (managers,

FIGURE 25.5.　HR FOR IMPACT

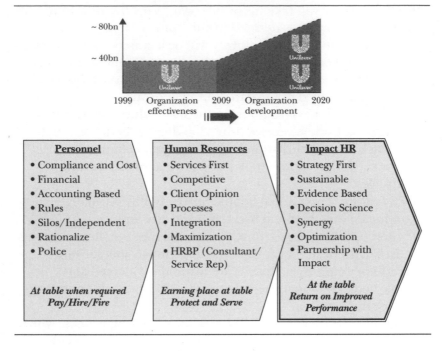

employees, factories, facilities, business units, training courses) and found ways to simplify.

Now that we are supporting a growth agenda, we have to move from a skill set focusing on restructuring to a new skill set focusing on organization development. In addition, assessing the readiness of each part of the business, we have also had to take stock of our own readiness as a function to deliver on this new direction. We have decided to improve our capabilities in this area and are using this opportunity to learn by doing. It has created a new sense of energy and purpose across our HR teams after nearly a decade focused on restructuring (Figure 25.5).

As we implement these growth-oriented actions, we also need to be mindful that we are not just delivering a program; our program must have very clear, measurable key performance indicators that lead directly to business impact and results. Although we just a few months into this new agenda, we are optimistic about our ability to make this transition, reskill ourselves, and help the business achieve this exciting vision.

PART SIX

CHARACTERISTICS OF TODAY'S CHRO

CHAPTER TWENTY-SIX

PREPARING CHROs TO EXCEED CEO EXPECTATIONS

Dave Ulrich, Ellie Filler

For decades, HR professionals clamored to be at the table. The table becomes a metaphor for being invited to and involved in key business decisions. HR's legacy was to develop terms and conditions of employment and to deliver efficient administrative processes that protect the company. HR's future will be to build on this legacy by being even more connected to the thinking, conversations, and actions of the CEO and business leaders.

CEOs today have a tough job. Business conditions have eroded as global recession and uncertain recovery make it more difficult to access capital, create customer loyalty, design new products, and invest in an unknown future. CEOs have to spend more time on consolidations than expansions, layoffs than hiring, and takeaways than bonuses. Personal transparency and accountability, erosion of personal retirement portfolios, and pressures from regulators and investors have made the CEO's job more challenging than ever before. And CEO jobs are increasingly perilous. The tenure of CEOs continues to fall as they are expected to manage all these nearly impossible tasks with insights and grace. More than ever before, CEOs are looking for support from their C-suite team.

When CEOs invite leaders to join them at the table, they need more than administrative support; they need strategic insights. Finance does more than close the books on time, information technology does more than manage data centers, and HR leaders must do more than manage terms and conditions of work. When surveys are done to determine what CEOs are most worried about, the top of thee lists often set out items like these: implementing a new strategy, creating a capacity for change, building leadership depth, innovating new products, ensuring talent, and building disciplines in the company to deliver what it promises. These concerns of the CEOs are the solutions that CHROs should bring to the strategic discussion.

HR PARTICIPATION AT THE TABLE

One HR leader was excited to be invited to key strategy meetings, and he was prepared to contribute when an HR issue came up (around recruitment, training, compensation, communication, or organization design). In the first meeting, the focus was on increasing revenue from emerging markets; no "HR" issues were raised. In the next meeting, the focus was on product innovation, and again no "HR" issues were raised. In the third meeting, the team talked about managing costs of delivery, and again he sensed that no "HR" issues were raised. He did not attend the next meeting.

HR value creation is less about the practices and systems of HR and more about how those practices can be used to increase share in emerging markets, increase innovation, and reduce costs. This means that CHROs can examine which emerging markets to enter, how to organize resources to enter those markets (for example, joint ventures versus independent operations), when to enter the markets, and how to build the infrastructure of the market.

HR often argues that it wants to be invited to the table. This is the wrong way of thinking. HR should not push itself to participate in strategy discussions. It should be pulled in because CEOs need what it has to offer. When CHROs see their work as delivering business value, they are not only invited to strategy discussions but contribute to them.

TALENT AND THE CREATION OF MEANING

CEOs realize that their talent and well-functioning organizations become the means to deliver on their strategic aspirations. In both good and bad times, top talent will have opportunities elsewhere, so strengthening the top players and ensuring their engagement becomes a primary CEO agenda. In addition, since memories outlast recessions, CEOs have to make sure that the actions they take while under the magnifying glass of a recession will bear good fruit as the recession turns into prosperity. When talent is treated poorly in a recession, memories will linger in the upswing. In *The Why of Work* by Dave and Wendy Ulrich, we suggest that leaders are meaning makers who have to help employees discover why they are working in both good times and bad. When CHROs help leaders become managers of meaning, they create sustainable organizations.

While CEOs are ultimately responsible for managing talent and organizations in turbulent times, they should have a close ally in their CHRO. In recent years, the HR field has shifted attention from only doing transaction work to the more strategic work of helping organizations build capabilities to respond to customers and increase confidence from investors. When talent becomes a primary competitive differentiator, CHROs should help their CEOs as personal coaches, organization architects, and allies in the creation of responsive organizations.

Too often in this era when CEOs need more help from CHROs, some HR leaders are retrenching, taking fewer risks, and returning to the administrative work as a safe haven and comfort zone. Quite often the pressure of operational work dominates their days. HR professionals typically want to have a seat at the table and clamor for opportunities to have a voice in key business decisions. In these economic times, good HR leaders do not have to push their way into key managerial decisions; they are being pulled in because the CEO is looking for help in building capabilities.

CHROs can bring into leadership discussions insights about both talent and organizations. They can work with leaders of other business functions to help assure customers and investors that they will have both the right individual competencies and organization capabilities to respond to changing times. Top HR leaders do not need to ply their way into managerial decisions; they need to recognize and respond to opportunities that present themselves. CHROs should have deep understanding about employees in the organization and offer creative solutions on how to find, motivate, engage, and keep them. It is also about assessing and creating organization capabilities that turn business strategy into results. They should be able to recognize current compensation demands like financial restraints on executive pay, yet find creative ways to engage and value top talent. They should be disciplined at removing work so that remaining workers are not expected to accomplish previous work loads. They should be adept at helping craft a simple strategic story out of complex financial and customer demands that unites employees inside with customers and investors outside. They should be knowledgeable about how to make that story become real through words, symbols, and HR practices. They should be able to define the leadership brand that connects customer expectations to employee actions. They should be constantly building and assessing next-generation leadership. They should be able to redesign organization roles and routines to streamline operations to ensure efficiency and accountability. They should be aware of the unintended consequences of their actions as they shape a culture that endures over time. They should be aware of the impact of how decisions are made and resources allocated in getting the best ideas and in involving others. They should be sensitive to the enduring values of the company and how to make sure that those values continually guide tough business decisions. The role of the true business partner that today is so often misused encompasses all of these factors at a time when business needs it most.

QUESTIONS CHROS SHOULD ASK

To make sure that CHROs can rise to these opportunities, we have prepared a list of questions CHROs should be asking themselves to be prepared to fully participate in strategic thought.

• *Do I really understand how my business makes money?* It is in vogue for HR work to be linked to strategy. As CHRO, I should look through the strategy to understand customers and investors and know what they need and why they give money to the firm. I should define my "customers" not just as employees inside the firm, but as the true customers outside who take money out of their purse and wallet and give it to the firm. I should link

HR practices to customer expectations, to be the employer of choice of employees, to make sure that criteria for compensation reflect customer requirements, to build future leaders by starting with what customers want and turn those desires into leadership actions. I should be business savvy and be able to see the line of sight from customer expectations to HR actions.

- *Do I have the ability to prioritize and focus HR investments?* Not everything worth doing is worth doing well. It is important to prioritize and focus on things that matter most. I need to lead my function with the same discipline that C-suite executives have in other functions. Pruning and tailoring HR initiatives shows that I can lead and make difficult decisions.

- *Do I have the ability to work as part of the executive team?* Complex problems will be solved not by individual contributors but by team contributors. Can I work productively with marketing to provide talent and organization to serve customers, with finance to manage costs and operate within budgets, with manufacturing to ensure efficiency, and with other members of my management team? Can I be a coach and architect for talent and organizational issues?

- *Do I have the business gravitas to sort out and take tough positions not only on HR but on the business?* Do I have a point of view and voice an opinion on business issues like globalization, innovation, and efficiency? Do I bring new insights to the discussion? When I talk about the business in strategy discussions, am I credible with my peers because they understand that I know the business?

- *Do I have the ability to make things happen?* Legacy HR has often been guilty of rhetoric and activity more than results and outcomes. It is not enough to have HR as policy police who regulate work and monitor government programs. I must deliver value by anticipating what can and should be done, find creative ways to do it, and have the tenacity and determination to make things happen.

- *Do I have the capacity to link internal organization actions to long-term shareholder investments?* As intangibles become an increasing share of overall market capitalization, I should be able to link quality of leadership, culture, speed of response, innovation, service, and efficiency efforts to business goals. I should be a regular participant in investor calls and presentations to help investors have confidence in our future earnings. I should be as comfortable talking to investors as to employees.

- *Do I balance our team's discussions so we cover both short-term demand and long-term aspirations?* Am I an insightful facilitator who makes sure that difficult issues are faced head-on, that the executive team is able to disagree without being disagreeable, and that strategic intentions become grounded actions?

- *Do I help transfer our firm brand outside the company into our culture inside?* Culture is more than a set of norms, values, and patterns; it is the right patterns, or those actions inside the company that reflect the top customer demands. A sustainable culture comes when the expectations of customers and investors transfer inside the organization to leadership behaviors, corporate initiatives, employee actions, and managerial processes. I should be constantly bridging the outside with the inside. Am I as comfortable talking with key customers as I am with key employees?

- *Do I have global instincts and recognize the trade-offs of local autonomy and global leverage?* Am I committed to making sure that our organization is fully diverse, respecting not only demographic differences (race, gender, age, orientation) but global differences as we make decisions? I should be able to make $1 + 1 = 1$ by finding global economies of scale and efficiencies and $1 + 1 = 3$ by being able to leverage knowledge, talent, customers, and products across global boundaries.

- *Do I not only manage talent and individual ability, but teamwork and organization capability?* I want to help build an organization that outlasts our current leadership team. An organization's capability is what it is good at and known for. This capability resides less in an individual person and more in the set of organization practices that outlive any single individual. Too often today, CHROs overrespond to cries for HR to manage talent, workforce, or human capital and underrespond to opportunities to shape organizations. I need to be the voice of the employee and the architect of the organization.

- *Do I have the enough personal confidence to challenge other leaders when appropriate?* I want to have enough trust with the CEO to tell the truth about managerial efforts and organizational initiatives.

I offer candor with personal concern and willingness to face challenges with calmness are personal traits I want to demonstrate.

The personal template we offer is a high bar for the CHRO. When a CEO interviewed two external candidates for the CHRO job, it became clear what is expected of today's CHRO. Both candidates were well trained, broadly experienced, and highly recommended. On being asked what he would bring to the company, the first candidate talked about his experience in hiring and promoting people based on rigorous competency models; on being able to manage the complexities of base salary, bonus, and stock options; and on having created a leadership academy for future leaders. The second candidate guaranteed the CEO that through HR investments, the organization would have 10 percent greater innovation than other competitors as measured by revenues from products and services created in the previous three years, reduce costs by 5 percent, increase employee productivity and morale, be first to market with new products services, and gain customer share from targeted customers. The first candidate focused on HR activities, the second on business outcomes. In demanding markets, CHROs bring to the table business success by focusing on outcome not activities.

The Competencies of Today's HR Professional

It is not enough for the CHRO to hurdle the value-added bar. In our research, we have discovered what HR professionals must do to pass the questions we raise and deliver the results CEOs demand. We have identified six competencies that you should see in HR professionals throughout the company:

- *Credible activist.* Your HR professionals should be credible in that they are personally trusted, but also are activists who take a position on what the business requires to succeed. This means that HR professionals need to learn to be active participants in ongoing business discussions that are not only on HR issues.
- *Business ally.* Your HR professionals should know the business. This means knowing the external world in which you operate, including the business environment, technological changes, industry trends, and government regulations. It means passing

a business literacy test on how your company makes money, serves customers, and differentiates from competitors.

- *Strategic architect.* Your HR professionals should help shape and deliver strategy. This means that they can help write a strategic story and then work to make it real through HR practices and leadership behaviors. In addition, they can manage the process of creating strategy and communicating it inside and outside the organization.
- *Operational executor.* Your HR professionals should be able to deliver the HR basics on time every time. This means that the administrative work of HR is accomplished with flawless execution.
- *HR practice expertise.* Your HR professionals should bring innovative and aligned HR practices into the firm. This means that HR professionals have current experiences on how to manage people (staffing, training, downsizing), how to manage performance (compensation and benefits), how to communicate and share information, and how to design an organization in both growth and challenging times.
- *Change and culture change.* Your HR professionals should be able to make things happen and change the pattern of work. This means that they have the ability to turn ideas into actions and to conceptualize and manage culture and be able to maneuver through others by getting them to see the short- and long-term horizon.

In difficult times, CHROs have unique opportunities to contribute to business success. CEOs who face greater challenges than ever before need what HR can offer. CHROs can ensure that aspirations turn into actions, that customer expectations show up in organization procedures, that individual competencies turn into organization capabilities, and that pressures for change are met with capacity to change. CHROs invited to the table of business dialogue have much to contribute.

REFERENCE

Ulrich, D., & Ulrich, W. (2010). *The why of work.* New York: McGraw-Hill.

CHAPTER TWENTY-SEVEN

DELIVERING GLOBAL TALENT IN A HIGH-VELOCITY WORLD

What CEOs Look For in a CHRO

James Bagley

The CHRO role is harder to fill than ever before because CEOs demand a leader who can create investor wealth. Whereas it used to be enough for a CHRO to maximize efficiencies, and the CEO was happy with well-managed operational functions like staffing and benefits, the HR equation has evolved over the past twenty years. The CHRO's responsibilities have expanded to include the creation of competitive advantage by attracting, developing, and retaining top talent. Instead of hiring an employee relations manager to run the function, CEOs look for a leader who can anticipate business problems and deliver human capital solutions that produce measurable results.

In today's business world, the requirement for a strategic business leader in the role of CHRO has not changed. What is different is the velocity of global competition. CEOs want the most creative, innovative talent, and the new CHRO must be able to find that talent—not just in his or her own country but on every continent; align them with the company's culture and values; and over months, not years, lead diverse people in international settings to execute as a unified team.

Although the pace of business has made finding the right CHRO a more complex problem to solve, the solution for organizations is the same: the companies with the best talent win. Knowing they need the business insight, HR solutions, informed courage, and a balanced culture that assure the board that the enterprise has the human capital it needs to thrive in the new global marketplace, CEOs look for a CHRO who can be

- A strategic business partner in the C-suite
- An HR expert who maximizes efficiency and competitive advantage
- A leader who anticipates problems, connects with diverse colleagues, and keeps people at ease
- A keeper of the culture who balances results with an environment that supports engagement and extraordinary performance

STRATEGIC BUSINESS INSIGHT FROM A TALENT MANAGEMENT PERSPECTIVE

CEOs want a CHRO who enters every conversation with a clear understanding of the organization's commercial challenges and opportunities. The CHRO should be able to talk about the company's capitalization, balance sheet, and products as fluently as he can discuss the nuances of the HR discipline. He can measure HR activities in relationship to business results and present the impact of his talent management strategy in the boardroom with the same authority that the chief finance officer has in discussing capital structure and financial forecasts.

Today's CHRO solves problems for the CEO that the talent leader has never seen before. A CHRO's greatest value is in anticipating issues before they become problems and developing human capital solutions that address those needs. For instance, a pharmaceutical company's drug is ready for release six months ahead of schedule. This means the CHRO may have only a few months to prepare two hundred street-ready professionals because how he finds and trains the new sales team will determine the ultimate success of that product.

The metrics a CHRO tracks to prove the effectiveness of his actions depend on the strategic direction of the business, and in every company, it is different. For example, after narrowing the target market for their investment products, an insurance company may intentionally reduce head count, even though such an approach seems paradoxical to valuing talent. In this case, the CHRO would measure the areas of the business where fewer people could still provide the same impact for customers, resulting in greater efficiencies and more value for shareholders. While the measurements a CHRO crafts are unique to each business, in every organization a CEO looks for the talent metrics to be tied to the business goals.

HR Disciplines That Create Efficiency and Competitive Advantage

Historically HR was about operations. Today it's about talent. The CHRO has to master everything related to acquiring, developing, and deploying top talent and be able to lead the function by delegating the work of the discipline to her team.

Even in today's HR, however, the need to run efficient operations remains at the forefront of every CHRO's responsibilities. The worst nightmare of a CHRO is that when she needs to be concentrating on talent issues like sales force ineffectiveness or globalizing the business, the CEO hears that health care claims are not being paid on time or an article about poor factory conditions for workers hits the front page. When a talent officer spends all her time managing operations, the CEO loses a leader who can focus on human capital strategies and the value that talent development brings to the business.

The core HR function of today's CHRO revolves around the performance of the organization's people. Competitive advantage comes from recruiting the best talent at all levels, providing them with the tools and capabilities to be successful, and maintaining a culture where effective people want to stay. Companies with the best talent end up with the most capital; develop the most innovative client-facing products, processes, and solutions; and have a positive, engaged workforce.

For example, by staying connected to the sales and marketing leadership of a company that is losing market share, the CHRO stays aware of the opportunities and challenges for personnel. The CHRO has the capacity to perform the analytics on the sales force and produce recommendations, supported by data, detailing whether the team is too small or underperforming. If a better talent pool is the answer, the CEO looks for a CHRO who can then recruit the new talent within the economics of that business and train and deploy the new team into the marketplace.

The CHRO also builds the talent models that allow the CEO and the board to make sound business decisions. Immediately after placing a new CHRO, the CEO told the candidate that he wanted to go into a new line of business. She then called me and asked for access to our specialists in that area. She knew that before she started hiring people, she had to present the CEO and the board with the overall cost from a human capital perspective—how many people, how much salary would attract them from other firms, and the time it would take to build the business—before they decided to go forward. The CHRO always validates the talent strategy before an organization makes decisions because the success or failure of the new direction will depend on the availability and performance of its people.

EXPERIENCED LEADERSHIP THAT DEMONSTRATES ATTENTION AND INFORMED COURAGE

CEOs want a CHRO who has operated at the board level and contributed to the financial and cultural success of previous organizations. The CHRO can tell the stories of the business problems he has solved using human capital solutions and provide data to prove the effectiveness of his strategies. The CHRO's perspective about what he achieved then matches the perspectives of others who worked with him.

The CHRO can also tell the story of how he supported his people. Not only does the best talent win, the CHRO with the best team wins. Top HR leaders possess the ability to gain the support of those around them and maximize the team's performance in a way that also creates a common, connected identity.

The CHRO can build the best team because he understands his impact on others. The CEO wants someone who is persuasive in front of groups and has ethos because he leads by example. He sees the big issues in the business and does not get overwhelmed in the details. Because of the CHRO's business acumen, he stays calm when others panic. He is not just a leader of HR, but in the company and community as well.

CEOs look for a CHRO who is always informed because he knows how to listen. Success in providing value to a CEO comes from understanding what he means versus what he says. The CHRO has the abstract reasoning to take in the CEO's ideas and quickly develop a thesis around the solution sets that will affect the business, and his ideas resonate with other leaders.

The CHRO is completely trusted by the CEO and others in the organization, and that trust is built on intentional, brave actions that consider what's best for the entire enterprise. For instance, the final candidate for the CHRO position at a Fortune 100 company had an offer in hand, but he wasn't sure the firm was the right fit. At the final meeting, the CEO made generous additions to the overall package. The candidate, seeing the CEO's commitment, immediately accepted—until the following morning. The person called me and said, "I can't accept last night's offer. I've looked at the proxy, what other people are being paid, and the culture. If I accept the additional compensation, I'll always be the person who got the big contract. I want the job, but for the original package." The candidate took the job knowing that what was best for the organization would produce greater personal compensation over time, and it has.

Trust is essential because CHROs hear the entire story—not only from the CEO but also from every other executive, and with details that could damage relationships and the company. An attentive CHRO has a sense of personal equilibrium: he can be a lightning rod for people to come to him, he can translate what he hears according to how it affects the business, and then he takes action in a way that maintains the trust of everyone who uses him as a sounding board.

The CHRO who is a respected leader also possesses the courage to offer solutions. When the CEO says, "I want to double the share price of the company," the CHRO needs to be able to provide an informed answer: "Exactly how do you expect to do that? I've looked at our equity and it's fully priced. Our P/E ratio is above that of our main competitors. The only way we can do this is through a merger. That's the only way we can double the share price."

A CULTURE THAT EMPOWERS THE TEAM

Compare two phenomenal cultures: the Peace Corps and the Marine Corps. For little pay, the talent in both organizations is convinced that they will save the world. Interestingly, the cultures could not be more different, and smart, capable people continue to be drawn to both institutions. The message in this comparison is that an organization's performance is most important and culture matters deeply: organizations must balance the desired results with the environment that people need to perform.

The CHRO is the keeper of an organization's culture that attracts, trains, and empowers talent. Building the culture starts with communicating a clear business strategy to every person in the organization so they understand how to contribute. The message begins with the CEO. The CEO sets the tone and describes the environment she hopes for—values like collaboration and open debate. And CEOs look for a CHRO who can help them communicate consistently. The CHRO provides the right words and venues for the CEO to articulate what success means in an organization.

After spreading the message, the CHRO connects the culture's values with the symbols of success. The CEO can intentionally and consistently talk about the outcomes and behaviors she wants, but employees emulate the highest-paid people in the organization. The company can say it wants to operate as a team, but if it pays an individual contributor the most money and he is held up as a hero, employees get a clear message of what the organization truly desires. Companies get the behaviors for which they compensate their people.

The personal style in which the CHRO cultivates a culture determines if the efforts produce results. The culture of the company and cadence of activities within a company are directly correlated to the life cycle of what that company produces. In retail, for instance, the pace is quick; decisions and changes happen quickly. When the CEO of a retail company says she wants an HR officer who can drive change, that person has to be nimble and adaptive. Conversely, if a company has a large capitalization and a long-cycle product, if the CHRO tries to make changes too abruptly, the HR chief will damage relationships and his ability to strengthen the overall business.

When the culture is truly producing business results, the CHRO has created an environment where there are no barriers for learning, innovation, and application of new ideas. The CHRO matches the performance review and feedback process and incentive and compensation plans to the CEO's value messages. People are recognized for behaviors that match the explicit cultural expectations. They aren't afraid to say, "Here's where we can do it better, and here's how." Employees know where to take problems and new solutions, and they see their contributions affect what the company produces and its overall success.

SHOULD A GREAT CHRO BE RAISED OR RECRUITED?

The immediate circumstances determine if the right person should come from natural succession or an outside organization. HR, which owns succession in any company, should be thoughtfully building succession within its own group—ideally, a CHRO surrounds herself with more talented teammates. When the head of total rewards, the head of talent, and the head of HR for the major business units (line of business or geographically defined) are as talented as the current CHRO and represent a diverse range of perspectives and experience, the CEO has a strong bench from which to develop talent.

When the right successor to the CHRO doesn't exist within HR, companies often put an internal, non-HR executive into the role. If a CEO is not convinced that an HR officer is sufficiently connected to the business, she often places an executive without HR training into the CHRO seat, surrounding that leader with subject matter experts. This approach can broaden an executive's experience, provide deeper insight into the entire company, and help prepare the person for a possible succession into the CEO's office.

The two powerful reasons CEOs hire outside their organization is that no successor is ready or a company has become too insular. It is obvious that a company without a succession plan needs an outside candidate to deliver human capital solutions that keep up with the velocity of business today. A company that has lost the edge of fresh insight and diverse perspectives, however, will also search outside the enterprise. When an organization needs new ideas and change, an external candidate, whether for the top HR job or one of the top lieutenants, can fill the technical, experiential, or relational gaps in the leadership team and provide the spark of new perspective.

THE MEASUREMENTS OF A CHRO's SUCCESS

In addition to business results like sales and profit, when a CEO can point to effective successions throughout an organization, whether through development or acquisition, the CHRO is effectively managing the talent needs. Ironically, one of the greatest marks of a CHRO's performance is recruitment of an organization's people by outside companies. Companies with strong CEO and HR leadership—organizations like General Electric and Goldman Sachs—become known as talent academies, and these alumni become highly sought-after candidates. The more aggressively other companies try to recruit people, the better the proof is that a CHRO is fully developing the organization's employees.

Qualitative evidence of effective talent management is just as important. CEOs look for a CHRO who has an awareness of everyone around him or her and an ability to connect individuals and teams. The best CHROs listen carefully to the board and the CEO, play the role of confidant and mediator in conflict, and align the company around the most important goals for the organization. CHROs know how to be direct and informative in a way that people want to respond to their ideas and feedback. They are sought after as speakers outside the organization. They can be the face of the organization, both within the company and to the market, personifying the company's cultural values. CEOs look for a CHRO who can lead with a style that sets an example and creates a balanced culture.

The role of CHRO is to deliver global talent, keeping pace with the high velocity at which needs and opportunities arise in today's organizations. The result of CHROs whose human capital solutions match what CEOs looks for is, in fact, simple to measure: they grow investor wealth.

CHAPTER TWENTY-EIGHT

WHAT DOES TODAY'S CHRO LOOK LIKE?

Demographic Characteristics of CHROs at the World's Largest Companies

Patrick M. Wright, Mark Stewart

Today's CHROs occupy a position of increasing status and impact on the firm. With talent and leadership becoming sources of competitive advantage, firms rely more than they did in the past on having CHROs who understand the needs of the business, understand the tools and techniques of HR, and have the analytical and integrative skills to merge these needs and solutions to add value.

However, little research has examined the characteristics of today's CHROs. How long have they been in their positions, and how did they get those positions? What work experiences prepared them by providing them the competencies and credibility necessary to function in these positions effectively? What educational backgrounds do these individuals have that gave them the foundational knowledge and skills they need? The purpose of this chapter is to provide a glimpse into the characteristics of CHROs at top companies.

DATA COLLECTION

Since 2006, researchers at the Center for Advanced Human Resource Studies (CAHRS) at Cornell University have sought to study the CHRO role. The survey was designed by the lead author (P.W.) with the help of a number of CHROs who comprise the CAHRS advisory board. In order to understand how U.S. CHROs compare to those outside the United States, we first developed a list of the Fortune U.S. 100 CHROs (based on the 2008 Fortune 500) and gathered information on their background from publicly available sources (for example, biographies on the company Web site, press releases regarding the CHRO's appointment, conference brochures where the CHRO spoke). We assessed how long they had been in their positions; whether they were hired from the outside or promoted from within; and their age, sex, race, and educational background. We then went through the same process for the Fortune Global 100 CHROs. Because forty-three of the U.S. CHROs were on the Global 100 list, we deleted them from that list and computed the relevant information on the subsample of sixty-six CHROs of companies headquartered outside the United States from Fortune's Global 100. (Note that one CHRO was missing from both lists. Berkshire Hathaway, as a holding company, does not have a traditional CHRO, and this company appears on both the U.S. and the Global 100 lists.) Of the sixty-six non-U.S. companies, we were unable to identify the CHRO for eight of them, resulting in fifty-eight CHROs. Finally, using the 2008 U.S. Fortune list, CAHRS conducted a survey of CHROs at the top 150 or so companies. (The list consisted of the entire 150, plus twenty-six companies that were members of CAHRS and fell in the 151–500 range.) The final section of this survey asked the CHROs a number of demographic questions (race, sex, age, education, and others), as well as questions about how they were promoted into the job and whether they had worked outside the HR function at some point during their careers.

Demographic Characteristics of Top CHROs

Tenure

In general, the CHROs at Fortune 100 companies are relatively new in the job, with a majority (over 50 percent) having been in the role for three years or less. The longest-tenured CHRO on the list has been in the position for sixteen years, while only five others have served longer than ten years.

While the U.S.-based CHROs seem relatively new in their role, they still had longer average tenure relative to their non-U.S.-based counterparts (4.1 years versus 3.3 years). The major cause of this difference is at the long end of the spectrum. For instance, 12 percent of both U.S. and non-U.S. CHROs had less than 1 year in their role. On the other hand, only one (2 percent) non-U.S. CHRO has been in the role for 10 years or more compared to five (6 percent) of the U.S. CHROs.

AGE

Generationally the U.S. Fortune 100 CHROs come largely from the ranks of Generation X and the baby boom—ranging in age from 35 to 66, with a median age of 53. This result mirrors that found in the survey as the respondents there reported an average age of 52.5. The U.S. and non-U.S. CHROs did not differ in their average age (53.1 for the non-U.S. group), but did differ in the range. U.S. CHROs ranged from 35 to 66 (with 4.5 percent being younger than 40), whereas the non-U.S. group ranged from 42 to 64.

SEX

CHROs at the U.S. 100 companies don't seem to be subject to a glass ceiling. Women hold 44 percent of the Fortune 100 CHRO jobs, and men hold 56 percent. This would indicate that the CHRO role seems to be the C-suite role that has the greatest representation of women among the largest U.S.-based companies.

However, sex differences did exist when comparing the U.S. CHROs with the Global CHROs. The starkest difference between U.S. and non-U.S. CHROs revolved around sex. While U.S. CHROs were almost evenly distributed between men and women (56 percent versus 44 percent), non-U.S. CHROs were highly skewed toward men (84 percent versus 16 percent). In other words, U.S.-based companies were almost three times as likely to have a woman CHRO (44 percent versus 16 percent) relative to companies based outside the United States. Thus, while U.S.-based companies may still strive to increase the balance between male and female C-suite executives, these companies, at least as far as the CHRO role goes, are far beyond their non-U.S. counterparts.

RACE

At one level, the racial composition did not differ between U.S. based and non-U.S. based (89 percent white versus 86 percent white, respectively). However, this initial comparison is quite misleading because race is so strongly tied to national origin among the global companies and many of the companies on the Global 100 list are based in relatively homogeneous countries.

Among the forty-three non-U.S. CHROs for whom we could find race data, none were black, whereas 7 percent of the U.S. 100 CHROs were black. In addition, the non-U.S. companies tended to have CHROs whose race represented their country (for example, Indian in a company from India, Korean in a company based in Korea), and the racial mix of these CHROs really reflects more of the country mix of the Global 100 list.

Thus, in a sense, similar to the results with regard to sex, the U.S.-based companies seem to have done a better job of developing a racially diverse set of CHROs.

EDUCATION

Our study of Fortune 100 CHROs supports the growing belief that next-generation HR leaders need some form of business education background, more likely at the graduate level than the undergraduate level. Only 20 percent of these CHROs have an undergraduate degree in business, with concentrations scattered across general business, management, finance, accounting, and marketing. Interestingly, 8 percent of the CHROs have undergraduate degrees in either political science or psychology, making these majors the most frequently represented. Six percent of CHROs have undergraduate degrees in industrial/labor relations or human resources (ILR/HR).

It appears that the Fortune 100 CHROs also gained their business credentials at the graduate level, with almost one-third (30 percent) having some type of graduate business degree (of which the majority are M.B.A.s). To round out the educational picture, 12 percent of these CHROs have law degrees, 11 percent have graduate degrees in ILR/HR, and 8 percent have doctoral degrees. On the whole, a majority (58 percent) of Fortune 100

CHROs have at least one graduate degree. The results point to a trend for CHROs to have an educational background based on a broad liberal arts undergraduate experience, followed at some point by a formal graduate degree in business.

CHRO CAREER PATHS

The previous section on basic demographic characteristics of CHROs does not tell us about the path that they took to achieve their positions. For instance, were they promoted from within or hired from outside? Did they spend their entire career in HR, or did they work outside the function at some point during their career? Again, we sought to combine information from publicly available sources with the direct responses from survey respondents to shed some light on these issues.

PROMOTION PATH TO CHRO

As the CHRO role has become more important and in many cases tied more closely to the CEO, CEOs have begun demanding more from their CHRO. One of the interesting issues raised by CEOs and executive search consultants specializing in HR searches deals with the difficulty in finding qualified successors to CHROs. They often complain that insufficient talent exists backing up the CHRO such that when the CHRO leaves, no one internally has the competencies necessary to replace him or her. In addition, anecdotally within the United States (based on discussions with executive recruiters focused on senior HR roles), it seems that often when a new CEO steps in, he or she soon wants to find a CHRO who is "his or her own." Whether due to a lack of internal talent or a desire for a CEO to choose a CHRO, many go outside the organization to search for the "best" available CHRO, and often the requirement for the new CHRO is having already served as a CHRO. If this situation exists across companies, then it suggests that firms must engage in poaching existing CHROs from other companies.

In a sign that top firms may be doing a less-than-stellar job of developing their own HR talent, examining the biographies and press releases of the Fortune 100 CHRO revealed that almost one-third (30 percent) were hired from outside their current firms. However, this statistic likely underestimates the true proportion hired from outside. This is because a number of firms in the past few years have brought in outsiders as potential successors twelve to eighteen months before the actual transition. In addition, some CHROs may have moved into their roles from other business functions rather than being promoted from within the HR function. Because most of our data relied on company press releases, such moves would have been recorded as an inside promotion yet would have indicated a lack of an internal successor.

We compared the advancement process between the U.S. and non-U.S. CHROs by examining the press releases and biographies of those in the CHRO role to determine if they had been promoted from within or hired from outside the firm. CHROs at U.S. companies were much more likely (30 percent) to be hired from outside relative to their counterparts at non-U.S. companies (18 percent). Again, this does not suggest that the U.S. CHROs are more or less qualified. However, it does seem to suggest that the U.S. culture may favor a more fluid and open labor market for CHRO talent relative to non-U.S. companies.

Again, trying to interpret the information gained from press releases makes it difficult to identify the specific process through which a CHRO gained his or her position. In an effort to obtain more direct information within the United States, we asked the CHROs in the CAHRS survey to indicate how they had come into the CHRO position. The data undeniably revealed a failure to devote adequate attention to developing successors within HR. In fact, almost half (44 percent) of the CHROs did not achieve the position from an internal succession process. They were directly hired from outside the firm (31 percent), hired from outside with the promise of being promoted into the CHRO role (3 percent), or promoted from outside HR within the firm (10 percent). In fact, only 36 percent reported that they had been promoted from within the HR function.

These results suggest that the old criticism of HR being like the shoemaker's children who go without shoes may be quite accurate. One would find it difficult to explain why the function that has responsibility for designing and overseeing the development and succession processes within the firm would not have sufficient development and succession going on within itself. Many CHROs have suggested that the role is so different from the roles that report to it that the only way one learns it is by being in it. However, the same could be said for other in the C-suite. Certainly aspects of the role become apparent only after being in it, but this does not excuse CHROs from seeking to provide such exposure to their potential successors. This suggests a formal and systematic approach for CHROs to develop their successors, including getting them exposure to board work and some formal training programs as well.

NON-HR WORK EXPERIENCE

One additional aspect of the demographic background of CHROs regarded the extent to which they had held roles outside the HR function at some point in their career. Anecdotally, a number of CHROs suggest that while useful, HR professionals need not take jobs outside HR at some point in their careers. They propose that it can provide a deeper understanding of the business and add to an individual's credibility, but that both of these objectives can also be obtained during a career entirely in HR. While this is true, the majority of CHRO respondents in this study (54 percent) have held roles outside the HR function, and only 26 percent responded that they had not held such a role. This should be tempered by the fact that 10 percent of the sample were actually promoted to the CHRO job from outside the HR function, so it may be closer to 40 percent of the CHROs who would be considered career HR professionals who had taken on non-HR jobs at some point during their careers.

As part of the CAHRS HR Leadership podcasts, many of the CHROs have been asked about the need to work outside HR during some point in their career. Some of those asked the question had such experience (for example, Bill Conaty, former CHRO at GE), while others did not. Obviously those without such experience suggested that while it might be helpful, it could not be considered necessary. However, more interestingly, those who had such experience tended to agree. For instance, Conaty suggested that the important point was that an individual learn the business. In addition, some of those who had such experience said that the value of such experiences stemmed not from new skills or perspectives, but from how the experience increased one's credibility in the eyes of their line colleagues. As John Murabito, CHRO at Cigna, said when asked what he gained by working outside the HR function early in his career, "I'm not sure I learned anything that I couldn't have learned somewhere else. However, having been in a line role made my line colleagues look at me differently, attributing more credibility to me than if I had not worked in such a role."

Thus, it seems that working outside HR does not hurt one's career and potential to become a CHRO, but neither is it a requirement for effectively executing the role.

CONCLUSION

In examining the demographic characteristics of CHROs, there are some promising and troubling implications. One promising finding is that CHROs in U.S.-based companies seem to be close to providing a diverse representation along both sex and race lines. Another is that most of today's CHROs have gained academic credentials in business at the undergraduate or graduate level. Third, a significant percentage of CHROs have worked outside the HR field. This provides them with a more business-based perspective and lends them credibility with their C-suite peers.

One troubling aspect is the low level of tenure among CHROs. We note that the data do not mean that, on average, a CHRO can expect to spend 3.3 years in the role, but rather than among current CHROs, the median tenure is 3.3 years. However, assuming a relatively constant level of turnover, this does suggest that over time, the average tenure should not stray far from this level.

Second, and relatedly, given the short tenure of CHROs, one would expect more attention to be devoted to building the competence of the potential successors. However, close to half (44 percent) of current CHROs did not attain their position as a result of an internal development process.

Given the increasing importance of human capital to the success of firms and the critical role that CHROs play in ensuring that the firm has the necessary human capital, it seems that much can and should be done to increase the pool of potential CHRO talent.

CHAPTER TWENTY-NINE

BRINGING IT ALL TOGETHER
The Four Knows of the CHRO
Patrick M. Wright

This book has brought a number of perspectives to bear on the current and future role of the CHRO. Current CHROs, past CHROs, consultants, researchers, and even executive search experts have shared their experiences and opinions about the challenges facing CHROs, the strategies for addressing those challenges, and the competencies necessary to succeed. In looking over these chapters, I would propose that they tend to identify four knowledge areas that play critical roles in the success or failure of a CHRO: know the business, know how to lead, know people, and know yourself.

KNOW THE BUSINESS

The first "know" has been oft repeated to HR professionals at all levels of the organization for over twenty years. The chapters by Dave Ulrich and Ellie Filler and by Jim Bagley describe how CEOs expect this type of knowledge. In addition, the chapter by Mirian Graddick-Weir describes the transition process of learning the business dynamics when moving to a new industry. Given the emphasis, one would not expect that it presents a challenge to those who have risen to the top seat in the HR function. Yet a constant theme throughout this book focuses on the need to know the business. In essence, this knowledge base consists of three areas.

First, one must know the nature of how the firm makes money. Business models differ between financial services and manufacturing firms, with each having different relative levels of fixed costs, different margins, and different infrastructures. When PepsiCo acquired the fast food companies of Taco Bell, Kentucky Fried Chicken, and Pizza Hut, one might assume that this was simply branching out into a different distribution channel for a food and beverage company. However, PepsiCo's beverage (Pepsi) and snack food (Frito-Lay) businesses differed greatly from the companies they acquired. The beverage and snack food business were high-margin businesses with relatively low fixed costs and a largely skilled and ambitious workforce. The fast food industry was an extremely low-margin business with relatively higher fixed costs and a largely low-skilled transient workforce. One reason for the failure of this merger was trying to run both kinds of businesses the same way. A CHRO who cannot identify the basic way that the firm makes money will end up embarrassed.

This embarrassment will stem from offering the wrong solutions, which leads to the second area of knowing the business. Once one understands the basic business model, one must next identify the ways that people in general, and which people in particular, can serve as a source of competitive advantage, competitive parity, or competitive disadvantage. For instance, in a high-margin business, one can invest in developing an overabundance of talent and letting the cream (the best of the best) rise to the top. In a low-margin business, identifying the right potential leaders early becomes of utmost importance so that the limited resources can be invested in those from whom the firm can generate the greatest returns. CHROs who propose the wrong HR infrastructure for the needs of the business will likely do so only once.

Finally, knowing the business entails knowing the rhythm of the business. Every business has regular cycles in terms of when in the year business is booming and when it is waning (for example, retail booms in November and December, but wanes much of the rest of the year). Ignorance of this cycle may lead to decisions that imply ignorance of the CHRO. Years ago, I was conducting research on the role of people in competitive advantage and the role of the HR function in creating that. In interviewing the sales leader in a large computer company, he noted that HR needed to "understand the business." Having heard this criticism a number of times, I asked him to give me an example. He suddenly got excited as he explained: "A few years ago, our HR function thought we needed to be an employer of choice. Looking around the area, they noted that almost all the companies gave their employees the week off between Christmas and New Year's Day, so they decided we needed to do the same thing." He then got a big smile on his face as he asked, "Do you know what the busiest week of the year is for us? The week between Christmas and New Year's Day! So we had to pay triple time to get employees to come in and work during their 'vacation!'"

KNOW HOW TO LEAD

Knowing how to lead an organization serves as the second "know" of the CHRO. A number of the chapters in this book have told stories of how a CHRO transformed an HR function or got the HR function on the same page as the business. For instance, the chapters by Sandy Ogg (Unilever), Ken Carrig (Comcast), and Hugh Mitchell (Shell) describe HR transformations. In addition, the chapter by Amy Kates, John Boudreau, and Jay Galbraith provides some guidance about structuring an HR function. While these stories can help provide guidance for what an effective HR function can and should look like, what they seldom reveal is the management competence necessary to create them.

In interviewing CHROs about their roles over the years, what quickly became apparent to me was that the leader of the HR function role consists of leading, not doing, HR. As more and more demands have been placed on CHROs (board work, counseling, and so forth), they have less and less time to focus on the details of HR processes, structures, and systems. This leadership role consists of defining direction, identifying talent, delegating responsibility, and holding individuals accountable.

Defining direction entails articulating the goals of the function in a way that makes it clear how the function will support the business and provides a vision and a strategy for how the function will get there. For instance, Hugh Mitchell's transformation of HR at Shell required an entirely different approach to how HR would be delivered, governed, and cost structured as the firm moved to a formal CEO model. People in the function need to understand where the function is headed and have a clear line of sight as to how it will get there.

Second, CHROs must choose the right team to lead the function in the defined direction. In my interviews of over one hundred CHROs over the past few years, I noted that they seldom described much of their role with regard to the HR function. In interviewing some of them, I finally tried to describe the role and suggested, "I get the idea that your major role in leading the HR function is to pick great people to lead the HR function." The response was a resounding yes, which leads to the third part of knowing how to lead.

Once the CHRO has the right talent on the team, he or she must delegate responsibility to those direct reports to manage their areas. After suggesting that the CHRO's role in leading HR was to pick great people to run the various pieces of HR, many have said, "I am being pulled in so many different directions that I don't have the time to get into the details of this process or this system. I can only really define what we need to accomplish, and then I have to let them figure out how to do it."

However, the final, and possibly most important, aspect of leading requires CHROs to hold those leaders accountable for their results. I was asked once about, across all my experiences with CHROs, the common characteristics that made them successful. I know all the CHROs who wrote chapters for this book, and I can guarantee they all differ in styles, backgrounds, and perspectives. But the common approach they all share is that they hold people accountable for their results. They might do it in a harsh way, or they might do it in a supportive way, but they do it. Those who don't deliver don't last long.

KNOW PEOPLE

Knowing people constitutes the third "know" for a CHRO. This does not mean knowing a lot of people or knowing the right people, but knowing the basic human condition that can guide people to fantastic success or unbelievable failure. Knowing people means knowing human nature and the implications for decisions and group dynamics. Dave Pace's chapter describes some of these dynamics, and Elease Wright's chapter describes some of her learnings in working with seven different CEOs. In addition, the Patrick Wright and L. Kevin Cox chapter presents some of the CEO weaknesses that CHROs identified.

I used to begin my interviews with CHROs by asking about how they would divide up their jobs into different areas of responsibility. They would articulate many of the types of roles discussed throughout this book (talent architect, strategic advisor, HR leader, and so on—all but counselor/confidant/coach). Then I would suggest that they play three major roles: executing strategy, influencing the formulation of strategy, and managing the dysfunctional dynamics of the senior team (I call it managing the formation of strategy). Overwhelmingly the response would be, "I've never really thought about it that way, but that last part is how I spend 90 percent of my time."

Strategy researchers often refer to two characteristics of executives that can lead to dysfunctional decisions: opportunism and hubris. Opportunism refers not just to self-interested behavior, but a willingness to engage in self-interested behavior no matter what the cost to others. Hubris refers to such an overwhelming level of pride that an individual thinks he or she can do anything successfully. Executive leadership teams consist of highly successful (thus, the potential for hubris) and highly ambitious (thus, the potential for opportunism) individuals who have been thrown together and must cooperate and compete at the same time. This is a recipe for disaster, not success.

However, an effective CHRO sees the landscape of the team, the land mines of various personalities, and the incoming missiles of competitive dynamics and then navigates the entire scene to try to bring about a successful process. This requires knowing which influence approaches will work with which individuals, how to communicate messages whether directly or indirectly, and when to intervene versus when to ignore. A CHRO who does this effectively acts as the catalyst for successful team functioning. A CHRO who does this ineffectively soon becomes sidelined, unable to have an impact.

KNOW YOURSELF

Finally, CHROs must know themselves. In particular, knowing one's self requires knowing the values that one holds and why one holds them. Increasingly we hear thought leaders calling for courage in HR leaders. Courage has been described not as the absence of fear but the willingness to do what is right in the presence of fear. Libby Sartain's chapter provides a strong foundation for this "know" because she notes that to have courage you have to know what you believe in.

The HR function in general, and CHRO in particular, have often been referred to as the conscience of the organization. While all leaders should play a conscience role, one cannot deny that most people look to HR to act as the primary referee of the organization's values, calling fouls on those who violate them. But organization values are often ambiguous, amorphous, or unheeded, so CHROs must often rely on their own internal values to guide them.

Many people say they got into HR because "they like people." While such a statement is somewhat naive, my experience is that the greater problem stems from its lack of clarity. They do not mean that they "like" people, but that they "value" people, seeing them as human beings with dignity and worth. Their statement really means that they want to see people grow and develop individually and corporately to achieve success through helping others achieve success as an organization. Thus, it is not a statement of preference but a statement of worldview.

As the focus on strategic HR has emerged, we have increasingly sought to find ways to use people as a source of competitive advantage. While the increasingly competitive marketplace requires effective and efficient allocation of resources, such an approach can lead to a worldview of people as impersonal assets. In fact, in his Nobel Prize speech, Gary Becker stated, "Human capital is so uncontroversial nowadays that it may be difficult to appreciate the hostility in the 1950s and 1960s toward the approach that went with the term. The very concept of human capital was alleged to be demeaning because it treated people as machines" (Becker, 1992, p. 10).

C. William Pollard, the former chairman and CEO of Service-Master, used to refer to the company's philosophy of people as the subjects rather than the objects of work. What he meant was that the purpose of the firm was not to use people as a means to achieve profits, but rather to use profitability to help people grow and develop. It reflects a worldview of the ultimate value of people as ends, not means—as human beings deserving respect and being treated with dignity, not as machines to be exploited of their useful life and then discarded.

I suspect that this worldview originally drove many CHROs into the field. Over time the trappings of success, the ambitions to move ahead, and the desire to be respected by one's peers and bosses can tempt them to lose this perspective and begin to forget who they are, where they came from, and why they got into HR. In essence, it is forgetting who one is. Those who succeed fight such an urge and constantly relearn the lesson of knowing themselves in order to courageously stand up for the values that originally led them into HR. It is the combination of knowing clearly what one believes and the courage to stand up for those beliefs that leads every successful CHRO to be willing to have that "put your badge on the table" moment. Only through knowing yourself internally can you define yourself externally.

CONCLUSION

This book describes today's CHRO role. The role continues to evolve; it is different today than it was ten years ago and different from what it will be ten years from now. Industries will die, be born, and transform. The competitive dynamics within industries will change. Technology will drive new products, processes, and ways of doing business. Competitors will emerge from around the globe. With each of these developments will come new expectations and demands from the CHRO role. However, what will not change will be the needs to know the business, know how to lead, know people, and know yourself. Those will form the constellation from which CHROs can navigate the landscape.

REFERENCE

Becker, G. S. (1992). *The economic way of looking at behavior: The Nobel lecture.* Palo Alto, CA: Hoover Institution, Stanford University.

INDEX

Abilities. *See* Competencies

Accountability: for decisions, 84, 85, 87–88, 90; demanded by CEOs, 160, 166; as principle for HR leaders, 19–20; and recovery from scandal, 103; for results, required of leaders, 66, 299; for talent demand, 81

Advisors: to CEO, 123–124; strategic, 8, 41, 42–45

Age, of CHROs, 290

Agenda: evaluating and refining, 226; for first ninety days, 245; setting, in first 100 days, 220–222, 225–226

Allen, R., 163

American Express, talent management system at, 76, 77–78, 81

Antoine, R. L., 1, 7, 32

Armani, 250

Assignment planning, 36–37

AT&T, 237–238, 239

Axelrod, B., 3, 11, 71, 82

Bagley, J., 10, 279, 296

Banwart, S., 8, 57

Barr, K., 51

Battles: avoiding personal in, 150–151; guidelines on fighting, 148–150

Becker, G. S., 301, 302

Board of directors, 171–182; chair of, as constituency of CHRO, 121–122; CHRO as liaison to, 42, 43, 50–52; CHRO as resource and counsel for, 24–25; CHRO as strategic partner with, 187–191; CHRO role with, 9–10, 183–184, 187; members of, with HR expertise, 183–184, 189–190; as pressure on CHRO, 6–7; support given by CHRO to, 184–187; tips on working with, 181–182;

understanding role of, 28. *See also* Compensation committee ("comp committee")

Bock, L., 49

Boeing, 87

Bolden, J., 66

Boudreau, J. W., 1, 8, 10, 83, 85, 87, 91, 92, 184, 188, 190, 191, 192, 198, 246, 248, 250, 251, 256

Brand, CHRO's personal, 31, 147–148

Brand, company's: ambassador for, 24; transferring, into culture, 276

Brannigan, M., 164, 167

Breen, E., 100, 106

Burke, S., 213, 219

Business knowledge: about executive compensation, 199–201, 203–205, 210; desired in HR professionals, 277–278; how to obtain when in new job, 241–242; needed by CHRO, 213, 215, 216–218, 224; overview of necessary, 296–298; as priority, 29; strategic, from talent management perspective, 280–281

Business leader, CHRO as, 24–26, 29

Business models: business partner/center of excellence, 251–255; new, and design of HR function, 247–250; required knowledge about, 297

Business partner, CHRO as, 26–27, 280–281

Business partner/center of excellence model, design of HR function in, 251–255

Capabilities. *See* Competencies

Career paths, of CHROs, 285–286, 292–295

303